DECISIONS

Second Edition Revised

Lawrence G. Wrenn

Canon Law Society of America
Washington, D. C. 20064

Copyright 1983 by Canon Law Society of America.
First edition copyrighted 1980.
All rights reserved.
ISBN: 0-943616-17-4
SAN: 237-6296

Multis passeribus
meliores estis vos

Mt. 10, 31

CONTENTS

Preface

PREFACE

This is not a new volume of *Decisions;* it is a second edition of the old volume.

In other words, much of the material that appeared in the first edition is simply reprinted here. Eighteen cases (Elster, Brant, Columba, Golab, Choucas, Pernice, Mewa, Gallo, Gazzera, Drossel, Grouse, Quaglia, Cormorant, Turnstone, Grebe, Gazza, Rail and Gelinotte) are reprinted exactly as they appeared in the first edition or with only very minor changes. Nine more cases (Chapon, Scoter, Wachtel, Willet, Darter, Eider, Wrona, Strzyzyk and Kestrel) are the same except for the law section.

There is, however, a fair amount of new material as well. Twelve cases (Passerine, Anhinga, Crake, Roitelet, Woodstock, Thrush, Seal, Cigno, Petrel, Kite, Siskin and Noddy) are entirely new. There are also twenty-two new law sections included in this edition—twelve of them are translations of rotal decisions; the other ten are my own. Most rotal decisions that predate the 1983 Code are, of course, dated to some extent. They nevertheless remain extremely important and are included here for that reason. The two indexes at the back of the book should be useful to the reader in locating all of the law sections in both the first and second editions.

Notably absent from this edition are the historic law sections of Serrano (4/5/73), Anné (2/25/69), Canals (4/21/70) and Rogers (1/21/69) which appeared in the first edition on pp. 8, 94, 133 and 144 respectively.

The canon numbers cited in this edition are from the new Code except where the context clearly indicates otherwise. The order of the cases also follows the new Code.

The first edition and this edition of *Decisions* are referred to in this book as D1 and D2.

Lawrence G. Wrenn

Hartford, Connecticut
February 16, 1983
Ash Wednesday

I
The Facts

Janet Passerine and Marc Finch, both Catholic, were married at the Church of St. Ignatius, Edgewood, Connecticut in the Archdiocese of Hartford, on the fourteenth day of June, 1975. Janet was twenty-eight years old at the time; Marc was thirty.

Janet and Marc lived together for about five years. The marriage seemed a reasonably happy one for most of that period but Marc had an extramarital affair in the summer of 1980. Janet discovered the affair quite by accident and was unable to forgive Marc. The couple separated in October of 1980. A divorce was granted in Edgewood county on September 21, 1981. No children were born of the marriage since Marc had had a vasectomy performed prior to marrying Janet.

On October 26, 1982, Janet petitioned this Court to declare the marriage null on the grounds that Marc Finch's vasectomy had rendered him impotent. Janet's petition was accepted and the Issue in Pleading was defined by the Judge on November 11, 1982, with the respondent's impotence being assigned as the *"caput nullitatis investigandum."*

II
The Law

A. Prior to May 13, 1977, the standard jurisprudence of the Rota and other church courts regarding male impotence required that, for a man to be potent, he had to be capable of ejaculating within the vagina "verum semen," i.e. seed produced in the testicles. If a man was incapable of that he could be declared impotent.

B. On May 13, 1977, however, the Sacred Congregation for the Doctrine of the Faith issued the following decree (CLD 8, 676-677):

> The Sacred Congregation for the Doctrine of the Faith has always held that persons who have undergone vasectomy and other persons in similar conditions must not be prohibited from marriage because certain proof of impotency on their part is not had.
>
> And now, after having examined that kind of practice, and after repeated studies carried out by this Sacred Congregation as well as by the Commission for the Revision of the Code of Canon Law, the Fathers of this

S. Congregation, in the plenary assembly held on Wednesday, the 11th of May, 1977, decided that the questions proposed to them must be answered as follows:

1. Whether the impotency which invalidates marriage consists in the incapacity to complete conjugal intercourse which is antecedent, of course, and perpetual, either absolute or relative?

2. Inasmuch as the reply is affirmative, whether for conjugal intercourse the ejaculation of semen elaborated in the testicles is necessarily requisite?

To the first question: *In the affirmative;* to the second, *In the negative.*

And in the audience granted to the undersigned Prefect of this S. Congregation on Friday, the 13th day of the said month and year, the Supreme Pontiff, Pope Paul VI, approved the above decree and ordered that it be published.

Given at Rome, from the offices of the S. Congregation for the Doctrine of the Faith, the 13th day of May, 1977.

This decree stated, in effect, that so called "verum semen" is not, in fact, required for potency.

C. After May 13, 1977, jurists generally agreed that this decree of the Congregation would definitely affect the jurisprudence of the courts. Two solid opinions arose, however, regarding the nature, and consequently the effective date, of the decree.

1. The first opinion is that the decree was an authentic declaration of the natural law stating what was always the true and proper sense of the law. The decree, therefore, is completely retroactive. The man whose ejaculate lacked a testicular component was, consequently, always potent. He was never impotent. The standard pre-decree jurisprudence was erroneous. Should, therefore, a case now come before the Tribunal claiming the nullity of a marriage, even of a marriage which had taken place prior to the decree, on the grounds that the man's ejaculate did not include a testicular component, the decision, according to this opinion, must be in the negative. The man was not impotent.

2. The second opinion is that the decree "explained a doubt," as the old C. 17 said, and that, therefore, it is not retroactive, and, in accord with the old C. 9, did not become effective until three months after the date of the AAS issue in which it was promulgated. Since therefore, this decree was promulgated in the July 31, 1977, issue of the AAS, it

2

would not, according to this opinion, be effective until November 1 of that year. Prior to that date the man who lacked a testicular component in his ejaculate would be impotent; after that date he would be potent.

D. Because of this difference of opinion, these two interpretations, though both well founded, are not certain but only probable. Prior to the decree, therefore, the man lacking a testicular component in the ejaculate was only probably impotent (according to the first opinion he was potent). Consequently, a Tribunal, which cannot be satisfied with probability but requires moral certitude, cannot declare such a man impotent; nor can it declare null a marriage involving such a man simply because he could not produce "verum semen."

III
The Argument

The evidence adduced in this case consisted, for all practical purposes, of the testimony of both principals plus a report from Reginald Philips, MD, the urologist who performed the vasectomy on Marc in 1970. Testimony was also received from two witnesses but the only relevant information they had to offer was that, as far as they knew, Janet and Marc had a "normal" sex life during most of the marriage.

It is clear from the evidence that in 1970, when Marc Finch was cohabiting out of wedlock with a certain Diane, he arranged to have Doctor Philips perform a vasectomy. In his report submitted to the Tribunal, Doctor Philips describes the standard vasectomy procedure and attests to the fact that the operation was indeed performed on Marc Finch on April 12, 1970.

Within a year after the operation Marc and Diane broke off their relationship. Marc came to regret having had the vasectomy and saw it as a short-sighted decision but he did not, in fact, ever visit a physician thereafter to inquire into the possibility of a reversal.

After meeting and becoming serious with Janet Passerine, Marc advised her of the fact that he had had a vasectomy four years previously. Both parties seemed to regret, at least mildly, that they would not be able to have children, but continued the courtship nonetheless and married in June of 1975.

It is clear from the testimony that Marc's sexual performance during marriage was satisfactory in every way except, of course, that his ejaculate did not contain a testicular component. It is true, of course, that, prior to the 1977 decree, a court would have declared their marriage null on the grounds that Marc Finch could not produce "verum semen" and was, therefore, impotent. Nevertheless, despite the vigorous argumentation of the advocate, the Court is convinced that, following the 1977 decree, Marc Finch could no longer be regarded as having been certainly impotent when he married Janet Passerine in 1975.

3

The allegation that the Passerine-Finch marriage was null on the grounds of the respondent's impotence has, therefore, not been demonstrated with moral certitude.

WHEREFORE

```
┌─────────────────────────┐
│           I             │
│       The Facts         │
│                         │
└─────────────────────────┘
```

Salvatore Anhinga and Ruth Bocian, both Catholic, were married in the Church of SS. Simon and Jude, Upton, Connecticut, in the Archdiocese of Hartford on the twenty-third day of June 1978. Salvatore was twenty-five years old at the time; Ruth was twenty-one.

Salvatore and Ruth lived together for about four years, but both parties drank to excess and spent beyond their means. They quarrelled a great deal and separated finally in May of 1982. No children were born to the couple because Ruth was unable to conceive. A divorce was granted in Upton on November 15, 1982.

On December 4, 1982 Salvatore petitioned this Court to declare the marriage null on the grounds of Ruth Bocian's impotence. The petition was accepted and the ground alleged in the petition was accepted as official in the *Contestatio Litis* conducted on December 29, 1982.

```
┌─────────────────────────┐
│           II            │
│        The Law          │
│                         │
└─────────────────────────┘
```

The jurisprudence that would apply in this case is summarized in a decision dated October 16, 1980, coram Raad as found in *Monitor Ecclesiasticus* 1981, n. 1, pp. 46-48.

3. Much has been said in older decisions about the so-called "excised woman" or "occluded woman" or about a woman fitted with an artificial vagina. See, for example:

Bejan, July 30, 1959 (51, 412)
Ewers, October 28, 1961 (53, 470)
Rogers, February 14, 1963 (55, 102)
Sabattani, February 11, 1963 (55, 127)
Mattioli, April 29, 1965 (57, 384)
DeJorio, October 13, 1965 (57, 640)
Filipiak, January 26, 1966 (58, 46)
Bejan, July 29, 1967 (59, 656)
DeJorio, October 11, 1967 (59, 678)

Pinna, January 28, 1969 (61, 96)
Lefebvre, December 16, 1972 (64, 79)
Davino, April 25, 1979)

However, after the May 13, 1977 decree of the Sacred Congregation for the Doctrine of the Faith, which answered in the negative to the question "whether an ejaculation of seed elaborated in the testicles is necessarily required for marital intercourse?" (AAS 69, 426; see also the decisions coram Raad of March 9, 1978, March 15, 1979, and February 15, 1979) and after the studies regarding marital intercourse conducted by the Pontifical Commission for the Revision of the Code of Canon Law (*Communicationes* 6, 1974, n. 2, pp. 177-198; see also paragraph 5 below), it is clear that an artificial vagina should now be considered the equivalent of a natural vagina.

4. Impotence consists in the inability to perform conjugal intercourse; in order for impotence to invalidate a marriage, it must be both antecedent and perpetual (Canon 1068, § 1).

A woman who lacks a natural vagina is most certainly impotent, but what if she is fitted with an artificial vagina? The insertion of an artificially constructed vagina before marriage removes impotence but, if it is done after marriage, it does not have a retroactive effect regarding the validity of a marriage already entered, and the marriage would, therefore, remain invalid. Because, viewed juridically, the impotence of that woman was perpetual, since the plastic surgery involved in the insertion of an artificial vagina is an altogether extraordinary means and remedy which a woman is not bound to use. As Monsignor Pinna said, in his decision of January 28, 1969: "Perpetuity is a legal concept, not a question of fact. In order to be invalidating, the defect under which a person suffers ought to be perpetual, that is to say, irreversible at the time of the marriage contract. In the case at bar, the absence of the vagina on January 4, 1960 was juridically perpetual, because it could be remedied only through an altogether extraordinary means, namely, through the construction of an artificial vagina. A woman could not be obliged to avail herself of this remedy, nor could she be compelled to do so by the man, For, as our expert, Doctor Noel, says: 'it would be a question of an operation which is extremely rare; feasible, but still rare. I have never performed it myself. It is a serious operation, one we would consider to be major', in which, at least in some cases (about 2%), the danger of death is involved. And even beyond the danger of death, other complications could also arise which would create a health crisis for the patient (see the decision of February 2, 1963 coram Sabattani (55, 137)), and nobody is bound to submit themselves to that sort of danger. Then, too, we must keep in mind that sometimes the operation will not be successful, that repeated incisions and lengthy preparations are sometimes necessary, and that oftentimes there are detrimental after effects, like sclerosis of the vagina, conglutination of the vaginal walls and abnormal scarring of the vaginal opening. But if, in fact, the woman did, *after* marriage, undergo this remedial surgery, then, even if the surgery was successful, the fact remains that, when the woman contracted marriage, she lacked a vagina altogether and so could not enter marriage, and, even though the vagina was later reconstructed, the marriage would still not be convalidated unless marital consent were renewed" (61, 104). Because, as Monsignor Pinna said in that same sentence "perpetuity is a legal concept and ought to be estimated at the moment the consent is given, and at that moment a diriment impediment due to irreversible impotence was indeed present, even though it was perhaps remediable by means of a difficult and extraordinary operation. Therefore, even if one were to grant (though not concede) that a true vagina could actually be artificially constructed, the marriage would still have to be validated" (61, 100).

5. The Pontifical Commission for the Revision of the Code of Canon Law made the following pertinent statement: "Regarding an artificial vagina, nearly all the consultors are of the opinion that, if the woman obtained the artificial vagina prior to marriage, she ought to be regarded as potent and therefore a marriage entered by her would be valid. If, however, the artificial vagina was obtained after the marriage, then the marriage is null but it can be convalidated" (*Communicationes* 6, 1974, n. 2, p. 196).

6. Even though a previous marriage was declared null, a new marriage should not be forbidden, since the woman, now endowed with an artificial vagina and therefore capable of having intercourse, has become potent in terms of any future marriage. Even our Defender of the Bond wrote, "But sometimes it happens that a woman is provided with an artificial vagina by which she becomes capable of satisfactorily having intercourse. In such a case, it is a question of using an extraordinary and therefore not obligatory means. But if the woman was, in fact, fitted, prior to marriage, with an artificial vagina, namely, one constructed plastically, she should thereafter be regarded as potent and a marriage entered by her would, therefore, be valid. If, however, the artificial vagina was constructed after the marriage was entered, then the marriage is null but can be convalidated. It is null because, at the time the woman contracted, she did in fact lack a vagina; it can be convalidated because now, at the present time, the woman should no longer be considered to lack a vagina even though her vagina is not a natural but an artificial one; consequently, if she is legitimately freed from the former bond, she ought not to be impeded from entering another marriage. See Canon 1068 § 2" (the Defender's Animadversions No. 2).

7. In such a case one could, in theory, admit the ground of a defect of the object of consent, as our distinguished advocate has proposed.

But, where the marriage is declared null on the ground of impotence, it cannot be declared null a second time on the grounds of a defect of the object of consent at the time the consent was given, for that would constitute a mere tautology. As Cappello said, "a marriage contract consists essentially in the mutual handing over and receiving of the right to intercourse; but an impotent person, by the very fact that he or she is impotent, cannot hand over that right; therefore, the object of the marital consent is lacking and, therefore, the contract itself, lacking its object, is null" (Cappello, *Tractatus canonico - Moralis de Sacramentis*, vol. V, De Matrimonio, 1947, p. 357, n. 347, 3°).

III
The Argument

Salvatore and Ruth met at Upton Community College in 1976 when they were twenty-three and nineteen respectively. Salvatore had entered the Navy after high school and did not begin college until after his discharge from the service. He was a junior when they met; Ruth was a freshman.

Within a few weeks of meeting, Salvatore and Ruth became romantically attracted to each other. It was at this point, before the relationship became really serious, that Ruth explained to Salvatore her physical problems. These problems are perhaps best summarized in the medical report of Phyllis Courlan, MD, dated January 28, 1983, and entered as evidence into the acts of this case. Doctor Courlan's report reads as follows:

> Ruth Bocian was the first child and grandchild, born in 1965. Amidst the joys and celebrations of her birth came a note of sadness when it was noted by her pediatrician that there was an abnormality of her genitalia.

> Ruth grew into a beautiful woman. She was graceful, attractive, and her academic achievements were high. However, side by side with Ruth's development into a young woman with much potential came the overbearing problem of her physical abnormality. At age thirteen she was admitted to the hospital for surgery which consisted of removing tumors from the pelvis which the pathologist reported as testes. Ruth had a condition which is called testicular feminization, which is an end organ failure resulting in a person who in appearance is a woman but whose chromosome count is that of a male and whose genital system is a cross between male and female.

> Ruth, who has the appearance of a woman will never menstruate, will never be able to bear children, will never, without medical intervention, be able to have sexual relations, as she does not have a uterus or vagina.

8

At age 18, in 1975, she is admitted again to the hospital and undergoes a plastic surgery procedure to provide her with an artificial vagina made from a graft of skin from her thigh. She has been receiving hormonal therapy in the form of estrogen to promote breast development since age 14.

Ruth's life has been enhanced and the aberrations of nature have been balanced by enabling her to function as a woman.

Ruth explained all this to Salvatore in November of 1976. Not all of it actually, because Ruth herself was never made aware of the chromosomal imbalance, but she did explain to Salvatore that she had been born without a vagina and that this had been surgically corrected the previous year. Salvatore expressed his appreciation for Ruth's honesty in apprising him of her condition, and indicated that he wished to continue the relationship.

The relationship did continue and after some months the couple began to have intercourse, which both seemed to regard as satisfactory. They became engaged at Christmas time of 1977, with plans to marry in June, following Salvatore's graduation.

The wedding went off as planned and the couple seemed to get off to a reasonably good start. Salvatore took a position with a small manufacturing firm about ten miles from Upton and the couple found an attractive apartment.

Their sexual life, however, gradually deteriorated. Ruth did not find intercourse particularly enjoyable herself and was afraid that she was not satisfying Salvatore. Ruth continued to attend college and to see her old friends while Salvatore developed new friendships at work. Together they did a great deal of partying and entertaining, mostly with Ruth's friends. Much alcohol was consumed and much money was spent. Eventually both partners began to suspect infidelity on the part of the other. Salvatore wanted Ruth to quit school, partly to "liberate" her, as he saw it, from her immature companions, and partly so that she could go to work and help out with their rather considerable debts. They quarrelled more and more and had sex less and less. Beginning early in 1982 they slept in separate bedrooms. They separated finally in May.

The evidence in the case consists of the testimony of both principals and that of four witnesses, plus the report of Doctor Courlan already quoted.

The witnesses knew of Ruth's operation and corroborated most of the problems encountered by the couple during their four years together. The testimony, indeed, suggests that the Anhinga-Bocian marriage may have been null, perhaps on the ground of lack of due discretion or lack of due competence.

The evidence does not suggest, however, in light of our present jurisprudence, that this marriage was null on the grounds of Ruth's impotence.

WHEREFORE

9

CHAPON - AUTOUR

Aldous Chapon and Lily Autour, both Catholic, married at St. Mark's Church on May 18, 1942 in Blanc City, New Brunswick, Canada. Aldous was twenty years old at the time and Lily was nineteen.

Aldous grew up in a town about eighteen miles from Blanc City but in 1940, about a year and a half before the marriage, he went to Blanc City to take a course as a machinist and while doing so he boarded in the home of Lily's aunt. Lily and her mother lived upstairs from the aunt and Aldous and Lily soon found themselves attracted to each other.

Several people in Lily's family had mental disorders. Her father, who had died in the early thirties, had been an alcoholic and had walked out on the family. Two of her father's sisters had been mentally ill and two of his brothers, who also had been alcoholics, ended their lives by suicide. Several of Lily's siblings (she had two brothers and three sisters) also had mental problems and our one witness described the family as "kind of cuckoo."

Lily herself showed some evidence of moodiness, blandness and paranoia before the marriage but Aldous loved her and did not consider it important. After the marriage, however, the indications began to increase and after the birth of their second child in 1946, four years after marriage, Lily had a complete schizophrenic breakdown and has been hospitalized ever since.

On December 1, 1972, Aldous, who had never divorced Lily (the divorce was granted in Hartford in November 1972) and who has faithfully visited her every month over the years, petitioned this Court to declare the marriage null. The Reverend Thomas J. Lynch was appointed Guardian for the respondent; the petition was accepted and on January 27, 1973, the *Contestatio Litis* was conducted and it was agreed at that time that the grounds on which the case would be heard would be lack of due reason.

A. Description of Schizophrenia

Schizophrenic disorders are a group of disorders manifested by characteristic disturbances of thinking, mood and behavior, and involving at least one of the following: delusions, hallucinations, or formal thought disorder.

B. Characteristic Disturbances

The disturbances that are most often associated with the schizophrenic disorders are in the following areas:

1. *Content of thought.* These disturbances are delusions of various kinds, persecutory, delusions of references, delusions about one's thoughts either being inserted into the mind or broadcast to the outside world, etc.

2. *Form of thought.* In the schizophrenic person the form of thought is determined not by logical and relevant associations but by incidental ones like sound or alliteration. Consequently the association between one idea and the next is not obvious. This is called loosening of associations. It often involves vagueness, talking past the point, empty repetitions and use of stereotyped or obscure phrases, and perhaps even incoherence. Other disturbances in the form of thought, besides loosening of associations, include neologisms, perseveration and blocking.

3. *Perception.* These are hallucinations, most commonly auditory but occasionally visual, gustatory or olfactory.

4. *Affect.* This usually involves either a flattening of affect (a lack of emotional responsiveness) or inappropriate affect (an emotional expression that is incongruous to the situation).

5. *Sense of Self.* This involves a disturbance in one's seeking of individuality and uniqueness. It is sometimes referred to as a loss of ego boundaries.

6. *Volition.* This involves inadequate interest or drive, or an inability to complete a course of action. Severe ambivalence regarding two opposite courses of action may lead to near cessation of goal directed activity.

7. *Relationship to the external world.* The schizophrenic tends to become preoccupied with egocentric, illogical fantasies. Severe forms of this are called autism.

8. *Motor Behavior.* This may involve grimacing, mannerisms, waxy flexibility, posturing, stupor or rigidity.

C. A Jurisprudence

The jurisprudence regarding the effect of schizophrenia on one's capacity to enter marriage is succinctly summarized in the concluding paragraphs of the November 20, 1969 law section, coram Pinto (61, 1026-1027). Para-

11

graphs 3 (dealing with lack of due reason) and 4 (dealing with lack of due competence) of that law section read as follows:

3. In order to contract a valid marriage, that degree of mental discretion is required which is proportionate to the marriage covenant, that is to say, the discretion ordinarily possessed by a young person reaching the age of puberty (see St. Thomas, *Suppl.*, q. 58, art. 5, ad 1 and ad 4). This degree of discretion, however, can be lost through a mental disorder, including the disorder called paranoid schizophrenia [the case before Pinto involved this particular type of schizophrenia] when that disorder is proved to have been present at the time of marriage, because schizophrenia causes schizophrenic, unrealistic thinking which is resistant to correction and which constitutes a pervasive phenomenon that affects the entire personality. In such a case, the intellect is unable to distinguish truth from falsehood, at least in certain areas. Consequently, both the ability to understand and the ability to choose are disturbed, the former directly, the latter indirectly.

It is incorrect to regard this illness as "semi-insanity." For mental illness, in present-day terminology, signifies not semi-illness but total illness, illness, indeed, which entirely removes imputability. The term "semi-insanity" should be used only in regard to the psychopathic personality (see Ferrio, Psichiatria Forense, 1959, pp. 784-785).

Suffice it to list the following rotal citations, according to which schizophrenia proven to have existed at the time of marriage renders that marriage invalid because the due discretion proportionate to marriage and, therefore, the marital consent itself, are lacking (see Canon 1081, § 1):

Coram Felici, February 26, 1952
Coram Brennan, February 24, 1959
Coram Lefebvre, October 17, 1959
Coram Sabattani, March 24, 1961

4. According to our most recent jurisprudence, moreover, a marriage is also invalidly celebrated when a contractant is incapable of obliging himself to, or of fulfilling the essential responsibilities of marriage, even though he could in a sense give consent at the time, that is to say, even though he had not yet lost the faculty of understanding and choosing. See, for example, the following decisions:

Coram Heard, January 30, 1954, n. 7 (encephalitis)
Coram Sabattani, June 21, 1957, n 5 (nymphomania)
Coram Mattioli, November 28, 1957 (schizophrenia)
Coram Lefebvre, December 2, 1967, nn. 9-10 (homosexuality)

12

Roman law (*Dig.* 50, 17, 195) recognized the principle, "There is no obligation to do the impossible"; and that principle was received into the Decretals in the words, "No one is obliged to the impossible." (*Sexti Decret.*, lib. V, tit. 12, De regulis iuris, regula VI, *Corpus Iur. Can.*, Edit. Friedberg, T. II, c. 1122).

Thomas Sanchez (*De S. Matrimonii Sacramento*, Lib. VII, Disp. 98, n. 2), when speaking of sexual impotence, said: 'The essence of marriage consists in the perpetual binding of oneself to, and handing over of the right to conjugal intercourse. Since a thing cannot possibly exist apart from its essence, it is repugnant to the nature of marriage that both marriage and perpetual impotence co-exist, and, consequently, given the nature of marriage, the marriage of an impotent person would be invalid." The same would be true if, at the time of the celebration of the marriage, a contractant certainly suffered from a schizophrenic condition which was gradually progressing to the state of insanity, at which point the person would undoubtedly be incapable of fulfilling any obligation. In these circumstances, one cannot undertake a *perpetual* obligation since he would only be capable of fulfilling the marital obligations for a time (see J. R. Keating, *The bearing of mental impairment on the validity of marriage*, 1964, pp. 109-200).

It should be noted though that, if one is truly suffering from schizophrenia, even if he might apparently be giving consent, he is, nevertheless, not capable of giving true consent.

III
The Argument

There were several difficulties in the processing of this case: 1) The petitioner, who is a kind, tender man, tended to belittle the problem. After hearing his testimony, the Judge appended a note to the testimony which read:

> Mr. Chapon impressed all members of the Court as being extremely sincere and totally credible.

> It was clear that he was not particularly perceptive about his wife's problems or rather that he could not easily own up to her weaknesses. At the time he saw Lily as the perfect girl but on the other hand he knew that her siblings regarded her as a little strange, that Lily was only imagining that the girls at work were speaking critically of her, that she had a couple of blackouts before the marriage, that she had a sort of "lifeless" personality and that she was only comfortable in controlled circumstances.

> But the session was like pulling teeth and we were all left with the

impression that Mr. Chapon's account was, if anything, moderate, conservative and even minimizing.

2) There was really only one witness, Mildred LaPlante, whose only knowledge of Lily comes from about 1933 when Lily was ten or eleven years old, 3) The first really psychotic episode postdated the marriage by four years, and 4) No records were available from McKenzie Hosital where Lily was confined.

Nevertheless the Court is satisfied that the marriage has been proved null. For the following reasons:

Mildred LaPlante, who was a childhood friend of Lily's, perhaps the only friend Lily ever had, said that Lily was "very moody" and "very nervous and shy" and "even back in those days she could be called kooky."

There was a considerable amount of mental unbalance in Lily's family, both on the part of her father and his siblings and also on the part of Lily's own brothers and sisters. So the genetic components of schizophrenia were certainly present. So were the sociological components. Lily had a rough childhood. When her father was drinking he was mean to the children and they hid from him, under the bed and in closets; and once, gun in hand, he threatened to shoot them. Lily was only six or seven years old at the time and the traumatic impact of that kind of experience is not difficult to imagine. Shortly thereafter her father disappeared and then for a period of a year or two she was separated from her mother and brothers and sisters and lived with an uncle. It was, furthermore, depression time and, all in all, a brutal experience for Lily.

It was no wonder she became withdrawn and moody and nervous. She graduated from grammar school and went to work but she made no real friends and spent a great deal of time in church and before the mini altars in her room. She continued to save and cherish the pieces of a broken statue that her father had thrown at her more than ten years before. She didn't date or go to dances. Her affect tended to be flat and she stayed by herself most of the time or went to the movies with a girlfriend.

At work she showed some ideas of reference in that she imagined the other girls were making fun of the way she dressed, but in fact she dressed fine and the evidence indicates that the girls were *not* talking about her, that she only imagined it.

There were also a couple of occasions before marriage when Lily "felt dizzy and didn't quite know where she was." (Aldous, 30).

After marriage, Lily did fairly well for a while but she did have some paranoid feelings about the lady in the adjoining apartment and at Christmas time, 1942, about seven months after the wedding, she broke down and sobbed for ten or fifteen minutes after a couple of glasses of wine and no other provocation. As

14

Doctor Roger Martin, our expert, said, she was operating "on a thin edge." She became very upset and couldn't sleep over the thought of assuming the responsibility of buying land and building, and in 1946, after the birth of the second child, the complete and final breakdown came. Lily has been institutionalized since then, for all these twenty-seven years, usually communicating with reality not at all but occasionally in a fragmentary way.

On the basis of the evidence prior to and at the time of the wedding, our esteemed expert, Doctor Roger Martin, has stated that he is "as reasonably certain as one can be without having examined her at the time" that Lily was schizophrenic on May 18, 1942 and that she lacked the psychic capacity for marriage.

WHEREFORE

I
The Facts

Kathleen Elster and William Pollastro, both Catholic, were married in the Church of St. Peter, Baker, Connecticut in the Archdiocese of Hartford on the twelfth day of April 1954. At the time Kathleen was nineteen years old and William was twenty-four.

The couple lived together for about twelve years. One child, a son, was born to them. They separated finally in March of 1966 and a divorce was obtained in Hartford on April 12, 1967.

On March 8, 1979 Kathleen petitioned this Court to declare her marriage null. Her petition was accepted and on April 30, 1979, lack of due discretion was assigned as the grounds on which the validity of this marriage would be investigated and adjudged.

II
The Law

The law on lack of due discretion is well outlined in the decision coram Ferraro of November 28, 1978, as reported in *Monitor Ecclesiasticus*, 1979, volume 2, pp. 167-176. The following is a translation of an excerpt from the "In Iure" section.

> 5. The essence of marriage, insofar as it is a true and proper bilateral contract involving responsibilities, is composed of three distinct elements; (1) the object or matter about which the contract is concerned, (2) the persons contracting, (3) the legitimate consent given by the persons.

> Marriage, however, is a unique contract, partly because the persons involved are not only the subjects but the objects as well, for, in marriage, the contractants are not only contracting about a thing or an action but about their very selves, who are entering a community of life together.

> 6. This being the case, in order to reach a proper judgment about the validity of a nuptial contract, the contract should necessarily be viewed under the above mentioned triple aspect, namely on the part of the subject, on the part of the object and on the part of the consent.

As regards the object, besides the other conditions which ought to affect it in order that it be a suitable contract being entered here and now, it is required that the object be possible both physically and morally, because no one is obliged to the impossible, nor could one be so obliged. Indeed, this impossibility is understood in a very broad legal sense to constitute moral impossibility.

Consequently, without doubt, a marriage can be annulled on the part of the object if the contractants are judged incapable of marriage because they are either physically or psychologically unable to oblige themselves to assuming and fulfilling the rights and obligations of marriage.

7. As regards the subject, it is required that the contractants enjoy the juridic capacity to enter the marriage contract. In a decision of February 8, 1977 by the undersigned Commissioner handed down on a case from Pittsburgh, the following three sources of nullity were cited: (a) the natural law, (b) the general principles of law and (c) the two norms found in the Code of Canon Law. The first of these two norms requires that the contractants be ''persons capable by law'' (Canon 1081 § 1); the other norm says that ''any one can contract marriage who is not prohibited by law'' (Canon 1035). Consequently, those people who lack the use of reason are excluded from entering a contract by the *natural* law, while those who are unable or at least not firmly able to enter specific contracts are excluded by *positive* law.

8. And finally the third aspect, the consent, where discretion of judgment or maturity is necessary in order to understand and choose marriage.

Consequently, a marriage contract can labor under triple nullity: by reason of the object, insofar as the substance of the issue presents itself as physically, psychologically, or morally impossible; by reason of the subject, insofar as the contractants are not ''capable by law''; and by reason of the consent, insofar as discretion of judgment is lacking.

9. As everybody knows, there is no problem in transferring these three elements of a contract into matrimonial jurisprudence. For, even though the three elements are logically distinct from one another, nevertheless, they are all intimately joined in the person of the contractant, namely in the substantial composite of body and soul which we call the human person.

Perhaps it is because of this intimate joining of the three aspects in the one person that jurisprudence, following canonical legislation, has preferred to neglect this triple distinction. But the distinction cannot be neglected without serious consequences and even confusion, because some grounds of nullity are only clarified by seeing them in light of this distinction. The ground of insanity, for example, involves all sorts of disturbances and implications both psychic and psychological.

10. But whether the marriage is investigated from the point of view of the contract or from the point of view of the person (both as object and subject) or from the point of view of the consent, the marriage would always be regarded as invalid once it is clear that the contractant antecedently and perpetually lacked the capacity (a) of discerning his own psychic fitness for the marital covenant, and (b) of handing over to his partner the right to interpersonal relations. Because in the *former* case, the contractant would not enjoy the estimative power or the critical faculty which are entirely necessary in order to enter a marital contract. And in the *latter* case, the contractant would hand over only a half of the right to the body, namely insofar as it is destitute of the right to those interpersonal relationships without which the conjugal partnership cannot exist.

III
The Argument

Both the petitioner and the respondent testified in the proceedings; five witnesses were heard; and the report of the Court-appointed expert, Doctor Helen Linotte, also forms part of the acts.

After studying all the evidence I am satisfied that Kathleen Elster's lack of due discretion has been proved. More specifically it has been proved that 1) most of Kathleen's motivation in entering this marriage was subconscious, subtle and misunderstood by her, so her critical faculty was, as it were, suspended, or working on faulty data; and 2) the marriage was engineered and manipulated by Kathleen's extremely influential mother, so Kathleen was a sort of puppet, without true psychological freedom.

Kathleen's mother is described as good looking but unfriendly. At the time of Kathleen's marriage the mother was forty-nine years old. Kathleen's parents had not got along and they divorced the year after Kathleen married. Kathleen had an older sister who was retarded. This seemed to embitter the mother and shape her attitudes.

Mrs. Elster always resented Kathleen, for reasons that were never clear to Kathleen. The mother was unreasonably strict with Kathleen and hypercritical of her. Kathleen could do nothing right. Even when she did well in school, as she invariably did, the mother belittled her. After Kathleen went to college the mother discouraged her from dating college fellows, but when William Pollastro, who had only an eighth grade education, came along, the mother said, "You had better marry him because you have a sister who is retarded."

The dynamics of this thinking are subtle. Some of the speculation worked out with Doctor Linotte was that the mother *wanted* her daughter to enter a stupid marriage and so fail in life—the "I went through it (an unhappy marriage and the pain of a retarded child) and so can you" syndrome. Or maybe Kathleen had a need to fail and thus be like her retarded sister and so be pitied as she was. Or perhaps Kathleen needed not only to fail but to fail precisely by executing mother's orders, in order to prove the mother wrong.

At any rate, Mrs. Elster obviously promoted this mismatch. Mr. Elster and practically everyone else saw immediately that Kathleen and William had nothing at all in common, culturally, educationally or socially, and that a marriage between them would be folly; but Mrs. Elster, for whatever reasons, nourished the relationship, took the young people on vacation and saw to it that they married.

Meanwhile a strange relationship developed between the 49-year-old Mrs. Elster, and the 24-year-old William. There is no indication whatsoever that the relationship was ever genital. Doctor Linotte thinks that perhaps Mrs. Elster saw William as a kind of son. After marriage Kathleen and William lived with Mrs. Elster. Kathleen and William got along poorly and periodically Kathleen would want to leave but always Mrs. Elster kept them together. Kathleen and William had a poor sexual relationship. William, according to Kathleen, had been unfaithful both before and after marriage and he became abhorrent to her. Meanwhile William and Mrs. Elster went off on weekends together. One witness noted that "William seemed to prefer the company of his mother-in-law to other young couples." According to William he wanted to move out of Mrs. Elster's house and get off on their own but the mother insisted they stay on. At the end, according to Kathleen, she and the son left while William stayed on in Mrs. Elster's house. According to the Instructor, William still visits Mrs. Elster to do little chores for her.

Back in the '50s, when this marriage took place, retarded children were regarded with some embarrassment and were hidden from society. Doctor Linotte notes that that promoted denial within people and taught them to hide things. Not only did this dispose Kathleen to ignore the folly of marrying a man so totally unlike herself (now she looks back and says, "How could I have been so stupid?") but it also disposed her to describe her second husband, whom she knew to be an alcoholic before she married him and whom she was on the verge of divorcing at the time of the description, as "a fine, good moral man."

This woman is, obviously, blind in one psychological eye and can hardly see out of the other. Her insight is extremely limited. As Doctor Linotte said, "She is in the throes of something beyond her ability to understand and cope with." She has some kind of compulsive need (Doctor Linotte considers Kathleen to have an obsessive-compulsive character) to enter stupid marriages that are doomed. In respect to her marriage to William, Mrs. Elster insisted that she marry him. Kathleen herself became convinced that, as the sister of a retarded person, she would have to marry the first person who asked her. Now she realizes that she was "just like a puppy following its master." After marriage Kathleen and William separated a

19

"half dozen times" but mother always insisted they get back together. And all the while mother and William carried on what was at best a strange relationship.

This marriage made no sense; and everybody, save Kathleen and her mother, realized it made no sense. Occasionally even Kathleen caught a glimpse of how stupid it was. Once, during the engagement William attended a wedding and took out one of the bridesmaids, and Kathleen thought to herself, "Now is the time for me to break the engagement," but mother applied more pressure and in no time Kathleen replaced the lid and repressed the truth which was so obvious to everyone else. Kathleen did not permit herself to admit the obvious. Her critical faculty was almost totally inoperative, and her will had become slave to mother's orders.

WHEREFORE

```
┌─────────────────────┐
│          I          │
│      The Facts      │
└─────────────────────┘
```

George Brant and Margaret Adler, both Catholic and both twenty years old at the time, contracted marriage in the Church of St. Philip Neri, Medford, Connecticut in the Archdiocese of Hartford on the seventh day of June 1975.

The couple lived together for something less than two years, separating finally in March of 1977. George was always egocentric while Margaret tended to be jealous and hysterical. George treated Margaret like a servant, belittled and insulted her and, in their short marriage, became attached to two other women. No children were born of the marriage. On January 12, 1978 a divorce was granted to George in Hartford County on the grounds that the marriage had irretrievably broken down.

On February 21, 1979, George petitioned this Court to declare the marriage null. His petition was accepted on March 12, and on March 30 the Doubt was Formulated as follows:

> Whether the Brant-Adler marriage has been proved
> null on the grounds of lack of due discretion.

```
┌─────────────────────┐
│          II         │
│       The Law       │
└─────────────────────┘
```

The law applicable in this case is well summarized in the decision of February 4, 1974 coram Pinto as found in *Monitor Ecclesiasticus* 1975, I-II, pp. 106-115. The following are selected excerpts from the "In Iure" section of that decision.

> 2. Since marriage is effected by the consent of the parties who mutually hand over and receive the perpetual and exclusive right to conjugal acts (Canon 1081), that person invalidly contracts marriage who is incapable of giving marital consent of this kind. A man and woman give this consent when they express between them the intention of entering a permanent society involving the procreation of children, and when they hand over the necessary rights.

> 3. The person who is most obviously incapable of giving marital consent is the one who, at the time of marriage, actually lacks the use of reason, because, as St. Thomas said, "there can be no consent where the use of reason is lacking." . . .

4. But also incapable of giving marital consent is the person who, even though he enjoys the use of reason, nevertheless lacks that degree of discretion of judgment which is proportionate to the contracting of marriage.

In the Decretals of Gregory IX (Book IV, Title II) the discretion of judgment proportionate to contracting marriage was presumed to have been attained at puberty since once puberty was reached marriage was allowed. Later the Code of Canon Law required that the woman be fourteen and the man sixteen in order to enter marriage. The Code did not, however, say that once that minimum age was reached, due discretion was necessarily attained. Rather the reasons for requiring the minimum age were (1) to avoid the degeneration of the human race, (2) to foster public morality, (3) because of differences in local customs. (Gasparri, *De Matrimonio*, I, pp. 292, 293, note)

According to St. Thomas, "children under the age of puberty do not yet enjoy sufficient discretion of judgment to oblige themselves to a perpetual bond because they do not as yet have a developed will." (Suppl. q.43, a.2,c.) Thomas is therefore speaking of a defect not of the intellect but of the will.

Modern psychology has gone somewhat beyond St. Thomas, for it holds that a child below the age of puberty is incapable of a will act which involves the conscience deciding, choosing, and evaluating various options. At puberty one acquires a certain consciousness of one's own self and one's independence from the outside world. (A. Gemelli *La psicologia della eta evolutiva*, 1956, pp. 280-281) But Gemelli adds "I do not mean to say that the adolescent is already mature enough for a volitive act and that he can implement it . . . Often such a person will not be capable of that . . . It is not really proper to speak about the will until the human personality has obtained its full development." And H. Thomae said, "there are many reasons for believing that only a psychic structure which has already obtained puberty can truly make authentic decisions." (H. Thomae, *Der Hensch in der Entscheidung*, 1960, p. 226 in the Italian Version)

The decision to marry has, of course, an altogether special character, particularly because it involves entering into a state of life to which nature itself inclines us. St. Thomas said that "in those matters to which nature itself inclines us, one does not need the same power of reason as in other matters, and therefore one could sufficiently decide to enter marriage before one could enter into other sorts of contracts without a guardian." Gemelli, however, notes that "as far as sex is concerned, the awakening of the physiological function takes place in the girl between the ages of twelve and fourteen and the boy between the ages of fourteen and sixteen but the psychological factor only comes along later . . . it originally appears as pure desire or as need or infatuation or as loving and being loved, apart from the inclination to the sexual act. Among girls this occurs between the ages of fourteen and sixteen and among boys between the ages of fifteen and seventeen . . . But only later, when they become young men and women, do the two factors, namely the physiological and the psychological, come together." (A. Gemelli, p. 318)

Finally, even though it is to be hoped, when one decides to enter an interpersonal, perpetual and exclusive marital relationship with another person, that that decision was made in a tranquil way, with foresight and interior maturation and after suitable experience, nevertheless, this unfortunately is not usually the case. In a survey taken up by H. Thomae, out of one hundred and eight married people who were questioned, ten expressly denied that any decision at all preceded their marriage, and among the others, marriage, it seems, was entered more because of an impulsive reaction than because of a genuine decision. Among those surveyed, a truly mature decision had apparently been reached in only a very few cases.

Therefore, while the use of reason refers to the speculative cognition of the intellect, so that he who enjoys it is capable of understanding, at least substantially, what marriage is and what its essential properties are, the discretion of judgment proportionate to marriage refers instead to the methodical decision of the will, which necessarily supposes the weighing of motives and the practical judgment of the intellect about this marriage to be contracted here and now . . .

Sanchez noted that for a valid marriage mature advice and previous deliberation about all the circumstances which could occur in marriage are not required, but that a collating of all the subjective and objective motives both for and against marriage is sufficient. This collation is indeed required because, as Sanchez stated, the process by which the intellect compares something with its opposite leads to the possibility of the will either accepting or rejecting that thing and choosing the object that presents itself as good to the reasoning intellect. Consequently, where this collation is not present, simple and perfect freedom is lacking. One does not need a great deal of time to deliberate in this way, even if the judgment is being disturbed by some passion. Indeed, deliberation can even take place imperceptibly. "The self-determination of a person pursuing an intuitive comprehension of reality can make a perfectly voluntary and conscious choice, even if it does not appear as a rationally deliberate election." (R. Zavalloni *La Liberta personale,* 1965, p. 369) But a person is incapable of this intuitive comprehension when he cannot choose with reasonable deliberation, because "an intuitive comprehension offers an instant evaluation of the alternatives to that choice." (R. Zavalloni, p. 370)

Furthermore, although man has many different potencies, we must never forget "that it is the human person who acts as the unique activator of those different potencies. A free act is the most typical expression of the human person and it involves one's entire personality." (R. Zavalloni, p. 367)

When all of this is taken into consideration, one must conclude that an adolescent who is rendered incapable, by some psychic disturbance, of freely choosing marriage, by that very fact, lacks the due discretion for marriage. It is obvious that this is indirectly verified where one lacks the use of reason because, as St. Thomas said, the will is a *rational* appetite. But it can also occur as the result of a mental disorder. Neither the intellect nor the will can be directly affected by a disorder because they are spiritual faculties. But since the underlying structure can be ill, the operation of the spiritual faculties can consequently be seriously disturbed.

A will act can be disturbed:

(1) in the phase of the *presentation* of motives through a defect either of perception or memory which does not permit the person to perceive all the motivating factors that would be pertinent to the decision making process.

(2) In the phase of the *election*.

(a) through a defect of the instinct, which can be too strong or too weak and therefore qualitatively disturbed,

(b) through a defect of the critical faculty which does not permit a correct evaluation of all the motivating factors,

(c) through a defect of the affectivity which paints the motives in false colors and therefore distorts their quality and intensity.

III
The Argument

Besides the petitioner, four witnesses were heard in this case. All were family members of the petitioner: both parents and his brother and sister. Although this would seem to lack objectivity, the Court found the witnesses honest, oftentimes quite critical of George Brant, and substantially credible.

The Instructor, Father Robert Tucker, contacted the respondent, Margaret Adler, but could obtain no real information from her. Margaret was extremely emotional when talking with Father Tucker, wept during their brief conversations, made two appointments with him but failed to keep both of them. Margaret was urged to try to put something down on paper or suggest witnesses who could help but she likewise failed to do this.

It seems, therefore, that the Court has obtained all available information. That information does, however, convince us beyond prudent doubt that the Brant-Adler marriage was null because George Brant, at the time, lacked the due discretion necessary for marriage.

The following factors, attested to by the petitioner and witnesses, lead us to this conclusion:

1. *Motive* — George's motive for marrying was not really to commit himself to share his life with wife and children; it was rather to prove to his overly protective mother that he was no longer a child, that he was capable of the adult act of marriage, to "get back" at her for treating him like a child. It was an attempt to prove his independence from mother, but it was reactive and artificial, and in fact proved only that he was still embroiled in the emancipation struggle of adolescence. George's mother is Korean and, though a devout and good woman, perhaps she exacerbated the problem by a kind of oriental insistence on parental respect, to the point where the independence of children is discouraged.

2. *Guilt* — George Brant, as a handsome, big man on campus type, went through his teen years with a different girlfriend a month. He led an active sexual life, again, no doubt, to prove his manhood. During his courtship with Margaret Adler they had intercourse and Margaret became pregnant. An abortion was obtained but it left George feeling guilty and this gave Margaret a great deal of leverage in insisting that George marry. George owed her. She was Catholic and he had made it necessary for her to have an abortion so to make things right he would have to marry her.

3. *Pressure* — On several occasions Margaret threatened to commit suicide if George did not marry her. On at least one occasion she put this in a letter, a letter that was later seen by two of the witnesses. Obviously this kind of pressure made it very difficult for George Brant to assess or evaluate marriage and the decision to marry with suitable objectivity.

4. *Partner* — George's choice of Margaret Adler as a lifelong marriage partner is indicative of the high level of immaturity involved in the decisionary process. It is clear that George saw Margaret not really as a marriage partner but as a sex partner—and this was true both before and after the marriage. Margaret Adler was a highly emotional, suicidal, hysterical woman, but it was almost as though her personality, especially the negative aspects of her personality, was not considered an important factor in the decision to marry—a clear indication that George's discretion was operating at an extremely low level.

5. *Reluctance* — George was a half hour late for the marriage ceremony. He had been delayed in a traffic jam and commented that he wished he had been delayed longer. He did not really love Margaret and was reluctant to marry her.

6. *Goals* — According to George himself, Margaret "wanted a long homey marriage with lots of kids but I did not because I did not want to be with her. I wanted to fool around while married and I told her that it would be good if we had sex with others to strengthen our own marriage." In short, George's understanding of marriage was not at all the Christian understanding of marriage.

7. *Immaturity* — The witnesses describe George Brant as egocentric, cocky, impulsive, flighty and stubborn. He was an impulsive buyer, purchasing one car after another, sporting equipment, clothes and eventually a house, though the house was not something he wanted at all but rather Margaret's dream. George spent long hours away from Margaret. He was employed as a golf professional, spent many evening hours teaching, and would often go off on fishing and hunting trips alone, or without Margaret. Generally he treated Margaret like a servant. He belittled and insulted her and became involved with two other women. The first woman was older and this was not a sexual relationship but nevertheless a relationship that caused Margaret to be justifiably jealous. Our expert, Doctor Edward Eider, regards the twenty year old George Brant as narcissistic and a "perpetual adolescent," at the macho stage of interpersonal relationships, running away from parental authority and trying to prove that he's not somebody's little boy.

8. *Brevity* — The marriage lasted less than two years. At the very end George visited with a counsellor but only to tell the counsellor that he intended to get a divorce. George felt he never should have entered the marriage in the first place and he was not interested in putting any more effort into it.

All of these factors, taken together, prove to this Court that the marriage of George and Margaret was null because George did not seriously project and assess what marriage to Margaret would mean, and then freely choose to embrace that state—that is to say, he lacked the due discretion for marriage.

WHEREFORE

I
The Facts

Maria Columba and Thomas Bittern were married on April 23, 1945 at the Cathedral in Livorno, Italy. At the time Maria was twenty-one years old and Catholic; Thomas was twenty-four years old and non-Catholic.

About five weeks later, Thomas, who was in the U.S. Army and who had been stationed in the Livorno area, was transferred to Naples in preparation for returning home at the end of the war. In August he shipped from Naples to the States.

Efforts were made by Thomas to bring Maria to this country but problems were encountered, and after some months he met and became involved with another woman. Early in 1946 Thomas wrote to Maria telling her the marriage was over.

On June 20, 1983 Maria petitioned this Court to declare the marriage null. Her petition was accepted, and on August 14, 1983 the *Contestatio Litis* was conducted, assigning Maria's lack of due discretion as the ground on which the validity of the marriage would be investigated and adjudged.

II
The Law

A. The Pertinent Canon

C 1095 - They are incapable of contracting marriage 2° who labor under a serious defect of judgmental discretion concerning the essential matrimonial rights and duties which are to be mutually handed over and accepted.

B. The Meaning of Lack of Due Discretion

1. Lack of due discretion is distinguished from ignorance (error of action) in that ignorance refers to an absence of *knowledge* whereas lack of due discretion refers to an absence, at least a temporary absence, of *maturity*.

2. Lack of due discretion is distinguished from lack of due reason in that lack of due reason refers to an absence of sufficient *reason* whereas lack of due discretion refers to an absence of *maturity*.

3. Lack of due discretion is distinguished from lack of due competence (marital incompetence) in that incompetence refers primarily to an inability to assume and fulfill the obligations and responsibilities of marriage (matrimonium in facto esse) whereas lack of due discretion refers primarily to an inability to give consent (matrimonium in fieri).

4. Stated positively, lack of due discretion is well described by Sabattani in his decision of February 24, 1961 (53, 118):

> The doctrine on discretionary judgment . . . can be summed up in these words of Jullien, 'since marriage is a very serious contract which is not only future oriented but actually indissoluble, in order to enter it validly a greater degree of discretion is required than would be necessary to consent to some action which only concerned the present, as, for example, the amount of discretion required to commit a mortal sin' (27, 79).

> Indeed, since marriage is 'a covenant filled with responsibilities in which the gift of one's whole life and being is pledged' (as Wynen said, 35, 171) then clearly 'greater freedom and deliberation is required for marriage than for other contracts' (from a decision of Grazioli 18, 111).

> And let it be remembered that a mere *cognoscitive* faculty, which consists in the simple mental apprehension of something, is not sufficient but that there is further required a *critical* faculty, which is the ability to judge and reason and so order one's judgments that new judgments can be deduced from them (see the December 3, 1957 decision of Felici and Lamas' sentence of October 21, 1959).

> A marriage, in short, is only valid when a person, using that critical faculty, can deliberately form judgments with his mind and freely choose actions with his will.

In order to consent to a valid marriage, in other words, the decision should be informed with a certain fundamental prudence. It should include, therefore, such qualities as good advice (eubulia), insight (synesis), a sense of the situation (gnome), deliberation, foresight, circumspection, appreciation, sound judgment and clear reasoning that enables the person to draw rational inferences from his insights and experiences.

More specifically, a person must be able to make at least a rudimentary assessment of the capacities of himself and his spouse, and to decide freely that he wishes to establish a perpetual and exclusive community of life with this person, a community that will involve a lifetime of fundamentally faithful caring and sharing.

C. Giving Consent vs. Expressing Consent

At the time of the marriage ceremony the parties *express* their consent. Presumably they *gave* their consent, i.e., actually consented to marry some time prior to that. At the time of the ceremony, besides expressing their consent, they may but need not actually renew their consent. It suffices if their consent previously given virtually perdures and is expressed at the time of the ceremony.

In order merely to express consent already given one does not need due discretion or a critical faculty or prudence. It suffices if he can simply place a human act. It would, therefore, be very difficult to prove a marriage null simply because one of the parties was, for example, drunk at the time of the ceremony. Because at the time of the ceremony one does not have to place a *prudent* act (consenting) but simply a *human* act (expressing consent).

When, therefore, a Court investigates the matter of due discretion, the investigation does not confine itself to the moment of the ceremony but rather concerns itself with the whole period of time during which the person decided to and consented to marry.

D. Proof of Lack of Due Discretion

Depending on the nature of the problem, various proofs are helpful in demonstrating lack of due discretion. If a mental disorder is involved then medical records will, of course, be pertinent. If, on the other hand, the problem is more a matter of being temporarily disturbed, then the Court must usually depend principally on the data provided by the declarations of the parties and the testimony of witnesses together with the observations of a psychiatric expert.

```
         III
   The Argument
```

In my judgment the evidence available in this case sufficiently demonstrates that Maria Columba lacked the due discretion for her marriage to Thomas Bittern.

This evidence, in brief, consists of 1) the testimony of the petitioner and respondent, 2) that of two witnesses: Clara Modugno (an Italian war bride) and Giuseppe Rutigliano (a friend of Maria's from her days in Italy), 3) a psychological report from Doctor Cohen, and 4) the observations of the Court Expert, Doctor Edward Eider.

The evidence may be viewed under the following headings: 1) Social Circumstances, 2) Family Circumstances, 3) Maria's Personality Makeup, 4) Maria's

Motive in Marrying, 5) The Relationship Between Maria and Thomas, and 6) Observations of the Expert.

1) *Social Circumstances* — This marriage took place in a combat zone and in a war torn country in the closing days of World War II. The people had endured several years of hunger and hardship of various kinds, and in recent months the area had been under heavy bombardment. American soldiers were lonely but appeared as liberators and redeemers to many of the Italian people. People lived on the edge of death, and the sentiment prevailed that one should find one's happiness today because no one knew what tomorrow would bring. The grimness of war was in some sense offset and made bearable by an unrealistic spirit of romanticism. They were not the best of circumstances in which to make a sound, well reasoned commitment to a lifelong marriage. Many decisions to marry in those days were seen later to be not much more than capricious and whimsical, perhaps even blind. Young women were dismayed to find out after the war that the handsome, bemedaled, fun loving, fighting hero they had married was, in fact, a brutal husband. Men discovered that their pretty foreign brides with the cute accent, with whom they had fallen in love at first sight, were, in fact, selfish and calculating. In short, when it came to choosing marriage, the conditions of that place and time, Italy in the spring of 1945, tended to promote a low level of discretion. They were confusing times. Many people found it difficult to remember what life was like before the war, and even more difficult to project what it would be like afterwards. As a result it was not uncommon even for fairly mature people to make ill advised, ill informed, ill considered marital decisions.

2) *Family Circumstances* — Maria was the only girl in a family of four. She had an older, a twin, and a younger brother. Both parents were protective and domineering. Her father and older brother, before they died, were forever checking on Maria to make sure she wasn't becoming involved with boys. As a result of this domination and control Maria was particularly immature for her years and sheltered. Her father died in the early years of the war. Her twin brother was killed in action in 1942 or 1943; and her older brother was severely wounded and a prisoner of war at the time Maria married. He died shortly thereafter. Maria's younger brother was a seminarian. Staying at home, therefore, meant, for Maria, remaining alone with her somewhat domineering mother. The family had suffered tragically from the war. The house was empty and sad. The prospects of remaining there were depressing.

3) *Maria's Personality Makeup* — The Instructor describes Maria as emotional, good hearted, simple, naive, frightened and timid. She now holds a responsible position with the Evergreen Insurance Company but the naivete is still in evidence, and Doctor Cohen, who evaluated Maria on the basis of a standard battery of psychological tests, noted that passivity, compliance and immaturity were all reflected in Maria's background history. In Doctor Cohen's opinion Maria was unprepared for marriage in 1945 and had little awareness of the consequences of it. Maria herself described herself as the equivalent of a fifteen year old when it came to maturity, and Clara Modugno was likewise of the opinion that Maria was

unprepared for marriage. Maria had never dated before. Thomas was the first boy ever to touch her hand. Maria was therefore ill equipped to distinguish love from infatuation.

4) *Maria's Motive in Marrying* — Maria says that at the time of the marriage there was bombing all around and she was confused. She had endured four years of war and hunger, according to Clara Modugno, and it is only reasonable that a large part of Maria's motive in marrying was to escape all the devastation and horror of war that had decimated her own family. It may also be that Maria at that time could not bear the thought of being left alone with her mother. And still another possible factor in Maria's decision to marry was that she had been introduced to Thomas by her young brother who was a seminarian. Maria was an extremely devout girl and to her a match made by a seminarian may have seemed at the time like one made by God. Basically, at any rate, Maria's motivation seems to have been largely, and perhaps understandably, escapist.

5) *The Relationship Between Maria and Thomas* — What suggests more than anything else that Maria was making a marital decision that was radically unsound and lacking fundamental discretion was her relationship with Thomas. They had known each other only four months and had virtually nothing in common. They were of different religions. They were never alone during the entire courtship and the language barrier was serious. Thomas spoke practically no Italian and Maria practically no English. By any reasonable, objective standard there was no way these two people could evaluate and assess their partners and their prospects for marriage together. But this did not seem to bother Maria. At least it did not dissuade her. She did have a vague impression that Thomas was moody, childish and giddy but again this objectively critical factor was discounted by Maria. A sure sign that her discretionary powers were not at work. Following the marriage two points are of interest: first that Maria does not remember whether the marriage was consummated (suggesting that she had a tenuous grasp on reality at the time), and secondly that, in the time they had together, Maria never once asked Thomas a personal question (suggesting that she could not have freely and deliberately decided to enter a lifelong, personal relationship with this man). Any prudent observer would have counselled against this marriage. Everything about it was wrong. Maria entered it because she did not, at the time, enjoy the ability to make a prudent, critical judgment.

6) *Observations of the Expert* — The Court-appointed expert, Doctor Edward Eider, is of the opinion that Maria probably understood intellectually what marriage involved but was unable to apply that intellectual understanding to her own situation. In our terms this means that Maria was perhaps exercising the cognoscitive but not the critical faculty. Doctor Eider, furthermore, is of the opinion that Maria was not so much choosing to marry as she was choosing to escape. He considers it virtually impossible, given the language barrier and circumstances of the time, that Maria could possibly have evaluated realistically the prospects of this marriage, because she could not possibly have known what kind of man Thomas Bittern was. She was, in short, rushing in where angels fear to tread.

It was, in other words, a foolish decision.

Given all of this evidence, the undersigned Judge has concluded that the marriage in question is null because Maria at the time lacked the degree of discretion required for valid marital consent.

WHEREFORE

I
The Facts

Daphne Crake, Catholic, and Herman Jay, Lutheran, were married at the Church of St. Charles, Auburn, Connecticut, in the Archdiocese of Hartford on the fourteenth day of May, 1973. Daphne was eighteen years old at the time; Herman was twenty.

Daphne and Herman lived together for about six and a half years and had two children, born in 1975 and 1978. Herman, however, had been unfaithful to Daphne at least as early as 1975 and, in January of 1980, he left her for another woman. A divorce was granted in Auburn on November 18, 1981.

On March 25, 1982, Daphne petitioned this Court to declare the marriage null. Her petition was accepted and at the Contestatio Litis conducted on April 21, 1982 the Judge assigned Daphne's own lack of due discretion as the grounds on which the validity of the marriage would be investigated and adjudged.

II
The Law

The law on lack of due discretion is neatly summarized in the decision coram Pinto of December 18, 1979 (see *Monitor Ecclesiasticus,* 1980, IV, pp. 375-376), of which the following is a brief excerpt:

> 3. A marriage celebrated by a person who is insane is, by the natural law itself, invalid because of a defect of consent (Canon 1982). A person is called "insane" when, having completed his seventh year, he either habitually or actually lacks the use of reason, either because of an illness or from some other cause (Canon 88, para. 3 and Canon 1089, para. 3). Such a person is incapable of a human act. In the Code of Canon Law those people who, even though they enjoy the use of reason and can, therefore, place a human act, nevertheless lack the discretion or maturity of judgment proportionate to the marital contract, fall under this same ground of nullity. According to Canon 1082, the knowledge that is necessary for marital consent is only presumed after puberty. But, since in marriage one undertakes obligations which constitute a perpetual state of life, the discretion of judgment that is proportionate to marriage demands the capacity firstly of understanding the essential obligations of marriage, at least in substance, and secondly of freely choosing to assume those obligations. As regards the capacity of *understanding,* a speculative or

abstract understanding is not enough; one must also have a practical understanding, which presupposes experience in living, about the particular marriage that is to be celebrated, with this person, in these circumstances, with some understanding of the particular difficulties both present and future, at least insofar as they can be foreseen, and with a sense of the responsibility and seriousness of the obligations that are being undertaken. As regards the capacity of *freely choosing* marriage, it is required that the decision to enter marriage be based on reasonable motives after sufficient deliberation and not on pathological motives, and it is also required that the will be able to order the decision into execution. See St. Thomas I - II, Q. 9, a. 1 et 2; Q. 13, a. 6; Q. 14, a. 1 et 3; Suppl. Q. 43, a. 2 et Q. 58, a. 5.

4. According to the Code (which maintained the discipline of the Decretals) the discretion of judgment proportionate to marriage *is presumed* after puberty (cf. Cardinal Gaspari, *De Matrimonio* I, 1932, p. 292, Nota I et II, n. 783). The schema on marriage in the new Code does not change the impediment of nonage, but the consultors wisely noted that this impediment only refers to biological maturity *(Communicationes,* 1977, p. 360). Psychological maturity comes later.

III
The Argument

The respondent, Herman Jay, has always been extremely anti-Catholic, and was not willing to cooperate in these proceedings. Absent his testimony, the evidence in the case consists of 1) the testimony of the petitioner, 2) the testimony of four witnesses, 3) a February 1980 report from Eric Ludlow, M.D. of McKenzie Hospital where Daphne sought therapy and 4) a report from Roger Martin, M.D., the Court-appointed psychiatric expert.

The evidence in the case may be summarized as follows:

1. Daphne's Family Background
Daphne always hated her father. She was also afraid of him. He was an alcoholic who had had several extramarital affairs that were known to Daphne. Daphne remembers hiding in the closet when she was little to protect herself against her father. She once threatened to kill him and was apparently always afraid that he would attack her. It is not clear whether this feared attack would involve sexual molestation but Daphne always kept a rock in bed with her so that she could hit her father should he come after her.

The mother often threatened to leave the father but instead she stayed on and worked outside the home to make ends meet. Since the mother went to work so early in the morning, the parents were unable to take care of Daphne, their only child, and, as a result, Daphne lived with her grandparents during the week and was only at home on weekends and holidays—which she hated because her father was always drunk.

Daphne, therefore, had her models. A man was mean, unfaithful and alcoholic; a woman was tolerant, long-suffering and depressed and was sometimes forced to neglect her children.

2. Daphne's Personality

Daphne was overweight, obese really, unpopular, lonely, immature, pathetic and extremely self-conscious. She remembers that in her high school yearbook she was never mentioned except for her picture. That made her feel bad, she said, because it was like being there for four years without anyone knowing it. She was so lonely that, as a teenager, she wrote herself a note once reminding herself that really *everyone* was alone. She used to take great consolation from that letter and, in moments of special depression, would take it out and reread it. She was so self-conscious that she absolutely hated to get dressed up. She carried this to such an extreme that, even though she was a religious girl, she would not attend Mass on Sunday because she did not like people looking at her. Instead she would attend a Monday night novena. She was a sad, lonely, pathetic young girl.

3. Daphne's Dating History and the Courtship

Daphne is described as immature and naive. She tells us that she never thought about sex and was afraid of boys. She had never dated a boy before Herman Jay.

Daphne and Herman met at a teen hangout in October of 1972. Herman was good looking and Daphne was thrilled that some man had finally shown her some attention. But Daphne was also afraid of Herman and, on first meeting him, gave him a false name and told him her father was a policeman. After knowing each other for three months they started having sex and became engaged. They married on May 14, 1973, after knowing each other for only seven months. It was a whirlwind affair that swept the attention-starved Daphne off her feet, giving her little time or space for reflection and deliberation about the important step she was taking.

4. Daphne's Choice of Partner

In her bewildered state, Daphne never came to realize or appreciate what kind of person Herman Jay really was. When she met him he was living on his own. He had, for some time, been in violent conflict with his father and when his mother had some sort of breakdown prior to the meeting of Herman and Daphne, Herman moved out of his parental home. Herman always treated his mother harshly. He was hostile to her and abusive and seemed to have no respect for her. He treated other women similarly and, largely because of this attitude, Daphne's family was opposed to her marrying him. Herman was also extremely hostile toward the Catholic Church and resisted being married in the Catholic Church. He signed the promises that were required at the time but apparently did so dishonestly. He later insisted that the children be baptized as Lutheran. He was also insistent that there be no ceremony in a church proper, so a small wedding ceremony was held in the rectory.

During the marriage Herman's disrespect for women was very apparent. He treated Daphne as though he had purchased her and owned her and he carried on a long-term extramarital affair during most of the marriage. He was rarely home after July of 1975 when the first child was born.

He also appeared to be cantankerous at work, going from one job to another every year or so, not to better himself necessarily but because he was never happy where he was.

5. *The Reports*
It is clear that, during the marriage, Daphne was very passive and tolerant of Herman's behavior. She complained very little and simply went along. It no doubt seemed to her that this is the way things were supposed to be: the man was supposed to be mean and unfaithful; the woman was supposed to accept everything. In *Doctor Ludlow's* report, it is noted that when Herman "left his own home he wanted to be very much the boss and she was very willing to allow this to be." At the time Daphne was counselling with Doctor Ludlow she needed her husband back, expressed no anger towards him, would accept him back on any terms, had "an almost child-to-parent relationship with him" and was concerned how she would cope without him. She was seen by Doctor Ludlow as a "very child-like, immature, passive-dependent type of person."

Doctor Martin, in his report, noted that the marriage was "ill-fated." Both people were insecure and tried to make security out of their union. Both parties, however, had poor relationships with their parents and poor role models, and both parties are probably neurotic. Even if they had availed themselves of counselling, Doctor Martin notes, the marriage could never have worked. The marriage could only have worked, says our expert, if both parties had been "made over."

Given all this evidence, the undersigned Judge regards it as proved that Daphne Crake lacked the due discretion for this marriage. She did not appreciate the fact that marriage is a "consortium," a partnership between two adults. She did not appreciate who she was or who Herman was or what a marital-type relationship between them would involve. Marriage for Daphne was an escape from an unhappy home and a father she feared (she kept her "protecting rock" throughout the first year of marriage) and it was also a kind of redemption from loneliness and from being a nobody, which is all she had ever known before meeting Herman. But she did not really *understand* with any reasonable degree of maturity what marriage really is, and she was so passive-dependent to begin with and so thoroughly off-balance by the whirlwind courtship that she was not psychologically *free* to make a genuine choice of marriage.

WHEREFORE

```
        I
    The Facts
```

Gwen Roitelet and Romeo Scricciolo, both Catholic, were married at the Church of St. Jerome, Fulton, Connecticut in the Archdiocese of Hartford, on the third day of June, 1954. Gwen had just turned sixteen that day; Romeo was eighteen.

Gwen and Romeo lived together for about four years but Romeo was unfaithful, violent and irresponsible. Two children were born of the marriage. The final separation occured in April of 1958. A divorce was granted in Fulton on June 3, 1963.

On August 3, 1982, Gwen petitioned this Tribunal to declare the marriage null. Her petition was accepted and the Issue in Pleading was, on September 4, 1982, declared to be the demonstrated invalidity of the Roitelet-Scricciolo marriage on the grounds of the petitioner's lack of due discretion.

```
        II
     The Law
```

1. Over the years, authors have taken three different positions regarding the degree of maturity required to enter a valid marriage. The most basic position is that if a person enjoys the use of reason and can place a human act, that person is capable of consenting to marriage (The Mortal Sin Norm). A second position required that the person reach the ordinary judgmental maturity of a young person arriving at puberty (The Puberty Norm). The third and most recent opinion is that, in order for one to be able to consent to marriage, one must enjoy a maturity of judgment that is due or proportionate to marriage (The Due Discretion Norm).

2. *The Mortal Sin Norm.* This is the view generally attributed to Thomas Sanchez (d. 1610). Some authors maintain that Sanchez himself did not actually endorse this norm, and that may be true. His words are ambiguous enough to warrant the conclusion *either* that he was only talking about the degree of understanding required for betrothal, not for marriage, *or* that he was only talking about the degree of deliberation (i.e. mere conceptual knowledge) required for marriage, not the degree of understanding (i.e. evaluative knowledge). But whether or not Sanchez himself championed this position, the fact is that some authors of note did, and that, historically, the Mortal Sin Norm was considered by some a legitimate jurisprudence.

3. *The Puberty Norm.* Thomas Aquinas (d. 1274) held that a person can sin

mortally before he can bind himself to something in the future. According to Thomas, it is not until the end of the second septennium that one can bind oneself to marriage. This, in general, was the norm that prevailed until fairly recent times.

4. *The Due Discretion Norm.* Cardinal Gasparri, in his 1904 edition of *De Matrimonio* (n. 881) spoke of a "defect of due discretion." For Gasparri, this norm did not, in fact, differ all that much from the age of puberty (Keating is of the opinion that he did not adequately distinguish due *discretion* from due *knowledge* - p. 152) but Gasparri did want in the contractant a "maturity of judgment proportionate to the contract" and he demanded that the contractant have a sufficient understanding of the properties of marriage. In a decision of August 28, 1911, Sincero quoted Gasparri and endorsed his position (3, 450). Monsignor Prior did the same in his decision of November 14, 1919 (11, 173) and gave as his reason the fact that marriage is a perpetual and irrescindible contract that binds the person to very serious obligations.

5. In the days of Gasparri, Sincero and Prior, marriage was seen as a contract by which the man and woman exchanged the right to those acts which are per se apt for the generation of offspring. In our own time, however, marriage is seen as a covenant by which a man and woman constitute a lifelong partnership (C. 1055) and by which they have the right to all those things which belong to a conjugal partnership (C. 1135). It is generally agreed (*Communicationes*, 1977, 2, p. 375) that that includes the right to an interpersonal relationship.

6. In our time, in other words, marriage is seen as essentially interpersonalist. Therefore, in order to enjoy the degree of discretion that is *proportionate to that covenant,* the parties, within the context of their own culture, must have a basic appreciation of the strengths and weaknesses of themselves and their partners; they must have made at least a rudimentary evaluation of what a marriage partnership between these two people will entail and what efforts will be required to sustain that partnership; they must be open to parenthood and its challenges and responsibilities; and they must be prompted to marry by healthy and reasonable motives, of which they have some fundamental awareness, rather than by pathological needs.

7. This is not to say, of course, that the decision to marry, in order to be valid, must be infallible, or even that it must be correct. Not every *erroneous* judgment is an *indiscrete* judgment. A woman, for example, might marry a sociopath. Shortly after marriage she realizes that she made an erroneous judgment. At the same time, however, she may well have exercised due discretion by dating the man for a reasonable period, observing him under various circumstances, obtaining appraisals from other people, etc. It is possible, in other words, that her entire assessment of the data was quite prudent. Prudent but inaccurate, because the sociopath had deceived her by supplying false data. Such a marriage might be invalid because of the man's lack of due competence but not because of the woman's lack of due discretion.

8. It *is* required, however, for a valid marriage that the parties enjoy 1) the degree

38

of judgmental maturity proportionate to entering this specific lifelong, inter-personal, intimate, heterosexual, caring partnership; and 2) the free exercise of that matured, judgmental faculty. See, for example, number 3 of the decision of December 18, 1979, coram Pinto as found in Crake-Jay, D2, pp. 33-34.

9. To sum up, therefore, it should be noted that the essence of marriage has, over the past twenty years, been redefined. Marriage used to be viewed basically as a contract involving corporal rights; it is now viewed as a covenant involving both corporal and personalist elements. Marriage, therefore, is now a more complex entity, and therefore, the discretion that is due or proportionate to that entity is also more complex.

10. It is in this light that C 1095 2° is to be read:
C. 1095 - They are incapable of contracting marriage 2° who labor under a serious defect of judgmental discretion concerning the essential matrimonial rights and duties which are to be mutually handed over and accepted.

11. Oftentimes, of course, a person lacks both due competence and due discretion. In such cases, our Tribunal customarily selects the ground on the basis of the particular circumstances. It may happen, for example, that the woman in a case is diagnosed by the expert as suffering from a Narcissistic Personality Disorder. If the woman was twenty-five years old at the time of the marriage and was married after a two year courtship, the Court will be inclined to judge the case on the grounds of lack of due *competence*. If, however, the woman was sixteen and pregnant and married after a five month courtship, the Court will be inclined to judge the case on the ground of lack of due *discretion*.

III
The Argument

The respondent, Romeo Scricciolo, did not respond to letters from the Tribunal but the facts have been clearly established by the testimony of the petitioner and four witnesses (the petitioner's grandmother, parents, and sister) and the Tribunal also consulted a psychiatric expert, Helen Linotte, M.D., who issued a report.

The evidence, which clearly demonstrates Gwen's lack of due discretion at the time of marriage, may be summarized as follows:

1. *Gwen's Age*. Gwen married on her sixteenth birthday. She had never dated anyone but Romeo and, as one witness said, she "thought puppy love was the marriage kind." Both her father and her Aunt Mina (who had reared her for several years) tried to dissuade her from marrying but to no avail. She was just a little girl on her wedding day and she remembers feeling kind of sad and crying as she drove off on her brief honeymoon.

39

2. *Gwen's Family Background.* Gwen's parents divorced when Gwen was three or four years old. The mother was an alcoholic and the father received custody of the children. While the father worked, he hired a baby sitter but the sitter was cruel to the children. She tied their hands and put mittens on them so that they wouldn't bite their fingernails. She blindfolded them while she fed them and the children were undernourished and suffering from rickets. She threatened them with a butcher knife and the children were petrified of her. When the father realized what was going on, the children were first given into the care of their grandmother for a short time, and then, for several years, their Aunt Mina took care of them. The mother, meanwhile, remarried a certain Roger Maxwell and when Gwen was twelve years old she went to live with her mother and stepfather. The mother, however, was at the height of her alcoholism at that time and life remained very unpleasant for Gwen.

3. *The Courtship.* At fourteen years of age Gwen began dating Romeo Scricciolo. She was lonely and starved for affection and she became infatuated with Romeo. He hit her several times and constantly pressured her to have sex with him but Gwen had been told that nice girls don't do that and she managed to put him off.

4. *Gwen's Personality.* Gwen was a totally unrealistic dreamer at age fifteen (dreaming was probably her only defense against the cruelty of the real world). Despite the fact that Romeo struck her several times and despite the fact that she knew he was always behind paying for his room at the boarding house where he lived, Gwen persisted in convincing herself that, after the marriage, Romeo would be a wonderful husband who would care for her and protect her for the rest of her life.

5. *Gwen's Choice of Mate.* As it turned out, Romeo was a violent man who often beat Gwen during the four years of marriage. He was unfaithful to Gwen and rarely wanted sex with her. He ignored the children and was financially irresponsible to the point where the utilities were turned off and there was no food in the house and foreclosure on the house was threatened. Our expert, Doctor Linotte, is certain that he suffered from some severe emotional disorder, probably sociopathy. There were evidences of all this prior to marriage but Gwen's perception of Romeo was blocked or severely blurred and she was unable to see this.

6. *Pressure on Gwen to Marry.* Besides the fact that Romeo slapped Gwen during the courtship, he would also threaten to commit suicide should Gwen ever suggest that they should break off the relationship. He would tell Gwen that he couldn't live without her and would kill himself if she left him. This obviously put a great deal of pressure on this fifteen-year-old girl.

7. *Gwen's Motive in Marrying.* Gwen's subconscious reason for marrying Romeo was, no doubt, to escape from the very unhappy surroundings in which she lived. Her mother was drunk a good part of the time and often "blacking out," and Gwen could not stand her stepfather, Roger Maxwell. He disgusted her by his eating habits and so Gwen ate apart from the rest of the family. Also, Gwen, in

effect, was the housekeeper for the family. She did the cooking, cleaning, washing and ironing, and she felt put upon. When she approached her mother about marrying Romeo, that was fine with the mother who was probably too preoccupied with her own problems to remind her fifteen-year-old daughter that she was too young to marry.

8. *The Opinion of the Expert.* Our psychiatric consult, Doctor Linotte, has observed that Gwen was emotionally impoverished in terms of her own needs being met throughout childhood and she unrealistically believed that Romeo held out some hope for the meeting of those needs. Gwen did not, in Doctor Linotte's judgment, enjoy the kind of maturity of judgment that would be necessary to opt, with any degree of genuine insight, for a lifelong partnership with Romeo Scricciolo, whose true character she was incapable of reading.

Given this constellation of evidence, I am satisfied that it has been proved that Gwen Roitelet entered this marriage lacking even the minimal degree of judgmental maturity and internal freedom required by our jurisprudence for a valid consent to marriage with its duties and responsibilities. I am, in other words, satisfied that the allegation of Gwen's lack of due discretion has indeed been proved.

WHEREFORE

I

The Facts

Rosemarie Golab and Lawrence Gans, both baptized Catholics, were married at St. Ignatius Church, Uniontown, Connecticut in the Diocese of Norwich on October 12, 1963. At the time Rosemarie was seventeen years old, and Lawrence was twenty-three.

Rosemarie had known Lawrence only a matter of months before the marriage. Her mother had been in and out of mental institutions all her life, and, as a result, Rosemarie had not received a great deal of supervision, nor any sex education. She had sex with Lawrence without realizing that it might result in pregnancy. She missed her menstrual period and had morning sickness but still it did not occur to her that she might be pregnant. Finally Lawrence's mother told her son to take Rosemarie to a doctor; it was only after seeing him that Rosemarie realized that she was with child.

The families then made arrangements for the two young people to marry. Rosemarie, according to reports, followed along in robot-like fashion. She was three months pregnant at the time of the wedding.

For Rosemarie, marriage was "hell." She lived with her in-laws and with their constant criticism and with Lawrence's jealousy and insensitivity. Finally, in January of 1969, after giving birth to their fourth child, Rosemarie suffered what her sister Eileen called a total collapse. For some time she could not even care for the children.

After her recovery, the marriage did not improve. Lawrence continued to be abusive and to treat Rosemarie as his servant girl, until finally, in June of 1971, Rosemarie had another apparent breakdown and, this time, attempted suicide.

That was the end of the marriage. A legal separation was obtained at that time, and three years later, on February 21, 1974, a divorce was obtained in Hartford.

On May 18, 1976 Rosemarie petitioned this Court, competent by reason of the residence of both principals, to declare the marriage null. Her petition was accepted and the Issue in Pleading was conducted on July 5, 1976, with lack of due discretion being assigned as the grounds.

The law on force and fear is well known. In order to be invalidating it must be grave, extrinsic, and causative.

Over the years some authors have suggested that the requirement of extrinsicality is excessive, and that fear should be regarded as invalidating even when there is no extrinsic force. Given the human condition, they say, the source of the fear, i.e., whether it be extrinsic or intrinsic, is not all that important. Intrinsic fear can be just as severe and just as paralyzing as extrinsic fear.

Generally, however, jurists have seen wisdom in the traditional approach. The ground of "vis et metus" is designed for application to a specific situation, namely one where there is not only "metus" but also "vis," that is to say, some extrinsic force. Where such a situation is not verified, one should look to another ground.

This seems fair enough. Particularly considering the fact that the adjacent ground of lack of due discretion picks up exactly where force and fear leaves off. Where, in other words, the fear is present to such a degree that it disturbs the subject's faculties and disables him from making a sound judgment and a free choice, then, even though the fear is intrinsic, the marriage is nevertheless invalid, not on the grounds of "vis et metus" but on the grounds of lack of due discretion.

Given sufficient pressures, even mature, experienced people can make stupid, disastrous mistakes. The ship's captain, for example, when suddenly faced with another ship bearing down on him from out of the fog, and with only a split second to make a decision, turns port instead of starboard. The ships collide and lives are lost. He might spend the rest of his life wondering why he failed to make the obvious and traditional turn to starboard, but the fact is that the pressure was so great that it robbed him of his wits.

Lesser pressure has the same effect on lesser people. Immature, inexperienced people can be robbed of their wits by a circumstance that would be quite manageable for the average person.

When all of this is applied to marriage, it can be said that, given sufficient pressure on a sufficiently immature person, the faculties of intellect and will can be so diminished as to render marital consent defective and the marriage null. To be more specific, it is entirely conceivable, and surely recognized by the principles of our jurisprudence, that when a young, immature girl discovers that she is pregnant, given certain attitudes on her part, and a certain attachment to her family, and given a certain amount of pressure, which may fall short of the "vis" required in a force and fear case, and given, on the one hand a certain time limit within which to make a decision, and, on the other hand, a protraction of the pressure, it is, I repeat, entirely conceivable that such a girl could, so to speak, turn port into marriage rather than starboard away from it. She could, in other words, be robbed of her wits, temporarily deprived of due discretion, and thus enter marriage irresponsibly and invalidly.

III
The Argument

It is clear from the acts of this case that at the time of marriage, Rosemarie Golab lacked the wits or what our jurisprudence calls the "due discretion" necessary to enter a valid marriage.

Rosemarie was raised in a home where the mother was mentally ill, and where the father and mother were constantly bickering. The police were often called to the house to restore order, and the children often had to go to the police station for questioning. Rosemarie was herself born in McKenzie Psychiatric Hospital, where, according to her sister Eileen, attempts had been made to abort Rosemarie by electroshock. When she was a little girl, Rosemarie would occasionally be awakened traumatically from a deep sleep by her poor sick mother beating on her.

As a result of the constant turmoil that existed in the Golab household, Rosemarie became a loner of a child who walked in the woods by herself and talked to the animals. Oftentimes the mother was confined to an institution. Which meant that Rosemarie would be virtually without supervision. But the situation was, in many ways, far worse when the mother was home because then the house was constantly filled with yelling and screaming.

At eleven and twelve years old Rosemarie would go riding with older boys, but she was never touched until she began having sex with Lawrence Gans at age seventeen. Rosemarie, however, was socially retarded and had a grossly diminished appreciation of the ramifications and consequences of sex. It appears that, for Rosemarie, sex was not much more than a pleasurable, exhilarating experience of the moment. It did not occur to her that this was the way a child was conceived. And when she did learn that fact of life, the hard way, it came as a very rude shock indeed, and left her numb and bewildered.

When Rosemarie, after visiting the doctor, finally realized that she was pregnant, she was, according to her own testimony, "totally numb." She commented, "It was like being told the dog's going to have puppies. Big deal. So what? I was going to have a baby. I was going through the motions."

And that is precisely what she did for the next several weeks. She went through the motions. Her "father paced like a wild bull, his fists clenched, literally steaming." Her mother was in shock. And Rosemarie herself doesn't "remember anything else." Her parents made arrangements for the marriage. Rosemarie asked her sister if "you *have* to get married if you're pregnant," but it was an academic question; in fact, Rosemarie went through the motions and did not make a free, deliberate choice.

According to Rosemarie's sister Eileen, Rosemarie was totally unprepared for marriage, and should have been playing with dolls rather than real live babies. Lawrence was or should have been just another boyfriend in Rosemarie's adolescence. When she married him, the time was, in fact, ripe not for marriage but for a change in boyfriends. Rosemarie was tiring of Lawrence around that time. But suddenly she was pregnant and her father was making preparations with the priest for the marriage. No alternatives to marriage were even considered.

From that time on, according to Eileen, Rosemarie was like a "robot." Tell her to do something and she would do it. She was "like in a daze," "mummified," "just numb," "in a fog, going through motions, not knowing what she was doing." She was "an animated corpse." Again, according to Eileen, the wedding pictures show Rosemarie with a dark, blank look on her face, so very different from the vivaciousness one might expect under different circumstances. And, according to Rosemarie herself, she was "just numb" on the wedding day, "not related to anything." She cried all the way up the aisle and "was just being led." Rosemarie said, "Everyone was doing everything for me. I didn't have to think—just do what I was told."

Perhaps to get through a ceremony it is not necessary to think, but to enter a valid marriage, a bride must make a free, deliberate, informed choice. A mummified, animated corpse, a numb robot in a daze cannot enter a valid marriage, because the due discretion is lacking. The Court is satisfied that such was the case in the Golab-Gans marriage.

WHEREFORE

I
The Facts

Brian Scoter and Louise Curlew, both Protestant, were married at the Reformed Church in Auburn, Connecticut in the Archdiocese of Hartford on the twelfth day of October 1955. At the time Brian was twenty-four years old and Louise was twenty-one.

The couple lived together for twenty-two years and had two children, born in 1958 and 1961. From the beginning Louise harbored an unreasonable dislike of Brian's mother and of the Scoter family in general. Though the relationship between Brian and Louise seemed to go fairly well for some years, it gradually deteriorated and by the later years Louise was alcoholic, abusive and violent. She obtained a divorce in Hartford, Connecticut on July 20, 1978.

On October 2, 1982, Brian Scoter, wishing to marry a Catholic woman, petitioned this Court to declare null his marriage to Louise. His petition was accepted and on December 17 the Issue in Pleading was declared to be

> Whether the Scoter-Curlew marriage has been proved null on the grounds of lack of due competence.

II
The Law

A. The Syndrome

The diagnostic criteria for the Paranoid Personality as found in DSM III are as follows:

1. Pervasive and unwarranted suspiciousness and mistrust of people as indicated by at least three of the following:

   a. expectation of trickery or harm
   b. hypervigilance, manifested by continual scanning of the environment for signs of threat, or taking unneeded precautions
   c. guardedness or secretiveness
   d. avoidance of accepting blame, even when warranted

46

e. questioning the loyalty of others

f. intense, narrowly focused searching for confirmation of bias, with loss of appreciation of total context

g. overconcern with hidden motives and special meanings

h. pathological jealousy

2. Hypersensitivity as indicated by at least two of the following:

a. tendency to be easily slighted and quick to take offense

b. exaggeration of difficulties, e.g., "making mountains out of molehills"

c. readiness to "counter-attack" when any threat is perceived

d. inability to relax.

3. Restricted affectively as indicated by at least two of the following:

a. appearance of being "cold" and unemotional

b. pride taken in always being objective, rational, and unemotional

c. lack of a true sense of humor

d. absence of passive, soft, tender and sentimental feelings

4. Not due to another mental disorder such as Schizophrenia or a Paranoid Disorder.

B. Jurisprudence

1. Canon 1095 3° notes that people who are not strong enough to assume the essential obligations of marriage, on account of psychological reasons, are incapable of contracting marriage.

2. This incapacity is often referred to as lack of due competence.

3. It should be noted that this Canon is included in the Code under the rubric of "Matrimonial Consent." Radically, therefore, the incapacity to assume obligations reverts to a defect of consent, since a person who is incapable of *assuming* obligations is likewise incapable of *consenting* to assume them.

4. For this ground to be operative it is not required that there be a mental disease or illness or disorder or even a psychic anomaly. It is only required that there be some psychological reason (causa naturae psychicae) that causes the inability.

5. It is clear that the "essential obligations of marriage" include "the right to the essential interpersonal relationship of the spouses" (*Communicationes*, 1977, 2, p. 375).

6. Although some judges tend to view Personality Disorders such as paranoia under the rubric of lack of due *discretion* (see, for example, the decision coram Anné of July 22, 1969, as found in CLD 8, 680-685), this Court generally (except

where the disorder was obviously distorting the contractant's power to understand and choose or where special circumstances indicate that the marital decision was made under pressure and/or with gross imprudence) views such disorders under the heading of lack of due *competence.*

7. It is clear that, when a Paranoid Personality Disorder is of sufficient severity it can truly incapacitate a person for assuming "the essential obligations of marriage."

III
The Argument

The evidence in this case is garnered from the testimony of both principals and four witnesses, namely the brother and sister-in-law of the petitioner, and a couple (Mr. and Mrs. Johnson) who were friends of both the petitioner and the respondent for twenty-five years.

Reflecting on this evidence, the Court expert, Doctor Mark S. Jaeger, has observed that at the time of the marriage Louise Curlew suffered from a severe Paranoid Personality Disorder which gradually unfolded during the course of the marriage, that it was sufficiently severe to interfere substantially with Louise's ability to function in marriage, that her disorder would have surfaced much earlier and the marriage ended much sooner had Brian been more aggressive and not so passive, that the disorder seems at present to be bordering on the psychosis, and that even if Louise had been motivated to involve herself in therapy early in the marriage, therapy, in order to be successful, would have had to be extensive and prolonged.

Louise Curlew was the eldest of three children. Her father had once held an executive position in a New York firm but lost that position because of alcoholism and became a delivery man. To outsiders the father seemed a friendly, perhaps at times a boisterous man, but within the family he was critical and cynical and difficult to please. Louise was always resentful that she was not reared in a happier home.

Four incidents that indicate the presence of paranoia in Louise around the time of the marriage are the following:

1. *The Family Reunion* — In September of 1955, about a month before the wedding, Brian drove his mother to New Jersey for a family reunion. Louise saw this as threatening and complained that Brian left her all alone to make preparations for the wedding. This was an incident Louise never forgot and brought up periodically over the next twenty-two years.

2. *Brian's Mother at the Wedding* — Prior to the wedding ceremony Brian's mother was crying and delayed arriving at her place for a brief time. Louise always

interpreted this to mean that Brian's mother disliked her, and this too was an incident Brian was never allowed to forget.

3. *The Lying* — Around the time of the marriage, Mary Scoter, a Catholic, was dating John Scoter, Brian's younger brother. Louise told Mary that the mother was bitterly anti-Catholic and that she would rather see John marry an Oriental than a Catholic. In fact the Scoters seem to harbor little or no religious prejudice and welcomed Mary into their family.

4. *The Letter Opening* — From the beginning of the marriage Louise used to open Brian's mail. Some mail from his family he would never receive so that oftentimes he would not even hear of family celebrations or occasions until after the fact.

These four incidents and others were apparently designed to sow seeds of discontent and mistrust among family members and to isolate Brian and lock him off from his family. In Doctor Jaeger's opinion, Louise did this, she kept Brian from his family, because she feared, unreasonably, that they would take Brian away from her. In all the years of marriage the elder Scoters had dinner at Brian's house on only three or four occasions. It was not unusual for several years to pass in between visits. Brian, in his extremely tolerant, "peace at any price" attitude towards marriage, would go for years at a time without contacting his parents. The two children of the marriage were deprived almost entirely of knowing their paternal grandparents, and yet, when it all came tumbling down, Louise blamed her mother-in-law for everything. Over the years Brian tried to reason with Louise and to discover why she was so opposed to his parents and family but Louise never really had a specific reason; she just felt his whole family was stupid.

Following the divorce in July of 1978, Louise, after years of ignoring the Scoters, showed up at their house at Christmas of 1978 and invited them to their granddaughter's high school graduation in June of 1979. At the same time, however, she has, in the past couple of years, been telephoning various members of the family at all hours of the night and day telling them that she plans to make Brian regret the divorce (even though she instituted it) and swearing revenge.

The divorce is interesting. Brian and Louise lived together right up until the time of the divorce. Brian was not represented at the divorce and claims that he did not even know about it ahead of time. The terms of the divorce required that he convey his interest in their very expensive home to Louise, that he pay $500 in counsel fees, that he pay $200 a month to support their daughter who was still a minor under eighteen, and that he pay $400 a month in alimony. Brian complied, moved into the YMCA and then found a furnished, one-room apartment where he lived for the next two years.

Although Louise seemed to function fairly well in the marriage, handled finances well without extravagant spending, and was a good mother to her two children, she gradually, and, according to Doctor Jaeger, inexorably, became unglued. Brian's extreme tolerance kept the lid on for an extraordinarily long time but it was only a question of how long. Eventually Louise would unravel.

In about 1963, when Louise thought she was pregnant for the third time, she became very angry and was extremely unpleasant to Brian for several months. Their sex life, which had been satisfactory prior to that time, began to deteriorate. Louise's jealousy and distrust of Brian became more evident. She began to drink more and more until, according to the witnesses, she became an alcoholic. The witnesses saw her now as troubled, loud, overbearing, rude, abusive, and argumentative, picking fights with everyone.

At home she became violent. She threw clothes out the window, broke lamps and even threatened Brian with a butcher knife.

She became a social climber, wanted to keep her reputation as the town WASP, resented Jews, and constantly needled Brian to be more and more successful. In fact Brian was highly successful in business. According to Doctor Jaeger, all of this needling was in fact a projection onto Brian of Louise's own profound sense of insecurity.

In her interview with the Instructor, Louise was very emotional and "weepy," blamed everything on Brian and claimed that she had no problem at all with alcohol, that she was only a social drinker, though the witnesses indicate that the contrary is true. The respondent indicated that she would make further contact with the Instructor but did not, in fact, oblige.

Given all the evidence, and especially in this case the insights of the psychiatrist into the nature of the problem and its presence at the time of the marriage, I am morally certain that Louise Curlew lacked the due competence for marriage.

WHEREFORE

CHOUCAS - JASKOLKA

I

The Facts

Celia Choucas and Herman Jaskolka, both Catholic, were married in the Church of St. Anselm, Reading, Connecticut in the Archdiocese of Hartford on the fifteenth day of June 1971. At the time Celia was twenty-one years old and Herman was twenty-four.

Celia and Herman lived together for about four years but Herman was always extremely distant and no relationship ever developed between them. Herman finally left Celia in March of 1975. A divorce was obtained in New Haven on the twelfth day of February 1976.

On November 3, 1978 Celia petitioned this Court to declare the marriage null. Her petition was accepted and, on December 21, 1978, the Doubt was Formulated with Herman's lack of due competence being assigned as the *caput nullitatis* of the instance.

II

The Law

A. The general law regarding lack of due competence is succinctly expressed in the following opening paragraphs of a decision dated May 11, 1978, coram Parisella, as contained in *Monitor Ecclesiasticus*, 1978, pp. 394-395:

> 2. The present case deals with the inability to assume conjugal duties which, as we noted recently, is considered in recent rotal jurisprudence as an *autonomous* ground of nullity. (See Navarrete's article in *Periodica*, 1972, 1, pp. 47-80, and my own decision of February 23, 1978). This incapacity, of which there is no mention in the Code of Canon Law, refers primarily to the three goods of marriage which, in the case at bar, refers especially to the perpetual and exclusive right to the body for those acts which are per se apt for the generation of offspring (Canon 1081 § 2).

> 3. But, besides referring to this biological element, the incapacity of assuming conjugal duties also includes the intimate community of life, that is to say, the conjugal, stable and interpersonal partnership or relationship which is brought about by the donation of the two partners (*Gaudium et Spes*, n. 48). In this matter, however, we should keep in

mind, in order to remain within the perimeters of acceptable juris-prudence, that the community (or communion) of life should be under-stood as referring to the *right* to the community of life. Only when so understood can the community of life be regarded as the substantial object of the marriage covenant. (See Canon 1081, § 2, and the decision coram Masala of March 12, 1975).

4. This incapacity of which we speak has been introduced into the latest schema of the revised Code as follows: "but if either or both parties by a positive act of the will exclude . . . the right to the communion of life . . . then they contract invalidly (Canon 303, § 2).

Anné was therefore correct when he observed, in his decision of February 25, 1969, that, for a valid marriage, the community of life can in fact be absent but not the *right* to the community of life. (See the following decisions: coram Serrano of July 9, 1976; coram DiFelice of January 17, 1976; coram Lefebvre of January 31, 1976; and coram Parisella of February 23, 1976).

B. As regards the particular disorder at issue, namely the Schizoid Personality Disorder, its diagnostic criteria are described in DSM III as follows:

1. Emotional coldness and aloofness, and absence of warm, tender feelings for others.

2. Indifference to praise or criticism or to the feelings of others.

3. Close friendships with no more than one or two persons, including family members.

4. No eccentricities of speech, behavior or thought characteristic of Schizo-typal Personality Disorder.

5. Not due to a psychotic disorder such as Schizophrenia or Paranoid Disorder.

6. If under 18, does not meet the criteria for Schizoid Disorder of Childhood or Adolescence.

III
The Argument

The evidence in this case consists of 1) the testimony of both Celia and Herman, 2) the testimony of three witnesses, all of whom knew both parties for several years, both before and during the marriage, and 3) the report of John Limpkin, M.D., the psychiatric expert appointed by the Court.

The principals and witnesses agree in their description of Herman's family background. He grew up in a family with strong, cold parents where the mother ruled the home. He was encouraged to have strong opinions and he stood by himself. He had no real friends and was seen as reserved, quiet, and calm. Because he gave the impression of being aloof, others stayed away and were kept at a distance. Herman rarely sought advice, was uneasy in groups and could not relax.

His personality was evident during the courtship with Celia. Because he seemed so distant five months before the wedding, the couple broke up. Herman preferred to be a bookworm; he did not socialize. He was, according to Doris Mulligan, isolated and aloof. He planned everything; he was never spontaneous. Two witnesses noticed during the courtship that the couple was like a pair of robots; there was no affection or caressing. Herman's family was not enthusiastic about the wedding.

It was clear on the honeymoon that Herman was different from what Celia expected. He had been interested in sexual relations before the marriage, but that interest declined. He told Celia that frequent sexual relations were characteristic of fairytales, not real life. He was reluctant to touch her or express his feelings, but rarely lost his temper or expressed any feelings or offered Celia emotional support. Communication in the marriage was superficial. Herman would only discuss work or objects, not problems or feelings.

Our expert, Doctor Limpkin, described Herman's personality as "porcupinish." When people came near him, he became extremely defensive and surrounded himself with a needle like protection. He did not want people near him ever, and surprises he liked even less. One of the witnesses, Doris Mulligan, said, for example, that one had to give three weeks notice before visiting the house. Doris' mother agreed that an "appointment" was necessary before going near the house and even then, as often as not, Herman claimed that he was either sick or too tired to entertain outsiders.

Although Celia and Herman lived together for about four years, all sex between them ceased after about fifteen months. Celia tried to interest Herman in sex after that and suggested that they obtain some counselling but Herman was not interested. His personality became more set and, by the beginning of 1973, whenever Celia entered a room, Herman would leave it.

The marriage ended in 1975 when Herman said that he was in love with another woman and wanted a divorce. He now says that neither he nor Celia were ready for marriage because they had not formed their attitudes and they spent time on separate endeavors. He has also indicated that he did not believe in permanent marriage.

Our expert, Doctor Limpkin, has diagnosed Herman as suffering from a Schizoid Personality Disorder with paranoid traits. The disorder, according to Doctor Limpkin, was moderate to severe but severe in terms of depriving him of the capacity for an intimate relationship, especially with someone like Celia who, the evidence shows, was a person who needed considerable affection and reassurance.

The evidence then, including the report of the expert, demonstrates that Herman Jaskolka suffered from a severe psychopathology which deprived him of the due competence for entering a marital partnership with Celia Choucas.

WHEREFORE

I
The Facts

April Pernice and Carl Ruff, both Catholic, were married at the Church of St. Olaf, Lincoln, Connecticut in the Diocese of Bridgeport on the fourth day of October 1962. At the time both parties were twenty-four years old.

The first separation occurred about nine months after marriage when Carl simply disappeared for a few days. There were several more separations over the next nine months and then, in April 1964, after only a year and a half of marriage, the final separation occurred. One child was born of the marriage. A divorce was granted in Bridgeport on March 10, 1966.

On October 10, 1978 April Pernice petitioned this Court, competent by reason of the petitioner's residence, to declare the marriage null. Her petition was accepted and the *Contestatio Litis* was conducted on November 29, 1978, with lack of due competence being established as the grounds on which the question of validity was to be decided.

II
The Law

A. For many years now rotal jurisprudence has held that in order to enter a valid marriage a person must not only have the intellectual capacity to understand the formal object of marriage but he must enjoy as well the volitional capacity to fulfill the object of the contract. Heard, for example, has said,

> Still, even if one wishes to insist that it has not been proved with certitude that the subject was, at the time of marriage, incapable of eliciting a human act, the marriage should nevertheless be declared null. For even if you admit that the man could have given consent which was in itself valid, still as far as marriage is concerned he was consenting to something of which he was incapable. He was incapable of obliging himself to the contract of giving over his body exclusively and perpetually to one woman. (46, 85)

And Felici noted that

> . . . for a valid marriage there is required that discretion of mind which

55

permits the person to perceive the peculiar nature and force of the marital contract and there is also required that strength of will which enables the person to give and receive the right and duties of marriage. (48, 468)

In the 1950s and '60s there was little or no ambiguity involved in the statement that a person had to have both the intellectual and the volitional capacity to understand and fulfill the formal object of the marriage. Gasparri (*De Matrimonio*, para. 7) and the other manualists had explained clearly what the "object" of marriage was. Just as in the sale of a house, the house itself is the material object and the ownership of the house is the formal object, so in respect to marriage, the object of the marriage contract is clear. The material object is the contractants themselves; the formal object is the mutual right and corresponding obligation to the body for those acts which are per se apt for the generation of offspring.

In the past decade or so, however, our jurisprudence has come to recognize that Gasparri's description of the formal object of marriage was an incomplete description; the present position is that the formal object of marriage comprises both the right to the body *and* the right to the community of life, that is to say, the right to an interpersonal relationship.

Our present jurisprudence, therefore, holds that unless a person is capable of exchanging the double right, the right to the body and the right to an interpersonal relationship (together they make up the formal object of marriage), he is incapable of the marriage covenant.

The formal object of marriage, furthermore, is a *ius perpetuum*. Consequently if a person, at the time of the ceremony, is incapable by reason of his personality makeup, *ob ipsam suam complexionem* (49, 503), *dotibus ipsis suis* (59, 803), of exchanging this perpetual right, then that person is incapable of marriage. It is not enough, in other words, for a person to be able to tolerate marriage for a month or a year or a decade. Rather, his temperament or character must be such at the time of marriage as to permit him to enter a lifelong union. To put it another way, the disorder may be incipient at the time of marriage but if it is destined under the circumstances to become debilitating and gravely disruptive of the marriage, then the person was incapable at the time of marriage of transferring the object of marriage. C. 1095 3° notes that that incapacity can be caused by certain "psychological reasons."

B. The "psychological reason" that is at issue in the present instance is the Schizotypal Personality Disorder described in DSM III as follows:

1. At least four of the following are required:

    a. Magical thinking, e.g., superstitiousness, clairvoyance, telepathy, "6th sense," "others can feel my feeling."

    b. Ideas of reference, self-referential thinking.

c. Social isolation, e.g., no close friends or confidants, social contacts limited to essential everyday tasks.

d. Recurrent illusions, sensing the presence of a force or person not actually present (e.g., "I felt as if my dead mother were in the room with me'), depersonalization or derealization not associated with panic attacks.

e. Odd communication (*not* derailment [loose associations] or incoherence), e.g., speech that is tangential, digressive, vague, over-elaborate, circumstantial, metaphorical.

f. Inadequate rapport in face-to-face interaction due to constricted or inappropriate affect, e.g., aloof, distant, cold.

g. Suspiciousness or paranoid ideation.

h. Undue social anxiety or hypersensitivity to real or imagined criticism.

2. Does not meet the criteria for Schizophrenia.

| III |
| The Argument |

Carl Ruff, the respondent, acknowledged receipt of a letter from the Tribunal but said that he did not "wish to synergize with the Tribunal in any way." However, the available evidence, namely 1) the testimony of three witnesses (the petitioner's sister, the petitioner's mother, and William Flynn, a friend of the respondent), 2) the testimony of the petitioner herself, and 3) a report from Anthony Canarino, M.D., the Court-appointed psychiatric expert, is, in the opinion of the Court, probative of nullity.

April and Carl met in 1960 when they were both students in law school. April's mother was opposed to her daughter marrying Carl because she considered him "strange" but April was in love and the couple married shortly after Carl began his final year of law school.

Aside from the fact that, according to April, Carl had a difficult time consummating the marriage, the first several months of marriage seem to have been rather uneventful. In July of 1963, however, Carl disappeared for a few days and this turned out to be the first of many such separations over the next several months.

The separations tell the real story—which is a story of Carl's solipsism and irresponsibility. The first separation, for example, took place when Carl collected his first pay check. On receiving his check, Carl simply took off for some days, spending what he earned on himself. This then became a periodic thing with Carl.

Carl was an only child whose parents were divorced. Carl's father abandoned his wife and Carl when Carl was eight years old. Carl always hated his father, and, when he was in high school, Carl changed his middle name, which had been his father's. His mother meanwhile manipulated Carl and often boarded him out so that, in fact, Carl was raised not so much by his parents as by assorted and sundry aunts.

Carl was extremely materialistic and appears to have married April because he thought she was wealthy. Carl was a big spender, borrowed a lot of money, pawned items, including April's engagement ring, and all the money he earned he spent on himself. April had to support herself and their baby boy, who was born in October of 1963.

Carl completely ignored the baby. He was on one of his "vacations" from marriage when the child was born; he never took any interest in the child at all, and after the separation he never paid anything towards the child's support. Carl has not seen his son now for several years.

Carl drank to excess during the brief marriage and would frequently get physically sick from it. He would often threaten to do harm to himself and to April and once he actually came after her with an enormous butcher knife.

The witnesses regard Carl as resentful, jealous, inconsiderate, self-centered, unethical, immature, irresponsible, heartless, disagreeable and even delusional.

The testimony of the three witnesses was consistent, concordant and adminicular and has satisfactorily established the facts.

Our expert, Doctor Canarino, reflecting on the facts, has concluded that Carl Ruff suffered from a severe Schizotypal Personality Disorder which deprived him of the ability to sustain a long-term interpersonal relationship.

Given the anamnesis and diagnosis, the undersigned Judge is morally certain that Carl Ruff was, in 1962, incapable of giving valid consent to marriage because he lacked the capacity to fulfill the object of that consent, in particular the ability to exchange the right to a marital partnership.

WHEREFORE

WACHTEL - CORVO

I
The Facts

Eric Wachtel and Wendy Corvo, both Catholic, were married at the Church of Our Lady of Lourdes, Auburn, Connecticut in the Archdiocese of Hartford on the 28th day of June 1962. Both parties at the time were twenty-three years old.

The couple lived together (with one fairly brief separation about a year after marriage) until February of 1965. At that point Wendy left Eric to live with a man with whom she had been carrying on an affair for several months. In November of 1965, however, Eric and Wendy reconciled. They lived together then—without affection but in peaceful coexistence—for another year, separating finally in October of 1966.

On December 27, 1979 Eric petitioned this Court to declare the marriage null. The petition was accepted and the *Contestatio Litis* was conducted on February 20, 1980 assigning Wendy's lack of due competence as the grounds on which the validity of this marriage would be investigated and adjudged.

II
The Law

A. The following resumé of our jurisprudence on lack of due competence is a translation of excerpts from a decision coram Pinto of December 18, 1979 (see *Monitor Ecclesiasticus*, 1980, IV, pp. 376-378):

> 5. A person is incapable of undertaking the essential duties of marriage not only when he cannot hand over those rights by which marriage is immediately directed to the social end that has been called "primary" (the traditional goods of children, fidelity and perpetuity) but also when he is incapable of handing over the rights by which marriage is immediately directed to the personal end that has been called "secondary," namely, the good of the spouses (cf. Pius XII, *Allocutio ad S. R. Rotam,* 3 oct. 1941, in A.A.S., 1941, 423; F. M. Cappello, *De Matrimonio,* 1961, n. 8-9). In order for a person to be substantially capable of this end, a conjugal partnership must not be morally impossible (cf. S.R.R. Decis. c. Pinto, 15 iul. 1977, n. 5 in *Monitor Eccl.* 1978, p. 150-152). The rights and duties which constitute the good of the spouses are described in the Code of Canon Law as "mutual help and a remedy of concupiscence" (Canon 1013, para. 1), and in the

schema on matrimony in the new Code as "the right to a communion of life," embracing those rights which pertain to the essential interpersonal relationship of the couple (can. 303, in *Communicationes*, 1977, p. 374-375).

7. . . . The right to the communion of life is the right to that constellation of acts by which, in different cultures and times, one partner demonstrates to the other, by whatever signs are required to show that conjugal partnership is not morally impossible, that juridically he considers her as his spouse (affectio coniugalis).

The capacity of obliging one's self to the handing over of this right supposes in the person who is marrying that, at the moment that he contracts marriage, he wishes himself to begin a heterosexual, intimate, exclusive and perpetual partnership directed to the mutual psychosexual perfection of the parties. Where, either because of a profound and instinctive homosexual tendency or because of some other abnormality of the instincts or character, the contractant is incapable of this, and where that incapacity cannot be remedied either by psychological or pastoral assistance, then it will be clear that there is an incapacity for assuming the conjugal state. The mere fact that the union of souls has not been attained is not sufficient, but if the contractant, who is incapable of obliging himself, cannot understand his own incapacity, then neither is he capable of giving consent.

B. The particular disorder that is at issue in this case is the Histrionic Personality Disorder, described in DSM III as follows:

1. Behavior that is overly dramatic, reactive and intensely expressed, as indicated by at least three of the following:

    a. self-dramatization, e.g., exaggerated expressions of emotions
    b. incessant drawing of attention to oneself
    c. craving for activity and excitement
    d. overreaction to minor events
    e. irrational, angry outbursts or tantrums

2. Characteristic disturbance in interpersonal relationships as indicated by at least two of the following:

    a. perceived by others as shallow and lacking genuineness, even if superficially warm and charming
    b. egocentric, self-indulgent, and inconsiderate of others
    c. vain and demanding
    d. dependent, helpless, constantly seeking reassurance
    e. prone to manipulative suicidal threats, gestures or attempts

Wendy grew up in a family where the father was a heavy drinker and a womanizer. He finally left the family and ran off with another woman when Wendy was twelve years old. He committed suicide early in 1963, some eight months after Wendy and Eric married.

Wendy was the eldest of three girls and the sibling rivalry was bitter and intense. This, indeed, seems to have been a major factor in Wendy's marrying Eric, or at least in her marrying him when she did. It seems that Wendy's younger sister announced that she was going to marry in August of 1962. When Wendy heard that, she proposed immediately to Eric and urged that the marriage predate her sister's. In the same vein, after marriage, Wendy's sister announced that she was pregnant. On hearing this news, Wendy, even though she had been practicing birth control prior to that time, complained that Eric was not man enough to make her pregnant.

Wendy and Eric met in 1956 when they were in high school. In 1958, when they were both nineteen, they became engaged, which seemed to surprise some of Eric's friends who were aware that Wendy had a reputation for promiscuity. To some extent this came to light in 1959 when Wendy, while engaged to Eric, began seeing a man eight years her senior. Eric broke off the engagement.

The following year, however, Eric and Wendy began dating again and they were reengaged in January of 1962. Between January and June the couple seemed to get along rather well but there were two major arguments: one over the fact that Eric discovered Wendy was seeing one of her old boyfriends on the side, and the second over the fact that Wendy, without advising Eric, made plans for an elaborate wedding.

In the first year of marriage Wendy had five different secretarial jobs. She felt people were against her, had great difficulty getting along with people and was either laid off from or quit one job after another.

Meanwhile she paid little or no attention to domestic chores and the house was a mess.

Wendy also complained constantly about Eric and his inability to provide for her in the style to which she was accustomed. In fact Eric was a steady worker, made a good salary; and the couple purchased a house after only a few months of marriage. And they had a new car. But Wendy was never satisfied and always wanted more.

After a few months Wendy shut Eric down sexually. She didn't seem interested. In the second year of marriage Wendy went to work for the Everglade Company.

She began staying out until two or three in the morning after a while, and it came out that she was seeing a fellow employee, fourteen years her senior. Eventually they were both fired from the company because of their scandalous behavior. Wendy lived with him from February to November of 1965.

When this man moved out of state in November of 1965, Wendy asked Eric to take her back, which, on the advice of a priest, he did. Within a year Wendy and Eric separated definitively and Wendy then lived with her Everglade friend again and had two children by him.

She is now in the process of being divorced from a third man, a man eleven years older than Wendy whom she married after knowing for only four months.

Wendy herself refused to cooperate in these hearings but two knowledgeable witnesses, including Wendy's mother, testified. Wendy is described as frivolous, given to lying, and as extremely jealous of her younger sisters.

The expert on this case, Doctor James Oriole, has diagnosed Wendy as suffering from a classical and severe Histrionic Personality Disorder.

It seems clear that this pathology deprived Wendy of the capacity to function in an exclusive, lifelong relationship with Eric Wachtel.

WHEREFORE

```
        I
    The Facts
```

Claudia Mewa and Owen Teal, both Catholic, were married on the twelfth day of May 1962 at Holy Redeemer Church, Edison, Connecticut in the Archdiocese of Hartford. Claudia was twenty-two years old and Owen was twenty-five.

After three years of marriage Claudia discovered that Owen was having an affair with a married woman (the woman's husband telephoned her about it). Claudia filed for divorce at that time but withdrew the file at the urging of a priest. The couple lived together then for eight more years, separating finally in March of 1973. Three children were born of the marriage. A divorce was granted in Hartford on June 3, 1974.

On November 9, 1977, Claudia petitioned this Court to declare the marriage null. Her petition was accepted and on January 4, 1978 the *Contestatio Litis* formulated the doubt as follows:

> Whether the Mewa-Teal marriage has been proved null on the grounds of lack of due competence.

```
        II
    The Law
```

A. The following is a translation of the law section of a decision given by Monsignor DiFelice on January 17, 1976. (*Ephemerides Iuris Canonici* 32, pp. 284-285)

> 2. When legitimately manifested between legally capable persons, marital consent (which can be supplied by no human power) makes marriage, and is "an act of the will by which the parties hand over and receive the perpetual and exclusive right to the body for those acts which are per se apt for the generation of offspring." (Canon 1081) Persons who are legally capable of contracting marriage are not only those people who are free of any impediments stated in the positive law of the Church but also those people who are not incapacitated by their own deficiencies from handing over and receiving the matrimonial rights and duties, which include the perpetual and exclusive right to the body for those acts which are per se apt for the generation of offspring. In order to be able to hand

over and receive that perpetual and exclusive right, people ought to enjoy the natural ability to enter that community of life and of conjugal love which was established by the Creator and endowed with suitable laws. As the Second Vatican Council teaches: "thus the man and woman, who are no longer two but one (Matthew 19:6) help and serve each other by their marriage partnership; they become conscious of their unity and experience it more deeply from day to day." (*Gaudium Et Spes*, n. 48) For perfecting this relationship during married life, that is to say during the *matrimonium in facto esse*, the contractants ought to be capable of fulfilling future conjugal responsibilities at the very time they manifest their consent, that is to say, at the time of the *matrimonium in fieri*.

Consequently, a contractant who, because of some serious psychopathology, is deprived of the oblative faculty which would permit him to make a life-long commitment of himself to his partner at the time of the celebration of marriage, is not able to hand over and to receive marital consent. Indeed, because of his undeveloped critical faculty, he cannot even appreciate what his problem is. In a recent decision on a case originating in Rome we wrote, "the marital capacities of a person are brought into clearer perspective by examining first the object of marriage and secondly the specific rights and obligations of marriage. The person who does not enjoy a sufficient critical faculty for evaluating the intimate community of life and conjugal love, that is to say, the person who is not capable of suitably estimating the rights and obligations of marriage, is incapable of handing over and receiving matrimonial consent."

3. The inability to hand over the right to the communion of conjugal life because of a psychopathology that affects interpersonal, conjugal relations stems from a defect of consent not only because the object of the consent is lacking, but also because there is a lack of due discretion on the part of the contractant. Because at the time he is pronouncing his vows he is already incapable of handing over and receiving the right to the community of life because of a preexistent character defect, and the manifestation of the consent therefore lacks the proper foundation or cause; and at the same time the contractant, because of a deficient critical faculty, is not even aware of this. He thinks that he is really handing himself over and receiving what is his but in fact he is not because he lacks the discretion proportionate to marriage, which is the only measure of sufficient consent. (46, 788 and 53, 117)

The inability to assume conjugal duties produces a double defect: (a) considered in itself, it takes away the objective force of the matrimonial consent since the contract lacks its object; (b) considered in its subject, it emasculates that consent since it removes the discretion proportionate to marriage. With consent entirely lacking on account of the lack of due discretion proportionate to marriage it is no longer a question of the defect of the *object* of consent since the consent itself doesn't really exist because of the incapacity of the contractant who is placing it. Consequently the inability to assume conjugal duties takes its juridic force for invalidating the marriage entirely from the lack of due discretion on the part of the contractant.

4. As regards proving nullity of a marriage on the grounds of lack of due discretion stemming from the inability of one of the parties to assume the obligations of marriage, it is important to remember that that incapacity must be both certain and concomitant. Very often the inability to hand over the right to a communion of conjugal life is confused with the intention of not implementing those rights or fulfilling those duties, or it is confused with problems that arise post factum.

In order to prove that there is a real inability to assume conjugal duties, it must be demonstrated that there was a serious psychopathology which rendered one of the contractants incapable of establishing a community of life with the other party. This has been often noted in rotal decisions, (see for example the following decisions: coram Anné, February 25, 1969; coram Lefebvre, March 1, 1969; coram Pompedda, October 6, 1969, coram Anné, February 6, 1963; coram Serrano, April 5, 1973; coram Pinto, February 6, 1974; coram DiFelice, January 12, 1974; coram Serrano, April 30, 1974; coram Masala, March 12, 1975). Mild characterological disturbances which are treatable, on the other hand, in no way remove the ability to assume conjugal duties, nor do they remove the discretion proportionate to marriage. (See for example the following rotal decisions: coram Pinto, March 18, 1971; coram DiFelice, March 8, 1975; and coram DiFelice, December 11, 1975)

B. Although this sentence of DiFelice appeared under the rubric "Incapacitas assumendi et adimplendi onera coniugalia," DiFelice, for the reasons given, reduces this to the ground of lack of due *discretion*. In our court it would be regarded instead as lack of due *competence*, but for us the distinction is basically a practical one. When, in other words, most of the evidence refers to the "Incapacitas assumendi et adimplendi" we call it lack of due *competence*; we reserve the term "lack of due *discretion*" for those cases where most of the evidence points to the inability of the party or parties to make a reasonably free, sensible evaluation of marriage vows.

The semantic problem, however, should not distract us from DiFelice's main point, which is that when a person is so affected by a psychopathology that he is incapable of those interpersonal relationships that are essential to marriage as a community of life, then he cannot validly enter marriage.

C. The psychopathology at issue in this case is the Narcissistic Personality Disorder, the diagnostic criteria of which are described by DSM III as follows:

1. Grandiose sense of self-importance of uniqueness, e.g., exaggerates achievements and talents, focuses on how special one's problems are.

65

2. Preoccupation with fantasies of unlimited success, power, brilliance, beauty, or ideal love.

3. Exhibitionistic: requires constant attention and admiration.

4. Responds to criticism, indifference of others, or defeat with either cool indifference or with marked feelings of rage, inferiority, shame, humiliation, or emptiness.

5. At least two of the following are characteristic of disturbances in interpersonal relationships:

  a. Lack of empathy: inability to recognize how others feel, e.g., unable to appreciate the distress of someone who is seriously ill.
  b. Entitlement: expectation of special favors without assuming reciprocal responsibilities, e.g., surprise and anger that people won't do what he wants.
  c. Interpersonal exploitiveness: takes advantage of others to indulge own desires or for self-aggrandizement, with disregard for the personal integrity and rights of others.
  d. Relationships characteristically vacillate between the extremes of over-idealization and devaluation.

III
The Argument

Owen Teal came from a home environment which tended to produce problems. The father had a drinking problem and died of cirrhosis of the liver in 1961. Owen has a sister who is divorced. Two of his brothers had had problems with the police. One of his brothers became intoxicated at Owen's wedding, caused a scene and had to be brought home.

Over the years Owen became essentially and radically narcissistic or solipsistic or enamored of himself. This, indeed, is our expert's, Doctor John Limpkin's principal diagnosis of Owen—that he suffered from a Narcissistic Personality Disorder. Doctor Limpkin noted, furthermore, that in Owen's case the disorder was egosyntonic, that is to say, that he was not conflicted by it, that he never really perceived the problem (Owen could never imagine anyone disliking him even though, in fact, he never made a close friend).

Owen's attitude towards sex is an interesting and rather classic example of this. Women, for him, were bodies. He talked about their bodies constantly, projecting how they would be as bed partners. Sex, for Owen, was a merely physical act, something that brought the great Owen Teal the physical pleasure he so richly deserved. He was forever flirting with women. He carried on affairs quite casually and when Claudia was devastated by his infidelity, walking the streets in the rain with her eighteen-month-old child, dazed and bewildered, Owen was unconcerned about Claudia and almost puzzled by her peculiar reaction—like he didn't really understand the problem or the fact that he had offended her.

When Owen was younger he had been a highly successful skier who had competed in two different Olympic Games. But what for most people would be a fond recollection and a moderate source of pride, became for Owen the great proof that he was, in fact, an heroic figure. Fate, alas, would blind the eyes of most mortals to his true stature. His cruel destiny would be that of an unsung hero. A sentiment expressed in the verse Owen submitted to the Court:

> Lost adrift in an endless sea . . . .
> Of emptiness, lost love and misery
> Why God! Does this have to be me
> Loneliness . . . . Fear . . . . Despair . . . .Misunderstood
> Why should I try to be good?
> Life is just a rat race. . . .
> Dog eat dog . . . .
> Why! Can't I play this game
> of the above rat race . . . .
> Why! Can't I keep up with this
> frantic pace. . . .

In his discussion with the Instructor, Owen expressed his anger that Claudia had petitioned for annulment, and he tried to express his perception of the marriage failure, but interspersed throughout was what the Instructor described as a long litany, repeated over and over again, of his successes and triumphs on the ski slopes. Owen seemed to miss entirely the fact that this litany was altogether out of place and inappropriate.

Owen always saw himself as numero uno, and his attitude was that, above all, one should take care of number one. If, for example, there was one piece of pie left at the conclusion of dinner, that naturally was for him, despite the fact that the children might like it. Even though Claudia worked as a nurse throughout the marriage (except for leaves of absence when she gave birth to the children) Owen always referred to everything as "mine," never as "ours." When he and Claudia went out, he always ignored Claudia and socialized with other people, backslapping fellow skiers or dancing with every attractive woman in sight.

Since the divorce Owen has shown a superficial interest in the children but he often drops them off at their grandmother's when he has visitation rights; he complains that the child support payments are too high; he has been late making the payments on several occasions and the check has bounced more than once. Owen is convinced that his children idolize him. He says that their daughter, Carol, would really prefer to live with him rather than with her mother, and he claims that Carol weeps when they part. Carol, however, has told her aunt (one of the witnesses) that she doesn't like her father much because he makes promises and doesn't keep them.

During the marriage, Owen seems to have maintained the same sort of relationship with his children. Owen worked during the day as a school teacher. Claudia, after the children came along, worked the three to eleven shift as a nurse, with the expectation that Owen would be able to babysit. Owen, however, bowled three nights a week, did not see that as excessive and would not expect the children to impinge on his time.

This, indeed, was the kind of relationship Owen maintained with everyone. He had no close friends, but got along fine with people on a superficial level, engaging in cocktail party type small talk as long as they praised him and did not evince boredom at his endless account of the great victories of Owen Teal, the Giant of the giant slalom. But if Owen did not get his own way, if people did not cater to his wishes, he pouted and sulked.

Doctor Limpkin regards Owen as suffering from a Narcissistic Personality Disorder, severe insofar as it affects his interpersonal relationships, with major sociopathic elements and some obsessive compulsive traits.

When the Instructor, Father Thomas Sas, initiated the interview with Owen, Owen expressed tremendous anger at the Church for even awarding Claudia a hearing, claiming that everything she and the witnesses said were lies. When, however, Father Sas invited Owen to complete a detailed marital history himself and to offer the names of people who would be objective witnesses, Owen said that he would think about it, but telephoned later to say that he decided it wasn't worth it. Doctor Limpkin regarded this entire exchange—the opening narcissistic rage and the later change of mind—as corroborative. The rage, according to Doctor Limpkin, is the defense against being seen, either by Owen himself or by someone else, as anything less than lovable; and the change of mind is the result of Owen's worst fear—that, even after naming his own witnesses, he will be proved wrong. This way he can blame the priests and psychiatrists of the Tribunal and the Church in general.

Given the facts (I am satisfied with the credibility of the two witnesses) and the opinion of the expert, I am morally certain that Owen Teal's Personality Disorder deprived him of the due competence for marriage.

WHEREFORE

I
The Facts

Isabel Gallo and Theodore Heron, both Catholic, were married at the Church of St. Andrew, Livingston, Connecticut in the Archdiocese of Hartford on the fourth day of September, 1955. At the time Isabel was nineteen years old and Theodore was twenty-two.

The couple lived together, with a few separations, for eighteen years, and three children (one of them stillborn) were born of the marriage. Throughout the eighteen years, however, Theodore was grossly irresponsible and the marriage lasted as long as it did only because of the extreme tolerance of Isabel. The final separation took place in 1973 and a divorce was granted to Isabel in Livingston on October 29, 1974.

On September 12, 1976 Isabel petitioned this Court to declare the marriage null. Her petition was accepted and the Formulation of the Doubt was executed on November 4, 1976, assigning Theodore's lack of due competence as the ground.

II
The Law

A. The jurisprudence regarding the Antisocial Personality Disorder was discussed in a decision coram Pinto of March 18, 1971 (printed in *Periodica*, 1972, pp. 439-445). The following is a translation of the opening paragraphs of the "in iure" section of that decision:

> 2. It is not sufficient in order to give marital consent that the contractant merely know that marriage is a permanent society between a man and a woman for the purpose of procreating children. But it is further required that the contractant have at least a pubescent's knowledge of the fact that in marrying he is handing over and receiving a perpetual and exclusive right to the body for those acts which are per se apt for the generation of offspring and that he freely intend to transfer that right.

> Consequently, if it is established with moral certitude that the contractant, because of some mental disorder at the time of the celebration of the marriage, lacked the aforementioned discretion because of a defect either of the intellect or of the will, the marriage should be declared null.

3. If a person actually gives consent but, because of a mental illness or disturbance, is incapable of giving and receiving the essential rights and duties of a marriage contract, namely those involving fidelity, perpetuity and openness to children, he contracts invalidly, providing, of course, his incapacity was both antecedent and perpetual.

Both Roman law and the Decretals respected the principle according to which no one can be obliged to the impossible. . . .

When modern authors apply to matrimony the principle "no one can be obliged to the impossible" they speak of the diriment impediment of moral impotence which is present when a person retains the capacity to exchange consent but because of some psychic defect or disturbance is rendered incapable of realistically assuming one or another or indeed all of the essential rights and duties of the marital contract. However, since moral impotence is derived from the natural law itself, it should follow the same rules as sexual impotence, that is to say, the incapacity ought to be both antecedent and perpetual. (can. 1068; Cfr. v.gr. P. Huizing, *Manual of Matrimonial Law,* 1963, J. R. Keating, *The Bearing of Mental Impairment On The Validity of Marriage,* 1964, and his article, "Sociopathic Personality," in *The Jurist,* 1965, pag. 429-438; J. T. Finnegan, "The Current Jurisprudence Concerning the Psychopathic Personality" in *The Jurist,* 1967, pag. 440-453)

As for Rotal jurisprudence on this point, Heard, in a decision of January 30, 1954, declared a marriage invalid saying 'even though the man could have given valid consent in itself, he was nevertheless incapable of the thing to which he consented in the marital contract. The respondent was incapable of obliging himself to an exclusive and perpetual handing over of his body to one woman' (46, 85). The same type of reasoning is also found in other Rotal decisions, for example, the one coram Sabattani of June 21, 1957 and DeJorio's opinion of December 19, 1961. In a decision coram Rogers of June 18, 1968 we read

'from the fact that a person seems to enjoy the use of reason we may not conclude that all the implications of his actions should be imputed to him since it could be that by reason of a psychic defect he was not capable of assuming the obligations of which he had some theoretical knowledge but about which he could not freely bring to bear his critical judgment.' In this case, as is evident, consent is lacking.

4. Our present understanding of the psychopath (in 1952 the American Psychiatric Association changed the term to 'sociopath') is the result of a long evolution. . . .

The psychopath (the psychopathic personality) . . . is normally defined by the Anglo-American school of psychiatry in this way: he is an asocial, impulsive and aggressive person who because of a distorted ability to love and a virtual absence of guilt is swept along by unrestrained desires.

He is called asocial because being restrained by no law or social norm, he habitually commits crimes and is dangerous to society. Not all delinquents, of course, are psychopathic. Sheldon and Glueck in their survey found that 48.6% of the delinquents they examined were in fact psychopathic (*Unraveling Juvenile Delinquency*, Cambridge, 1950). The psychopath is distinguished from other delinquents in that he experiences neither guilt nor love. So he is not really subject to correction.

The psychopath is not psychotic because the latter has withdrawn from reality and lives in a world of his own making, sometimes being exhilarated by it and sometimes depressed. And he differs finally from the neurotic because the neurotic experiences anguish whereas the psychopath does not.

B. The Antisocial Personality Disorder is described in DSM III as follows:

1. Current age at least 18.

2. Onset before age 15 as indicated by a history of three or more of the following before that age:

   a. truancy (positive if it amounted to at least five days per year for at least two years, not including the last year of school)
   b. expulsion or suspension from school for misbehavior
   c. delinquency (arrested or referred to juvenile court because of behavior)
   d. running away from home overnight at least twice while living in parental or parental surrogate home
   e. persistent lying
   f. repeated sexual intercourse in a casual relationship
   g. repeated drunkenness or substance abuse
   h. thefts
   i. vandalism
   j. school grades markedly below expectations in relation to estimated or known IQ (may have resulted in repeating a year)
   k. chronic violations of rules at home and/or at school (other than truancy)
   l. initiation of fights

3. At least four of the following manifestations of the disorder since age 18:

   a. inability to sustain consistent work behavior, as indicated by any of the following: 1) too frequent job changes (e.g., three or more jobs in five years not accounted for by nature of job or economic or seasonal fluctuation), 2) significant unemployment (e.g., six months or more in five years when expected to work), 3) serious absenteeism from work (e.g., average

71

three days or more of lateness or absence per month), 4) walking off several jobs without other jobs in sight (Note: similar behavior in an academic setting during the last few years of school may substitute for this criterion in individuals who by reason of their age or circumstances have not had an opportunity to demonstrate occupational adjustment)

b. lack of ability to function as a responsible parent as evidenced by one or more of the following: 1) child's malnutrition, 2) child's illness resulting from lack of minimal hygiene standards, 3) failure to obtain medical care for a seriously ill child, 4) child's dependence on neighbors or non-resident relatives for food or shelter, 5) failure to arrange for a caretaker for a child under six when parent is away from home, 6) repeated squandering, on personal items, of money required for household necessities

c. failure to accept social norms with respect to lawful behavior, as indicated by any of the following: repeated thefts, illegal occupation (pimping, prostitution, fencing, selling drugs), multiple arrests, a felony conviction

d. inability to maintain enduring attachment to a sexual partner as indicated by two or more divorces and/or separations (whether legally married or not), desertion of spouse, promiscuity (ten or more sexual partners within one year)

e. irritability and aggressiveness as indicated by repeated physical fights or assault (not required by one's job or to defend someone or oneself), including spouse or child beating

f. failure to honor financial obligations, as indicated by repeated defaulting on debts, failure to provide child support, failure to support other dependents on a regular basis

g. failure to plan ahead, or impulsivity, as indicated by traveling from place to place without a prearranged job or clear goal for the period of travel or clear idea about when the travel would terminate, or lack of a fixed address for a month or more

h. disregard for the truth as indicated by repeated lying, use of aliases, "conning" others for personal profit

i. recklessness, as indicated by driving while intoxicated or recurrent speeding

4. A pattern of continuous antisocial behavior in which the rights of others are violated, with no intervening period of at least five years without antisocial

behavior between age 15 and the present time (except when the individual was bedridden or confined in a hospital or penal institution).

5. Antisocial behavior is not due to either Severe Mental Retardation, Schizophrenia or manic episodes.

| III |
| The Argument |

Theodore Heron, the respondent, was notified of these proceedings and invited to respond but declined to do so, noting that the proceedings were absurd since the marriage lasted several years and children were born of the marriage. However, four witnesses testified, one of them being an attorney who had counselled Theodore on occasion, another a former business associate of Theodore. All four witnesses were knowledgeable and honest, and the facts are clear. The facts were presented to Doctor Roger Martin, the Court-appointed psychiatric expert, and Doctor Martin's report is also part of the acts of the case.

Theodore's problems in life began fairly early. His father drank to excess and was not a steady worker while the mother, who was quite self-sufficient, was always very protective of little Theodore, assuring him, no matter how much hot water he got into, that he was a good boy but that other people were not always nice to him.

Theodore had trouble getting through high school. He was absent a great deal and did not apply himself, and though naturally bright and quite charming, he stayed back a couple of years. It took him six years to graduate. He twice registered in college but dropped out both times from sheer lack of interest.

He was likewise a dropout in the business world. During the eighteen years of marriage he had forty-two different jobs. He was a car salesman for several firms and would do very well but then lose interest. He opened a restaurant with a partner but went bankrupt. Many of his sales jobs were very short lived, and he was often unemployed.

He ran up two hundred dollars worth of parking tickets. He gambled and was constantly in debt. The utilities were always in danger of being turned off. He failed to pay his income tax for several years. He kited checks and forged his wife's name to a loan he was unable to repay. He falsely misrepresented himself as representing a baking company and was arrested for that. He lied at the drop of a hat. He used people, associated with prostitutes and had a prolonged affair with a woman in 1965. Isabel left him for a year while he was having this affair and during the affair the girl's mother committed suicide. The girl finally ended it and, when she did, Theodore came back to Isabel because the girl had been supporting him and now he felt left out in the cold. Seemingly he had no remorse for any of his behavior.

He was callous and indifferent to Isabel and the children. When Isabel was in her eighth month of pregnancy with their first child in January of 1956, she developed complications and was in danger of losing the child. They had, however, planned a Florida vacation at that time and, rather than lose their reservations, Theodore left Isabel and went off to Florida by himself. The next day Isabel delivered a stillborn child. In 1965 their seven year old son was struck by a truck while riding his bicycle. He was hospitalized for a full week but his father only managed to drop in to see him twice for a couple of minutes each time. For the most part Theodore simply ignored his children. He never became involved with them, and even when Isabel had to go to work to feed them, Theodore was off buying himself a new car or a designer suit he couldn't afford. Since the separation he has seen his children only a few times and has never supported them financially.

Our expert, Roger Martin, M.D., has diagnosed Theodore as suffering from a severe Antisocial Personality Disorder which deprived him of the capacity for love and for responsible loyalty to any other human being.

Given the diagnosis as well as Theodore's miserable eighteen year record of failure in marriage, this Court is satisfied that his lack of due competence for marriage, i.e., his inability to enter a marital partnership characterized by caring, sharing and respect for others, has been demonstrated.

WHEREFORE

I
The Facts

Sylvia Gazzera and Ivan Tanager, both Catholic, were married on the 20th day of June, 1960 at the Church of St. John, Merrick, Connecticut in the Archdiocese of Hartford. At the time Sylvia was twenty years old and Ivan was twenty-four.

The couple lived together for seventeen years and had two children but Ivan was irresponsible, sadistic, violent and an alcoholic. The couple separated finally in March of 1977 and Sylvia obtained a divorce in Hartford on February 15, 1978.

On December 1, 1978 Sylvia petitioned this Court to declare the marriage null. Her petition was accepted on January 28, 1979 and the *Contestatio Litis* was conducted, assigning lack of due competence as the grounds on which the validity of the Gazzera-Tanager marriage would be investigated and adjudged.

II
The Law

A. The law in this case is well summarized in the following law section of an affirmative decision dated January 31, 1976, (*Ephemerides Iuris Canonici*, XXXII, pp. 285-287) given by the Dean of the Rota, Monsignor Lefebvre.

> A declaration of nullity is being sought in this case "because of the incapacity of assuming perpetually the obligation of heterosexual consent as described in Canon 1081, § 2."

> This incapacity consists in the impossibility of exchanging either the object of the matrimonial contract or an essential element of that contract, which can only result in an invalid union, since "no one is held to the impossible," as St. Thomas reminded us when he said, "Just as in other contracts, no real obligation results when one obliges himself to something that one cannot give or do, so the marriage does not really result when one of the parties is not able to perform the marriage act" (S. Th. Suppl. q. 58, a.1.c).

> The aforesaid incapacity can be the result either of a mental disorder or of an abnormality which is not really an illness but which is caused by various factors that experts regard as blocking the possibility of entering an interpersonal relationship. This abnormality, though not really an illness, may be called emotional immaturity.

75

As regards the *first* cause of incapacity, namely a *mental disorder*, it should be remembered that marriage is a perpetual and exclusive partnership of the entire life of a man and woman ordered to the generation and education of offspring. It begins with the matrimonial contract which effects, among other things, a community of life, the right to which is granted at the time of the contract, as explained in the decision on February 25, 1969, by Monsignor Anné.

Some people say that this right to a community of life may be regarded as an essential element of the marriage contract only relative to the law under revision and not to the present law. But this is incorrect because the Second Vatican Council (*Gaudium et Spes,* 48) clearly determined that the community of life ought now to be understood as the object of the marriage contract.

The community of life is, of course, not actually realized in every case, and can in fact be lacking, but this does not mean that the *right* to it is not given in the contract. The right to the community of life, incidentally, is not something independent of the right to the conjugal act with its essential properties, but the term "community of life" better describes those qualities which make up marriage, including perpetuity, exclusivity, and the ordering towards children.

The husband and wife, furthermore, should not be understood simply as individual persons completely independent of each other, without their having a certain "otherness" or "relatedness," because "relatedness" is the whole point of marriage. It is the thing that unites the spouses, and it is a basic presupposition in marriage, for without it the marital union would be deprived of its foundation.

Relative to this point, it should be noted that "for a marriage to be valid both spouses should be objectively capable of an interpersonal relationship" (O. Fumagalli Carulli, *Intelletto e Volunta nel Consenso Matrimoniale in Diritto Canonico,* Milano, 1974, p. 306). For since the subjective element, i.e., the subjective ability of the parties, arises from a consideration of the "relatedness" of the parties, it is not possible to consider the consent of each party independent of the other at the time of marriage. A later loss, i.e., a post-marital loss, of the subjective element, would not, of course, affect validity.

Which is why the subjective element ought to be regarded as part of the object of the matrimonial contract.

As regards the *second* cause of incapacity, namely the one we shall call *emotional immaturity*, there are certainly many dangers, for some people will use the term in a vague and very broad sense, and so will apply it to disturbances which are entirely accidental. But it is evident that "emotional immaturity" understood in this sense does not render impossible an interpersonal relationship.

Still, in other cases, the seriousness of this emotional immaturity cannot be denied as, for example, when "the limitation of one's interest is to one's own person (narcissism or egotism) or to the narrow area of one's own activities and accomplishments, which is a very special kind of egoism that includes susceptibility, vanity and stubbornness" (Ey, Bernard and Brisset, *Manuel de psychiatrie*, Paris, 1974, p. 632). In such a case it may be determined that "it is practically impossible, indeed sometimes absolutely impossible, for this moral weakling to overcome his problems and so he attempts to resolve them by inappropriate solutions that amount to neurotic defense mechanisms."

Consequently, it can sometimes happen that there is "an absolute incapacity" which, though it may be rare, can nevertheless have very serious consequences.

Having said that, however, it should be noted that the decision of the lower court in this case tends to extend this principle unduly. Because it says that "an emotional disturbance," which it describes as "serious," "could seriously damage or annul completely the required evaluative knowledge." And it goes on to say that this could result from "any coercive or sociopathic obsession, or indeed any sociopathic type disorder, or any serious characterological defect." It even goes on to add that "any disturbance of the personality or any character defect which makes it impossible for a person to fulfill his or her proper marital role, that is, to fulfill the responsiblities of marriage, would seriously limit or completely annul one's capacity to contract marriage."

All of which is quite unnuanced and unscientific.

As Ms. Carulli said in her excellent study quoted above, "Given the serious psychic fragility of so many people, especially at the time of marriage, an overextension of the principle would result in many marriages being considered null. Besides the fact that this contradicts the basic principles of capacity as applied to marriage, it also seems to deny what the Church has always admitted, namely that even people of very limited abilities have a natural right to marry" (Carulli, *op. cit.*, p. 336)

Furthermore, Cardinal Staffa in his letter to Cardinal Alfrink, dated December 30, 1971, said, "the incapacity to contract marriage because of a lack in interpersonal relationships and in psychological maturity is wrongly called a moral impotence anterior to marriage and cannot be looked upon with moral certitude as an incapacity anterior to the marriage." [Monsignor Lefebvre gives as his citation "Docum. cath., t.

69, 1972, p. 19. An English translation of Cardinal Staffa's letter appeared in the *Jurist*, 1973, pp. 296-300. The letter in general and the section here quoted in particular (p. 299, 5) are critical of certain Dutch decisions which were, in effect, declaring that, even though the parties initially enjoyed a capacity for marriage, still, somewhere in the course of the marriage, the relationship broke down and the marriage should therefore be declared dead.]

The underlying problem must, of course, be antecedent, and it must also be perpetual, since otherwise it would not be a genuine constitutional incapacity, or it would be only a temporary one and therefore a merely relative one. But one cannot really be called incapable where the possibility of cure remains. For the invalidity of marriage, therefore, it is required that the malady be incurable, as stated in Canon 1068, § 1, and as foreshadowed by St. Thomas when he spoke of a "simply incurable defect of nature" (S. Th. Suppl. q. 58, a.1.c).

There could be a disturbance resulting from an emotional problem that would be of such seriousness, given the circumstances in which the matrimonial consent was given, that it would indeed affect the matrimonial consent. If that disturbance were sufficiently grave, to the point where the importance of the contract would be unappreciated, then the consent, and consequently the marriage itself, would be null. But then we are not really talking about the incapacity of assuming conjugal duties but rather about a lack of due discretion.

Proof of incapacity is not always easy, as Anné noted in his decision of March 11, 1975, unless, perhaps, it is a question of grave disturbance of the psychophysiological substratum, as in cases of serious homosexuality, nymphomania or paranoia. But in all other cases, a thorough investigation is required not only of the life style of the party at the time of the engagement and marriage, but also of the character, general mentality and psychology of the person during his adolescence and youth, as well as of the way he conducted himself in other, more general, facets of his life. Without a complete and accurate anamnesis, and the judgment of psychiatric and psychological experts, a judge may not legitimately conclude that a party suffered from an abnormal personality that rendered him incapable of assuming the obligations of marriage.

B. As regards the Borderline Personality Disorder, DSM III lists the following diagnostic criteria:

At least five of the following are required:

a. Impulsivity or unpredictability in at least two areas that are potentially self-damaging, e.g., spending, sex, gambling, drug or alcohol use, shoplifting, overeating, physically self-damaging acts.

b. A pattern of unstable and intense interpersonal relationships, e.g., marked shifts of attitude, idealization, devaluation, manipulation (consistently using others for one's own ends).

c. Inappropriate intense anger or lack of control of anger, e.g., frequently loses temper, always angry.

d. Identity disturbance manifested by uncertainty about several issues relating to identity, such as self-image, gender identity, long-term goals or career choice, friendship patterns, values and loyalties, e.g., "Who am I?", "I feel like I am my sister when I am good."

e. Affective instability: marked shifts from normal mood to depression, irritability or anxiety, usually lasting hours and only rarely for more than a few days, with a return to normal mood.

f. Problems tolerating being alone, e.g., frantic efforts to avoid being alone, depressed when alone.

g. Physically self-damaging acts, e.g., suicidal gestures, self-mutilation, recurrent accidents or physical fights.

h. Chronic feelings of emptiness or boredom.

III
The Argument

Although the respondent, Ivan Tanager, chose not to cooperate in these proceedings, two excellent witnesses were heard, and the facts are adequately demonstrated.

Ivan grew up in a large family with ten siblings, a father who drank and was often out of work, and a mother who was dominant and who acted as Ivan's protector against his brothers and sisters, with whom Ivan had a poor relationship.

Ivan was a slow learner and had truancy problems in school. He only went as far as sixth grade. Later on, as a teenager, he went with a tough crowd and had occasional problems with the police.

Ivan started dating Sylvia in April of 1959, a little more than a year before the wedding. Two months before the wedding (at which time no definite plans for marriage had been made) Ivan's mother died. He wept bitterly, complained that it should have been his father rather than his mother, disappeared for a couple of weeks, and on his return asked Sylvia to marry him.

During the courtship Ivan would occasionally not show up for a date and would simply dismiss it by saying he had forgot, but to Sylvia he did not seem bad. She knew nothing of his background or his drinking.

The honeymoon came as a great shock to her. Ivan wept on the wedding night over his mother's death and did not consummate the marriage. As it turned out sex was a major problem for Ivan. He had intercourse only about twenty times in all the years of marriage and even on those occasions he was usually drunk, or Sylvia virtually forced him to have sex.

It was also on the honeymoon that Sylvia became acquainted with Ivan's drinking. He was drunk practically the entire honeymoon and he stayed out each night until four or five in the morning.

Periodically throughout the marriage Ivan would disappear for varying lengths of time. This absenteeism was one of the reasons (others were that he would drink and get in fights at work) for Ivan losing jobs. At any rate he seemed to have dozens of them during the course of the marriage.

No matter how much he made, however, there was never enough money. He gave Sylvia $70 a month for rent, utilities and food while he gambled and spent the rest. He took out loans and they went hopelessly in debt.

Ivan went out to bars every night, often drove under the influence and was involved in thirteen accidents during the marriage, one of them a hit and run.

Ivan was always a violent man, beat Sylvia and tried to choke her and was a monster to the children who were terrified of him and who eventually needed psychiatric help.

Other bizarre incidents include his wanting to burn the hospital bed which Sylvia was occupying as a patient in 1962, because she was going to die and should be cremated; and his own suicide attempt late in the marriage.

The expert on the case, Doctor Walter Taube, has diagnosed Ivan as suffering from a severe Borderline Personality Disorder, resulting largely from a deprived familial background and childhood.

Given all the evidence, including the opinion of the expert, it is clear that Ivan Tanager lacked the due competence for marriage.

WHEREFORE

```
┌─────────────────┐
│        I        │
│    The Facts    │
└─────────────────┘
```

Sandra Drossel and Stacey Grive, both Catholic, were married at the Church of St. Stephen, Florence, Connecticut in the Archdiocese of Hartford on the twelfth day of June, 1968. At the time Sandra was twenty years old and Stacey was twenty-four.

Sandra and Stacey lived together for about six years but Stacey never really became involved in the marriage and was, from beginning to end, irresponsible. No children were born of the marriage. The couple separated finally in May of 1974 and a divorce was granted in New Britain, Connecticut on March 23, 1976.

On December 1, 1977 Sandra petitioned this Court to declare the marriage null. Her petition was accepted on December 22 and the Doubt was Formulated on January 15, 1978, with lack of due competence being assigned as the grounds.

```
┌─────────────────┐
│       II        │
│    The Law      │
└─────────────────┘
```

A. Since the late 1940s rotal jurisprudence has at least germinally recognized the fact that a marriage could be null not only by reason of lack of due discretion but also by reason of lack of due competence. In a decision of February 21, 1948 Canestri spoke of a person being affected by a "moral impotence" in that a psychopathology deprived him of the ability to meet the obligations of marriage (40, 64)

Throughout the 1950s and '60s, during which time the essence of marriage was understood to consist only of the right to the body for those acts which are per se apt for the generation of offspring, the notion of lack of due competence was restricted to those cases in which a person was incapable of meeting those obligations which referred to the "three goods" of marriage: the *bonum prolis,* the *bonum fidei* and the *bonum sacramenti.* In a decision of June 21, 1957 (49, 500-513), for example, Sabattani dealt with a case in which the issue was whether a woman afflicted with nymphomania could assume the obligations of the *bonum fidei.* For a history of the development of this jurisprudence see *The Bearing of Mental Impairment on the Validity of Marriage* by John Richard Keating, Rome: The Gregorian University Press, 1964.

In a decision of February 25, 1969, however, a decision which history may regard as the most influential of our century, Lucien Anné noted that, in fact, the essence of marriage includes not only the *biological* element (the right to procreative intercourse) but the *personal* element as well (the right to the community of life). In light of this now generally accepted insight, the phrase "lack of due competence" (*incapacitas ad onera essentialia*) took on a whole new meaning, and now refers both to the right to procreative intercourse and to the right to a caring, interpersonal relationship.

When, therefore, a person is, by reason of some psychological cause, deprived of the capacity for those interpersonal relationships, he should be regarded as lacking the due competence for marriage.

B. As regards the particular psychopathology at issue in this case, namely the Avoidant Personality Disorder, DSM III describes its diagnostic criteria as follows:

1. Hypersensitivity to rejection, e.g., apprehensively alert to signs of social derogation, interprets innocuous events as ridiculing.

2. Unwillingness to enter into relationships unless given unusually strong guarantees of uncritical acceptance.

3. Social withdrawal, e.g., distances self from close personal attachments, engages in peripheral social and vocational roles.

4. Desire for affection and acceptance.

5. Low self-esteem, e.g., devalues self-achievements and is overly dismayed by personal shortcomings.

C. As regards the value of the psychiatrist's report, suffice it to quote the following from Parisella's decision of July 13, 1968 (60, 564-565), "In order to determine how much authority and importance should be attached to the report of the experts, rotal jurisprudence has always taught that it is wrong for a judge to disagree with their conclusions except for very serious contrary evidence—a *peritorum conclusionibus iudici recedere nefas sit nisi propter gravissima contraria argumenta.*"

D. One of the classic instances of the use of a peritior in a case before the Rota is found in the decision coram Morano of April 30, 1935 (27, 280 ff). In that case, one peritus opined *against* insanity; the other peritus and the peritior *for* insanity. The judges voted with the maior pars for insanity, i.e., for the nullity of the marriage, not only "*ob auctoritatem numeri*" but also "*ob intrinsecas rationes*" (p. 284).

I
The Facts

Stella Willet and Hugh Partridge, both Catholic, were married on the twelfth day of June 1952 in the Church of St. Brendan, Kirkland, Connecticut in the Diocese of Bridgeport. At the time Stella was nineteen years old and Hugh was twenty-five.

The couple lived together for about eleven years and had two children but the relationship between Stella and Hugh was always more that of mother-son than husband-wife. They finally separated in March of 1963 and a divorce was obtained in Bridgeport on May 19, 1964.

On August 15, 1979 Stella petitioned this Court, competent by reason of the petitioner's residence, to declare her marriage null. Her petition was accepted and at the *Contestatio Litis* conducted on October 8, the Issue in Pleading was defined as follows:

> Whether the Willet-Partridge marriage has been proved null on the grounds of lack of due competence.

II
The Law

A. Our law sometimes refers to the breakdown of a marriage as a "naufragium," a shipwreck (see, for example, the "Instructio Pro Solutione Matrimonii in Favorem Fidei" of December 6, 1973, II, 3). This is not an altogether useless analogy. It suggests that the parties to a marriage are, as it were, co-captains of a vessel, that if they are to be regarded as competent officers they must have assured themselves that the vessel is seaworthy and they must, furthermore, be equipped with the kind of temperament and knowledge that will enable them to cope with at least the ordinary contingencies of the sea, the storms and the doldrums to which every ship is eventually subject. A captain would not, of course, be regarded as inept if his ship was torn to pieces by a freak storm but he surely would be regarded as incompetent if he recklessly endangered the ship by steering into a storm or storm area or if he compulsively chased a whale into dangerous waters or if he rammed an iceberg while failing to provide the proper watch.

In marriage, as in sailing, in other words, competence involves not only sanity but first of all certain basic skills which permit one to steer clear of hazards and at order to avoid any possibility of having to rely on self, e.g., tolerates abusive spouse.

3. Lacks self-confidence, e.g., sees self as helpless, stupid.

III
The Argument

Hugh Partridge is now fifty-three years old. According to the witnesses, he has lived with his mother since separating from Stella sixteen years ago and has never remarried. It is reported that for many years he has been a very severe alcoholic who looks like a "bum." After the divorce he had great difficulty with employment and lost several jobs, mostly because of his alcoholism. He did not respond to correspondence from the Tribunal Instructor.

The evidence in this case consists of the testimony of the petitioner, the testimony of two witnesses (a sister of the petitioner and a cousin of the petitioner) and a report from the Court-appointed expert, Walter Taube, M.D.

I am satisfied that the total evidence demonstrates that Hugh Partridge, in 1952, lacked the capacity to exchange with Stella the right to a true marital partnership, i.e., the right to self revelation, understanding and caring. In other words, he lacked the competence for marriage.

Hugh Partridge's parents were divorced when he was very young. Hugh was an only child and he was thereafter reared and spoiled by his overprotective mother. The mother had a constant fear, while Hugh was a child, that the father would one day kidnap him (which was probably a touch of paranoia on her part) and whenever little Hugh was late returning home from school, the mother sent her brothers out in search of him.

Even after Hugh was an adult, mother made all the decisions for him and continued to give him everything he wanted. All of this developed in Hugh a dependence on women and a special attitude towards the function of women in his life.

Perhaps because the mother was so concerned about Hugh's being kidnapped on the way to or from school, Hugh left school in the seventh grade and so was never prepared for anything more than menial work.

Stella and Hugh met in 1949 and kept company for about three years before marrying. Stella had come from a broken home herself and, after her parents divorced, she lived with a variety of uncles, aunts and grandmothers. She was insecure herself and was attracted to Hugh mostly by his looks and the fact that he had a car. Even then, Hugh drank a lot and gambled and fairly often he would be late for a date or not show up at all. Three times during the courtship Stella broke off with Hugh because of his behavior but each time they got back together.

Even during the courtship the mother-son relationship was in evidence, with Stella forgiving Hugh's childish behavior and taking care of him, even to the point of taking his shoes home and shining them so that Hugh would look nice.

After marriage, as one witness said, Hugh just wanted to go hunting or fishing or playing cards, while Stella cleaned house and cooked for him. Stella did take care of Hugh, even laying out his clothes for him to wear, but she also gave orders which Hugh dutifully obeyed. When she told him to mow the lawn, he mowed the lawn.

Although Hugh was steadily employed during the marriage, he never made much money and, except during the time of childbirth and caring (the children were born nine years apart—one in the beginning of the marriage and one towards the end), Stella worked full time. Even then they did not have much money but Hugh still continued to gamble quite heavily throughout the marriage and whenever he wanted anything his mother intervened and purchased it for him.

The witnesses saw Hugh as shy, withdrawn, moody and dependent. His friends, one witness said, were anybody who had money in his pocket, but he did not like to socialize and would occasionally even leave the room when visitors came.

It was not so much what Hugh did in the marriage as what he didn't do. He was a peaceful, non-violent person and a "faithful" husband, in the minimalist sense of that word. But at the same time he never became a real husband to Stella. He did not communicate with her or treat her as a partner in the consortium of marriage. He watched television or went out gambling and drinking (Stella often went to fetch him at the local Italian club). He took his vacation during hunting season and managed to cut himself off from his family in his hobbies and in everything he did.

He refused to go anywhere with Stella, so eventually she took to going out bowling with some girlfriends. On one such evening she met a man with whom she became friendly and whom she saw fairly often, though there was no sexual involvement. One night she told Hugh about her friendship and the next day Hugh waited for the older boy to come home from school and told him he was leaving and that the boy could stay with mother or come with him. The boy chose to stay with mother and Hugh left and never returned.

Our expert, Doctor Walter Taube, has diagnosed Hugh as suffering from a severe Dependent Personality Disorder. Hugh, according to Doctor Taube, was, in marrying Stella, looking not for a wife but rather for someone to mother him. The passivity increased as the marriage went on, and the alcoholism became progressively severe, especially since the separation.

Given all the evidence it seems clear that Hugh Partridge was, at the time of marriage, not strong enough to assume the essential obligations of marriage, namely *self revelation* (Hugh was not aware that he was looking for a mother rather than a wife), *understanding* (he had little understanding of Stella's need to be a wife) and *caring* (he was incapable of genuinely disinterested affection for a wife).

WHEREFORE

I
The Facts

Harold Woodstock and Priscilla Swan, both Catholic, were married at the Church of St. Robert Bellarmine in Freeport, Connecticut in the Archdiocese of Hartford on the twenty-second day of June, 1978. Harold was twenty-five years old at the time; Priscilla was twenty-four.

Harold and Priscilla lived together for about three years but quarrelled frequently and led a strange, strained existence. No children were born to them and they separated finally in July of 1981 (they had also been circumstantially separated for four months in 1980). A divorce was granted in New Haven on February 8, 1982.

On November 4, 1982, Harold petitioned this Tribunal to declare the marriage null. His petition was accepted and the *Contestatio Litis* was conducted on November 30, with Harold's own lack of due competence being established by the Judge as the *caput nullitatis investigandum*.

II
The Law

A. Catholic jurisprudence regarding lack of due competence has developed over the years.

Older jurisprudence tended to see no middle ground between 1) marriage as a basic social unit of reproduction and education (which is *sufficient* for validity) and 2) marriage as a warm, happy experience (which is *superfluous* to validity). Pinto, for example, in a decision (E.I.C. 1977, 3-4, p. 335) of October 28, 1976 (within a year he modified his position—see Quaglia - Macreuse, D2, p. 113) said: "The duties which regard the mutual assistance of the spouses, even though marriage is, by its nature, directed to this assistance, as well as other duties stemming from positive law, even though they are extremely important in order for a marriage to go reasonably well (ut illud *bene* sit) are nevertheless not essentially necessary for a valid marriage (quod matrimonium simpliciter *sit*)."

More recent jurisprudence, however (see, for example, Pinto's more recent decisions as well as those coram Lefebvre, Ewers, Anné, Parisella, DiFelice and Serrano, among others) sees the older jurisprudence as positing an artificial and unnuanced dichotomy that does not reflect life.

The challenge to the jurist working today in the field of marriage is, first of all, to examine marriage as a continuum with its many gradations, and secondly to establish guidelines for the detection of a cutoff point between validity and invalidity in individual instances. In general, today's jurist recognizes that, at the very least, there exists a trichotomy rather than a dichotomy. In general, in other words, he sees at least three stages on the continuum: 1) marriage as a joining of bodies, 2) marriage as a joining of souls (one that includes some personalist elements as essential for validity) and 3) marriage as a warm, happy experience.

The difficult question, of course, is: *how* personalist must a marriage be in order to be valid? Obviously, it *does not* have to be romantic and fulfilling in order to be valid, but it *does,* in the opinion of most jurists, have to include some fundamental interpersonal recognition and sharing and, at the same time, exclude the substantial destruction of one or both parties.

For a valid marriage, in other words, the parties must be capable of exchanging "the right to those things which pertain to the partnership of conjugal life" as C. 1135 puts it. In our culture, those things which pertain to the partnership of conjugal life are the three acts of self revelation, understanding and caring.

1. *Self revelation* means that a person must first of all enjoy a basic ego identity, i.e., he must see himself as one fairly consistent person, have a reasonable degree of respect for that person, and convey a knowledge of himself to his spouse.

2. *Understanding* means that he must see his spouse as a separate person, and appreciate her way of feeling and thinking, without distorting it excessively by his own attitudes, needs or insecurities.

3. *Caring* means that a person must, with reasonable maturity, pledge himself to a lifelong community with his spouse, not because he wishes to possess her, but because of the special reverence and affection he has for her, and because he wishes to share his life with her.

B. The particular disorder pertinent to this case is the Compulsive Personality Disorder. DSM III describes the diagnostic criteria of that disorder as follows:

At least four of the following are characteristic of the individual's current and long-term functioning, are not limited to episodes of illness, and cause either significant impairment in social or occupational functioning or subjective distress.

1. restricted ability to express warm and tender emotions, e.g., the individual is unduly conventional, serious and formal, and stingy.

2. perfectionism that interferes with the ability to grasp "the big picture," e.g., preoccupation with trivial details, rules, order, organization, schedules, and lists

3. insistence that others submit to his or her way of doing things, and lack of awareness of the feelings elicited by this behavior, e.g., a husband stubbornly insists his wife complete errands for him regardless of her plans

4. excessive devotion to work and productivity to the exclusion of pleasure and the value of interpersonal relationships

5. indecisiveness: decision-making is either avoided, postponed, or protracted, perhaps because of an inordinate fear of making a mistake, e.g., the individual cannot get assignments done on time because of ruminating about priorities

---

III
The Argument

Priscilla Swan did not cooperate in these proceedings, declining to answer any mail from the Tribunal. The evidence, therefore, consists of 1) the testimony of the petitioner, 2) the testimony of five witnesses and 3) a report from Helen Linotte, M.D., the Court-appointed psychiatric expert.

Harold Woodstock sent a marital history to this Tribunal in February of 1982. The history was, in general, self serving and accusatory. The problem with the marriage, according to Harold, was that Priscilla was frigid and the marriage was not, therefore, truly consummated. He described himself as "intelligent, industrious, conscientious, affectionate, open, honest and disciplined."

On August 12, 1982, Harold wrote the Tribunal the following letter:

> Dear Rev. Wrenn,
> I wonder if it would be possible to have my case heard within the next couple of months.
> Two weeks ago I met the woman I am certain that the Lord intends me to marry. The circumstances surrounding our initial encounter are rather astonishing. I mentioned in my marital history that in late July of 1981 I had the experience of having a strong "premonition" that my marriage would be resolved and that I would have a replacement for my ex-wife. I was made aware that the woman I had just met the previous Friday was Priscilla's intended replacement on the last Tuesday of July, 1982, the anniversary of the premonition. We are perfectly suited to each other in every way. I look forward to telling you in person exactly what has transpired.
> Thank you for your consideration.
>
> Sincerely
> Harold Woodstock

Some of the reasons that led Harold to conclude that this new woman in his life was intended by God as Priscilla's "replacement" were that they both liked the same food, both drove the same model car and both were from New England.

So it was clear to the Tribunal early on that Harold Woodstock had emotional problems.

Harold Woodstock was the oldest of six children born to overprotective, strict parents. Harold was not allowed to date until he was a senior in high school. When he was in college, however, his roommate was a ladies' man and Harold says that he took notes on his roommate's modus operandi. Harold too became a ladies' man. In the five years from age nineteen to age twenty-four, Harold says that he dated two hundred girls and had sex with twelve or thirteen of them.

Harold and Priscilla met in July of 1977, shortly after Harold had been discharged from the Navy. The couple met at a pool and shortly thereafter began having sex daily. Priscilla became emotionally attached to Harold very quickly but Harold felt that he could break off with her at any time. Priscilla, however, pressured Harold to marry, cooked meals for him and professed to be madly in love with him. Within four months of meeting they were engaged.

Harold apparently was not quite sure that Priscilla was the ideal sex partner for him, despite the fact that they were having daily sex, so he made her promise before marriage that they would have sex together every day of the marriage. Priscilla consented.

The couple went to visit Father George O'Brien, a Bridgeport priest and an old friend of the Woodstock family. Father O'Brien, who was engaged for years in Cana work and who served as a witness in these proceedings, knew that Harold was emotionally unstable and the couple was ill matched, and he strongly advised against the marriage. The couple did not return to Father O'Brien but went instead to another priest who arranged the marriage for them.

After marriage the couple continued to have sex daily for a time but by late 1979 they were having intercourse only a couple of times a month and since Priscilla had had sex only half-heartedly during the three years of marriage Harold decided that the marriage wasn't really consummated.

Priscilla certainly had problems of her own. She had been reared in an extremely strict family where the parents regarded at least some of Walt Disney's movies as objectionable. Priscilla had attempted suicide when she was twenty-one years old over a broken romance, and she was hot tempered and perfectionistic.

The couple could not relate. Harold treated Priscilla like a thing or a sex machine, as apparently he views all woman (he actually referred to his present lady friend as a "replacement" for Priscilla—as though the old machine was being replaced by the new). Priscilla, naturally, responded poorly to this attitude and the couple quarrelled constantly over trivial matters. When Priscilla found sex painful or uncomfortable Harold was totally oblivious to her feelings. She, meanwhile, humiliated him in public and threw tantrums when everything was not in absolutely perfect order.

Our expert, Doctor Linotte, has diagnosed Harold as suffering from a severe Compulsive Personality Disorder with sociopathic traits and a sophisticated, subtle but strong sadistic quality. Priscilla, according to Doctor Linotte, suffers from a somewhat less severe Mixed Personality Disorder, with Compulsive and Hysterical features.

It is clear from the total evidence that Harold Woodstock lacked the capacity for sustaining a lifelong marriage characterized by *self revelation* (the man has almost no understanding of his own personality problems), *understanding* (he consistently treated Priscilla not as a person but a thing) and *caring* (his basic approach was one of hostile sadism rather than of "affectio maritalis").

WHEREFORE

```
        I
    The Facts
```

Ralph Darter and Alma Crane, both Catholic, were married on August 12, 1961 at the Church of St. Marie, Goldsboro, Connecticut in the Archdiocese of Hartford. Ralph was twenty-two years old at the time; Alma was twenty-five.

Ralph and Alma met in the fall of 1960, by which time Alma had already received her master's degree in psychology and was employed in a children's mental health center. Alma had apparently decided that it was time for her to marry, and that Ralph would make a suitable husband, and they were married within a year.

The couple lived together for fifteen years, and had three children, all boys, born in 1965, 1971 and 1973. Alma was always a cold, clinical sort of person who treated her husband like a casual acquaintance. When she finally terminated the marriage in 1976 in order to marry a fellow psychologist and father of seven children, she felt that it was, in a way, a pity to leave Ralph, but, after all, "we can't devote our lives to other people."

A divorce was obtained on May 15, 1977. On June 6, 1980 Ralph petitioned this Court to declare the marriage null. On July 1, 1980 Ralph's petition was accepted and on that same day the Doubt was Formulated in the following terms:

> Whether the Darter-Crane marriage has been proved null on the grounds of lack of due competence.

```
        II
    The Law
```

A. The jurisprudence in a case of this sort is discussed in the ratification decree dated December 15, 1979, coram Colagiovanni (*Monitor Ecclesiasticus,* 1980, 1, pp. 55-58), the "in jure" section of which reads as follows:

1. The sentence of first instance, recalling the kind of freedom that is necessary for marital consent, a freedom that is excluded when a person is psychologically pressured towards one option, quotes the well known decision of January 26, 1971, coram Anné, regarding grave psychological incapacity for eliciting consent and/or for assuming marital obligations. That decision of

Anné was certainly an excellent one but it is also true, as our diligent and insightful Defender of the Bond has noted, that "the more recent jurisprudence of our Tribunal has added a great deal to the study of this ground of nullity," and that this ground, if it is not properly understood and wisely applied, can lead to abuse and to unwarranted and overly broad extensions and applicatons. Certainly, as our Defender of the Bond noted, "we cannot expect that all first instance tribunals around the world be aware of all Rotal decisions" but neither can we approve of a law section which consists simply of one page of photocopied material that makes reference to one or more rotal decisions and then concludes with a brief description of the mental disorder in question as found in the *Diagnostic and Statistical Manual,* with no attempt whatever to reflect on the special modality of the ground under discussion. Such a practice is particularly unacceptable in our time when there are so many ways of rethinking and of deepening our juridical insights. Such a practice, furthermore, leads to the kind of automatism that genuine law and jurisprudence should studiously avoid, since their true function is not only to categorize reality but also to serve as a mirror of life.

2. During the last century, certain psychiatrists (Prichard, *Treatise on Insanity* London, 1835; and Koch, *Die psychopathischen Minderwertin,* 1891), noting that some people who are neither completely nor even partially insane nor lacking the use of reason, nevertheless act *abnormally,* called such people "psychopaths" insofar as they reflect peculiar and abnormal varieties of the normal personality (eine krankafte Spielart der Norm). This statement, however, gives rise to two difficulties: the first in defining the meaning of "personality," and the second in trying to determine what must be included in the term "normality."

Personality may be defined as "the dynamic organization in the bosom of the individual of those psychophysical systems which determine the behavior and the thinking that are characteristic of the subject" (G. Allport, *Pattern and Growth in Personality,* Holt Rinehart & Winston, New York, 1965; Italian translation Zurich, 1969, p. 24) or, in the words of A. Gemelli: "the human personality is made up of a complex of: a) the organic functions which are apparent in one's constitution; b) the dispositions, which includes tendencies, inclinations, affects, and especially functions variously described as pertaining to one's more earthy or practical nature; and c) the higher sentiments, that is to say, the intellective and volitive functions." Gemelli further notes, however, that "all those elements of the personality are not disparate or juxtaposed; on the contrary, together they constitute a living, unified totality and they contribute to the life of the person in whom they come together as a vital synthesis." (*Introduction to Psychology,* Vita e Pensiero, 1949, p. 433).

3. If this coordination of all the "phenomenological" elements (Gemelli, op. cit. p. 433) is blocked in its interior harmonization and in the implementation of choice into action, then not only is one or another faculty disturbed but also

the free dynamism of the entire personality is restricted both in its ability to judge the object and also in its ability to make the judgment and choice one's own. For, as St. Thomas said, "the human person, in judging what has to be done, can make a free decision only to the degree that he understands both the end and the means to the end, and also only to the degree that he understands the relationship between the two; a person must therefore be aware not only of his motives for acting but also of his motives for deciding" (St. Thomas, *De Veritate*, q. 24, a. 1; cf. Contra Gentes, L. II, c. 48).

This passage is talking about the "critical faculty," which is mentioned often in rotal decisions, and which can be disturbed if one or other of the elements that constitute "personality" (instinct, sense, character, temperament, affect, emotion . . . that is to say, the endotrophic basis of personality) departs from the "norm" in such a way that that vital synthesis about which St. Thomas was speaking cannot be attained.

The second difficulty here, as we noted, is in defining and circumscribing "normality," by departing from which one is called "abnormal."

Professor B. Callieri notes: "As is obvious, those parameters on which a norm depends are, in individual instances, influenced by the particular culture and environment in question and indeed by the personality of the psychiatrist or psychologist who is working within them. The above mentioned criteria, therefore, almost always carry with them a certain "cultural relativism," to the point where, in many places, there is an attempt to reduce the concept of a personality disorder to a simple (or complex) series of characteristics which seem unacceptable within a given relational system, or, as they say in English, within a given "frame of reference." (*De personalitatibus psychopaticis uti causa nullitatis matrimonii*, lectio pro manuscripto in "cursu renovationis canonicae 1979-1980" apud Pont. Univers. Gregorianam). While clinical psychiatrists and psychologists have vacillated between abstract normality and statistical normality, and have wavered between the school of individual subjectivism and the school of social conformism, our jurisprudence had steadfastly required that that critical faculty be proportionate to the nature and essential obligations of marriage (cf. A. Di Felice, *La "Discretio judicii matrimonio proportionata" nella giurisprudenza rotale*, in *Perturbazioni psichiche e consenso matrimoniale nel diritto canonico*, Roma 1976, p. 25 ss.; M. Pompedda, *Nevrosi e personalita psicopatiche in rapporto al consenso matrimoniale*, op. cit. pp. 58 ss.) relative to the formal object of marital consent (Canon 1081, para. 2).

4. This formal object of marital consent, however, essentially implies a "relational" aspect, that is to say, that rights and duties be handed over and accepted by the other party (and the offspring); and people with personality disorders can be seriously disturbed in their personality precisely in reference to this "relational" aspect of the person (cf. G. Winokur R. R. Crowe, *Personality Disorders*, in *Comprehensive Textbook of Psychiatry*, ed. 2, vol. II,

Baltimore, 1976; W. Mayer Gross - E. Smater - M. Roth, *Clinical Psychology*, Cassel, London, trad. ital. Sansoni, c. IV; Bleurer, *Trattato di Psichiatria*, trad. ital. ed. Feltrinelli, 1967, p. 606; Sheldon J. Korchin, *Modern Clinical Psychology*, Basic Books, N.Y., 1976, trad. ital. ed. Borla, 1977, p. 174, ss.). Which explains why all of this has juridic importance in our tribunals. It is, however, illicit to extend unduly the influence, seriousness and modality of such abnormalities when they do not bring about true illness. Callieri, indeed, has said that "we should emphasize as forcefully as possible, following Schneider's lead, that personality disorders do not constitute the matter of diagnosis nor can they be said to constitute a disease, but they simply manifest different *abnormal variations* of personality" (B. Callieri, lect. cit. p. 9). Nevertheless, although a personality disorder does not constitute a disease in the strict sense, it can still pose an obstacle to the formation of marital consent and it can be of the same seriousness as a true and proper mental disease. On this point, that is, as regards the power of the personality disorder to undermine consent, the German and the Anglo-American schools of psychiatry agree; they differ only as regards the terminology that should be applied to the individual anomalies of personality.

In order to bring about uniformity of terms, the American Psychiatric Association compiled in 1968 the "Diagnostic and Statistical Manual of Mental Disorders" (DSM II) revising the first summary that was published in 1952 (DSM I); practically at the same time the World Health Organization (OMS) published the "International Classification of Disease."

DSM I divided "Personality Disorders And Other Non-psychotic Mental Disorders" into four categories: A) Personality Disorders (paranoid, cyclothymic, schizoid, explosive, obsessive-compulsive, hysterical, asthenic, anti-social, passive-aggressive); B) Sexual deviation; C) Alcoholism; and D) Drug Dependence.

But equivocations and confusions still remain, either because the Anglo-American psychiatrists use DSM I on one occasion and DSM II on another, or because they follow the classifications of European psychiatry. Still another problem is that some people have characteristics that fit into many categories: a personality implies "a psychosomatic unity in which different processes of mental and behavioral life are mingled in a complex way" (S. Schneider, *Personal Adjustment and Mental Health*, Rinehart & Co., N.Y., 1955, trad. ital. S.E.I., 1959), so the elements which disturb the same personality can be commingled in varying grades.

5. It is understandable, therefore, that, when different juridic aspects come together in the same case, they are discussed according to the same terminology. The schema of the Revised Code, for example, under Canon 55, says: "They are incapable of contracting marriage . . . 2) who labor under a serious defect of discretion of judgment about the marital rights and duties that are to be mutually handed over and received . . . 3) who, because of a

serious psychosexual anomaly, are not able to assume the essential obligations of marriage"; and both of these categories are considered distinct from
those under number 1) who "are afflicted with a mental *disease* or grave
disturbance (of the spirit) in such a way that, since they lack the use of reason,
they are not able to elicit marital consent." It is clear, therefore, that those
who are under numbers 2) and 3) are not afflicted with a *serious disease
removing the use of reason.* Nevertheless "in the meeting of May 18, 1977,
the majority of the Commission members wanted the words 'on account of a
grave psychosexual anomaly' to be changed to 'on account of a grave psychic
anomaly'" (Coram Pinto, d. 20 April, 1979, in *Monitor Eccles.*, 1979, IV,
p. 384).

6. The personality disorders used to be attributed to constitutional or structural
causes; today, however, it is recognized that along with those causes there
can also be influences of faulty education, especially in the family and
primary community which deter the normal maturation or evolution of the
personality. (cf. Morton Schatzman, *Soul Murder: Persecution in the Family*,
Random House, N.Y., 1973, vers. ital. *La Famiglia che uccide*, Feltrinelli,
1973; N. Cameron - A. Margaret, *Behaviour Pathology*, Houghton-Mifflin,
Boston, vers. ital. Giunti, pp. 241-242). Thus is brought about an inclination
of the mind and a disposition of the will towards an erroneous appreciation of
matrimonial rights and duties in such a way that a lack of due discretion,
mixed with the intention of pursuing something other than marriage, can
result. Since, moreover, those people are weak of will, fragile in their emotional makeup and euphoric in their drives, they sometimes "are drawn not to
marriage but unknowingly to something other than marriage" (c. Davino, 18
dec. 1975, Gorzovien, P.N. 11.164; n. 2), which is all the more true when
there is some family pressure put upon them to marry. It is therefore difficult to
determine which element is the principal one in this confluence of many
factors that result in the lack of marital consent, but "the important thing is
always the facts and not terminology" (c. De Jorio, diei 13 maii 1964, vol. 56,
p. 353; c. eodem diei 5 dec. 1964, vol. 56, p. 901, c. eodem diei 28 jul. 1976.
. .) which is even more true when you are talking about terms that connote
psychopathological categories according to different psychiatric schools and
indeed, as Callieri notes, according to different psychiatrists.

7. Proof in these cases is obtained through certain conclusions of experts that are
based on a picture of reality that is learned from witnesses who refer to
established facts about the abnormal way of thinking or at least of acting on the
part of the disabled person. The judge, however, "should pay careful attention
not only to the conclusions of the experts, even where they agree, but also to
other circumstances of the case (cf. Canon 1804, para. 1) adverting to those
things "which are essential for contracting validly" but not "to those things
which are to be hoped for but which do not in themselves enter into the nature
of consent, and whose absence, therefore, does not affect the validity of the
consent (coram Davino, February 5, 1975).

B. The diagnostic criteria, as listed in DSM III for the particular Personality Disorder at issue in the case at bar, namely the Passive-Aggressive Personality Disorder, are as follows:

The following are characteristic of the individual's current and long-term functioning, and are not limited to episodes of illness.

1. Resistance to demands for adequate performance in both occupational and social functioning.

2. Resistance expressed indirectly through at least two of the following:
   a. procrastination
   b. dawdling
   c. stubbornness
   d. intentional inefficiency
   e. "forgetfulness"

3. As a consequence of 1 and 2, pervasive and long-standing social and occupational ineffectiveness (including in roles of housewife or student), e.g., intentional inefficiency that has prevented job promotion.

4. Persistence of the behavior pattern even under circumstances in which more self-assertive and effective behavior is possible.

5. Does not meet the criteria for any other Personality Disorder, and if under age 18, does not meet the criteria for Oppositional Disorder.

III
The Argument

Mr. and Mrs. Ralph Darter rarely argued. You would hardly say that they were a romantic, starry-eyed couple; all sex between them, by edict of Alma, had to be after one o'clock in the morning, and, generally Mr. Darter was treated by his wife almost like a complete stranger. But still they rarely argued.

Perhaps to a casual observer, Alma's control of herself might seem an admirable trait. When she received second and third degree burns on her hands in an accident, and when she suffered a miscarriage, she remained calm, cool and collected. And she rarely argued, rarely even uttered a harsh word. Surely there is something admirable in that.

Too bad, of course, that she was so inhibited emotionally, that she was so distant and clinical all the time. But better that, perhaps, than the hot tempered wife who would be throwing dishes at her husband.

At least Alma was not hostile and aggressive. Or was she?

Our expert, Doctor Roger Martin, reports that this was precisely Alma's problem—aggressiveness. She was, says Doctor Martin, aggressive to the point of being emotionally ill. But she expressed her aggressiveness passively.

She rarely argued or uttered a harsh word. But she treated people like things or cases. Everything, for her, was a psychological plan. She always had to be in control. No person or institution could be allowed to control her. Not even her own emotions could control her. The Catholic Church would like to control her and her thoughts and beliefs, and therefore it must be kept at arm's length. No need to quarrel with it, of course. Just keep it at arm's length. Her mother would probably like to control her too, so her mother was treated like a "business acquaintance." Her husband and children would very likely make excessive demands on her were they free to do so, so they would be treated like everyone else. Ralph, therefore, was treated like a "casual acquaintance." . . . "There was no affection or lack of affection." (Richard Lewis, 25). Mr. Lewis was of the opinion that Alma didn't really treat Ralph badly, but obviously, when you treat your husband like a casual acquaintance you treat him badly.

The children, meanwhile, were treated like objects, or, at best, subjects in a textbook written by Alma Darter. At the time of the separation, the twelve-year-old boy apparently wanted his mother to love him, but Alma found this too demanding, characterized his behavior as manipulative, gave him over to his father, and rarely sees him. In effect, of course, this cuts the boy off not only from his mother but from his two brothers as well, but Alma considers this for the best.

Eugene Kennedy described the syndrome of passive aggression this way (it fits Alma perfectly):

> These people are extremely difficult to deal with because, although conflict is never on the surface, cooperation is never there either. One of the reasons that it is difficult to help passive aggressive personalities is that the payoff on the unconscious level of their own dynamics is one that they do not easily give up, even when their behavior is pointed out quite directly to them. They can, after all, maintain a rather serene picture of themselves as well-controlled, quite proper and non-violent human beings. They are not, however, peaceful or peace loving personalities. They are extremely disruptive of the lives of others while they remain remote and inaccessible to healthy styles of relationships. Indeed, the passive aggressive person may be one of the most violent and harmful persons in our whole population, the one who cops out quietly, leaving hurts all around him.

This seems an accurate description of Alma. This is precisely what she did in the marriage. She copped out, leaving hurts all around her, because, after all, "we can't devote our lives to other people."

Throughout the marriage, Alma was regarded by virtually everybody as a "cold fish." Her profession became her entire life, which permitted her to maintain a safe distance from demanding personal relationships. As a clinical psychologist she was a superb listener, but more like a computer, analyzing the data, than a sympathetic, helping fellow human being. Emotions were, to Alma, a sign of weakness. Beliefs were contrived, convenient supports. Both of these she criticized in Ralph, whom she regarded as sentimental and as an obsessive-compulsive Catholic.

For the last year and a half of the marriage Alma began to drink to excess, perhaps even to get drunk, every night. And towards the very end, she talked to her lover on the phone, openly, before Ralph. Even then, however, she did not really wish to discuss the matter with Ralph but rather announced simply that she was getting a divorce. As Richard Lewis said, the marriage "became inconvenient" for her so she terminated it.

Doctor Martin diagnosed Alma as suffering from a severe Passive-Aggressive Personality Disorder and he observed that "this was not a marriage; it was a socio-psychological experiment as far as Alma was concerned and Ralph was the object."

Alma herself made a couple of appointments with the Instructor on this case but cancelled them at the last minute because of "emergencies." She promised to write but was never heard from again. However, four witnesses were heard, all of whom corroborate the marital history and personality profile as described above.

It is clear to our expert and also to this Court that this was not a marriage because Alma, by reason of her psychopathology, lacked the due competence for marriage.

WHEREFORE

I
The Facts

Clarence Thrush and Edna Goshawk, both Catholic, were married at the Church of the Resurrection, Jamesville, Connecticut in the Archdiocese of Hartford on the third day of June 1953. Clarence was twenty-seven years old at the time; Edna was twenty-two.

Clarence and Edna lived together for twenty-six years and had five children but there was always much fighting and quarrelling, and Clarence buried himself in his work as a lawyer while Edna pursued her own separate interests as well. The couple separated finally in May of 1979. A divorce was obtained in Litchfield on February 20, 1982.

On October 28, 1982 Clarence petitioned this Tribunal to declare the marriage null. His petition was accepted and the Doubt was Formulated on November 11, 1982, with Edna Goshawk's lack of due competence being identified by the Judge as the grounds for investigation.

II
The Law

A. The skeleton of the present jurisprudence on lack of due competence is expressed in C. 1095 3° which reads, "They are incapable of contracting marriage who, because of psychological reasons, are not strong enough to assume the essential obligations of marriage."

B. It is generally accepted that "the essential obligations of marriage" are not merely biological or materialistic, e.g. the ability to have intercourse or to earn a living or to be a housekeeper, but are also spiritual or personalist. The capacity to marry, in other words, involves more than the ability to cohabit or coexist under the same roof with a legal partner and offspring. Some relationships, as is well known, are intrinsically and essentially pathological. Witness, for example, the twisted and sick, though often highly durable, relationship between the masochist and the sadist. Such a relationship one would not dignify with the term "marital." A truly marital relationship must be a basically healthy one. While it need not be highly romantic, it must be basically constructive rather than destructive. It must, in other words, enjoy a certain quality.

The task of the jurist is to calibrate this quality of life within marriage and to determine, with reasonable precision within a given culture, the point or level below which a marriage can no longer be regarded as genuine.

Within our present culture it may be said that a person must be judged "unable to assume the essential obligations of marriage" if he or she is incapable of the three acts of self revelation, understanding and caring.

1. *Self revelation* means that a person must first of all enjoy a basic ego identity, i.e., he must see himself as one fairly consistent person, have a reasonable degree of respect for that person, and convey a knowledge of himself to his spouse.

2. *Understanding* means that he must see his spouse as a separate person, and appreciate her way of feeling and thinking, without distorting it excessively by his own attitudes, needs or insecurities.

3. *Caring* means that a person must, with reasonable maturity, pledge himself to a lifelong communion with his spouse, not because he wishes to possess her, but because of the special reverence and affection he has for her, and because he wishes to share his life with her.

C. Canon 1095 3° notes that incapacity or incompetence for marriage can result from "causes of a psychic nature." This obviously is an extremely broad term which could embrace all sorts of psychological reasons.

Although it would probably not include what DSM III (p. 305) refers to as "Personality Traits," because, generally, they are not severely impairing, it certainly would include "Personality Disorders." According to DSM III, *"Personality Traits* are enduring patterns of perceiving, relating to and thinking about the environment and oneself, and are exhibited in a wide range of important social and personal contexts. It is only when personality traits are inflexible and maladaptive and cause either significant impairment in social or occupational functioning or subjective distress that they constitute *Personality Disorders.* The manifestations of Personality Disorders are generally recognized by adolescence or earlier and continue throughout most of adult life."

This last point is an important one. Personality Disorders are so called precisely because they are part of the warp and woof of one's personality. They are with a person from the time his or her personality is formed early in life. They do not emerge, as though de novo, later in life, though, in some people, they may become more and more apparent with the passage of years and under the continuing stress of life.

They are, likewise, rather resistant to treatment, partly because they are, as indicated, part of the fabric of one's personality and partly because they are frequently egosyntonic, i.e. not perceived by the person as a source of distress or difficulty.

D. One final point: the right that is exchanged at the time of marriage is a "ius perpetuum"; this means that, in order for a person to be capable of marriage, he or she must be capable of exchanging a *perpetual* right. It is not enough, in other words, for a person to be capable of living in marriage for a limited period of time. Rather, if a person, by reason of his character or personality makeup, is, at the time of marriage, incapable of entering a *perpetual* union, then he or she is incapable of marriage.

III
The Argument

In the judgment of this Court, Edna Goshawk was, at the time of marriage, not capable, because of her Personality Disorder, of exchanging, in June of 1953, the perpetual right to a genuine marriage, i.e. to a union characterized by self revelation, understanding and caring.

Although the Defender of the Bond argues forcefully in favor of the validity of this marriage of twenty six years, the Court is, nevertheless, convinced that Edna Goshawk's ability to sustain perpetually a relationship that enjoyed at least the basic minimum quality of marital life required for validity, was wanting.

The evidence in this case consists of 1) a lengthy affidavit from the petitioner, 2) a report of a telephone conversation with the respondent (she would consent to no more), 3) affidavits from eight witnesses and 4) a report from John Limpkin, M.D., the psychiatric expert assigned to the case by the Tribunal.

Doctor Limpkin has diagnosed Edna Goshawk as suffering from "a moderate mixed narcissistic/borderline personality disorder with obsessional traits." Because the Borderline Personality Disorder is among the more severe of the disorders, Doctor Limpkin, furthermore, speaks of Edna's "always present severe psychopathology."

Doctor Limpkin, whom we have all come to regard as an extremely astute and always careful diagnostician, based his opinion, as usual, on a considerable amount of information garnered from the testimony.

The witnesses, in general, saw Edna Goshawk as bossy, flighty, acquisitive, greedy, manipulative, argumentative, abrasive, haughty, conniving, spiteful, aloof and hypercritical.

Edna was reared in a home where the mother was always hollering and demanding and belittling of her husband in public. As one witness said, the mother was "a tough customer." In later years when the poor husband became ill and was confined to a convalescent home, Edna's mother did not even visit him. As a child Edna was spoiled by her father but, in general, it seems, her role model in life was her bossy mother, and for many years Edna too had a poor relationship with her father.

Edna and Clarence met in 1951 when Clarence was in his final year in law school. They argued a great deal during the courtship (although Clarence is not, by nature, an argumentative person) but, despite the arguments, they married after a courtship of two years. Edna, according to at least one witness, was considerably motivated by the prestige that would come from being married to a lawyer.

At the very end of the marriage Edna, it was clear, was emotionally disturbed. She attempted suicide on at least one occasion and fired off a pistol inside the house because, in her confused mind, she wanted to demonstrate a point. She was then hospitalized for at least a year and has since become extremely withdrawn and is on medication.

This, however, occurred only at the end. For twenty-six years she functioned well enough to carry on, to some extent, both inside and outside the home. It appears, however, that it was, inexorably, a deteriorating situation, and that it was only a matter of time before the marriage would come apart.

Meanwhile, moreover, the marriage, it must be said, never really enjoyed that minimal quality of marital life required for a valid marriage. Edna was not really capable of self revelation, understanding and caring.

Self revelation. Edna never really faced up to the fact that she had a serious emotional problem. She denied it until she could deny it no longer, at which time she was hospitalized; but, by then, it was too late. Throughout the marriage, she had alienated everyone, instituted several law suits against people who rubbed her the wrong way, destroyed otherwise viable business relationships, was a political gadfly, was intolerant of other people's opinions, and, in general, went through life like a spoiled child. As one witness observed, people came to fear her. The self of Edna Goshawk, in other words, was never a well integrated, consistent person.

Understanding. Edna was an insensitive, intolerant person who, it appears, drove her husband out of the house and away from her because of her need to control and dominate. She was not an open, understanding, flexible person who appreciated her spouse and his considerable strengths. Instead, she demeaned and belittled him. In 1959, for example, when a neighbor and friend was being sued and was in need of a lawyer, Edna would not permit Clarence to serve in that capacity, claiming that he was incompetent—which he certainly was not.

Caring. This was another problem for Edna, whose own needs were so preoccupying that she really had little or no energy left to devote to others. She was not, as the evidence shows, entirely inept as a mother, at least on a short term basis (though here too the children were not well adjusted and Edna tended to alienate them over the long haul) but her ability to be affectionate and intimate and to truly care for a spouse was not within her competence. A husband, as she had learned, in an ingrained way, from her mother was someone to be bossed around, not someone to be respected and to share a life with.

The marriage failed, therefore, because Edna lacked the psychological resources needed to enter and sustain a truly marital union. By reason of her disorder, in other words, she lacked the due competence for marriage.

WHEREFORE

I
The Facts

Elizabeth Grouse and Vincent Veery, both Catholic, were married at St. Mary's Church, Lawton, Connecticut in the Archdiocese of Hartford on the twentieth day of May 1973. At the time Elizabeth was twenty-five years old and Vincent was twenty-three.

Elizabeth and Vincent lived together for about two and a half years without having any children. The marriage never seemed to succeed and Elizabeth more and more came to regard herself as a failure. The couple finally separated in February of 1976 and a divorce was obtained in Litchfield on January 20, 1978.

On October 16, 1979 Elizabeth petitioned this Court to declare the marriage null. Her petition was accepted and at the *Contestatio Litis* conducted on December 12 it was agreed that lack of due competence would be the grounds on which the validity of the marriage would be investigated and adjudged.

II
The Law

A. The jurisprudence regarding lack of due competence is well summarized in the following excerpt from the decision of January 15, 1977, coram Ewers (*Ephemerides Iuris Canonici*, 1977, n. 3-4, p. 356):

> It can happen, however, that someone, although not forming a positive intention of any kind, would nevertheless lack the strength to commit himself because of an inability to assume the essential obligations of marriage. For it happens in such cases that the person entering marriage, while he *wants* to give genuine marital consent, fully knowing and considering the nature of marriage, nevertheless at the same time is found to be *incapable of fulfilling* what he sincerely pledges to do. Since this person is actually unable to promise that over which he has no power, his marital consent is, in fact, futile and inefficacious because of that fundamental incapacity for consent which prevents him from assuming the obligations of marriage, and specifically it takes away the very possibility of an interpersonal relationship between the parties of the marriage union.

Psychosexual anomalies would stand out as the stronger and more serious causes of such a condition, but likewise it could be a serious defect of discretionary judgment on account of which the person consenting to marriage is prevented from being capable of handing over and accepting the rights and obligations of marriage. Indeed, whenever a mental illness or a personality disorder or an abnormal nervous condition are not proved, only with much difficulty will the judge be able to arrive at the conclusion of basic incapacity of any kind; and yet it can happen that the whole personality of someone consenting to marriage, along with a certain set pattern of behavior before or after the wedding, would strongly support concluding to a moral state in that person which would demonstrate that he was certainly incapable of assuming the obligations of marriage. In which case, such a marriage ought to be considered and declared null.

B. As all of this applies to an anxiety disorder or neurosis, the following points should be noted:

1. Description

Anxiety Disorders, sometimes referred to as Neuroses, are maladaptive emotional states resulting from unresolved, unconscious conflicts and typified by anxiety and avoidance.

The principal types of Anxiety Disorders are Phobic Disorders, Panic Disorder and Obsessive Compulsive Disorder.

2. The Paradox of the Anxiety Disorders

The neurotic process involves a kind of paradox, because, although most human beings tend to be highly pragmatic in doing what works, the neurotic tends to get caught in a vicious, self-defeating circle. Which is why the Anxiety Disorders are by definition, maladaptive. The circle begins with a situation, which the neurotic sees as a problem and which causes stress. The first sign of stress causes fear. The fear is then avoided and the avoidance brings relief. But the avoidance also reinforces the whole causal chain. That sweet feeling of relief, that immediate gratification hooks the person and establishes a pattern of avoidance but, in the long run, of course, the constant avoiding only confirms in the person's mind that he really is an inferior human being incapable of coping with life.

3. A Jurisprudence

When the four usual areas of investigation are applied to the Anxiety Disorders, the following observations might be useful:

a. Severity

The degree of impairment from Anxiety Disorders varies a great deal and is sometimes confined to a specific problem quite unrelated to one's ability to function in marriage. A person, for example, might have a neurotic phobia of heights or elevators.

When it is a pervasive problem, however, resulting in such things as avoidance, rigidity, lack of insight and egocentricity, it can, understandably, deprive a person of the basic capacity for self revelation, understanding and caring.

b. Antecedence

Anxiety Disorders have a fairly early onset, usually around the time of adolescence. In practice, at any rate, such a disorder can be presumed to have been antecedent if it was disruptive of the marital relationship in the early years of the marriage.

c. Perpetuity

A severe disorder present at the time of marriage must be presumed legally perpetual. The person suffering from such a disorder is in severe psychological pain and often avails himself of therapy. Even with therapy, however, the disorder often destroys the marriage before competent functioning can be restored, and this constitutes legal incurability.

d. Relativity

The low threshold of the other spouse to relate to even a moderately impaired neurotic partner could, in practice, result in relative, that is, mutual incompetence. Also an insensitive, non-supportive partner can, of course, exacerbate a neurotic condition and make it virtually impossible for the anxious person to function in a marital relationship.

III
The Argument

Both principals testified in these proceedings along with two knowledgeable witnesses. Reports were also obtained from McKenzie General Hospital where Elizabeth was treated for an anxiety disorder: a) from November 1972 to May of 1973; b) during October and November of 1973; c) during February and March of 1975. And finally a report was received from John Limpkin, M.D., the Court-appointed psychiatric expert on this case.

The diagnosis assigned Elizabeth both at McKenzie General Hospital and by Doctor Limpkin is Anxiety Disorder or Neurosis. Doctor Limpkin feels certain that it was of such severity at the time of marriage that Elizabeth was not capable of functioning in marriage.

Elizabeth grew up in a strict Irish Catholic family. Her mother was "extremely nervous," according to Elizabeth's own description of her, and the father was somewhat removed from the family in that he worked ten or twelve hours a day as a bus driver. The parents rarely socialized outside the home and demanded that their children adhere to strict moral and religious practices. Every night during Lent the entire family recited the Stations of the Cross in the home.

Early on it was discovered that Elizabeth was extremely deaf and she has, for most of her life, worn two hearing aids.

Elizabeth and Vincent met in their early teens and dated off and on for the next ten years. Both dated others as well and, as a matter of fact, Elizabeth had a serious romance with another young man in the early '70s. In the summer of 1972 she broke off with him, however, deciding that Vincent was, after all, the man she truly wanted to marry.

But in October of that year Elizabeth had a severe anxiety reaction accompanied by tachycardia. That same month she gave Vincent a kind of ultimatum, telling him that they had been dating for ten years now, that she was twenty-four years old and should be getting married soon, so if he was not interested she would move to California and start a new life. Vincent was not really eager to marry her but felt some obligation to her and finally gave her an engagement ring in December.

The anxiety reaction was very severe. Elizabeth was out of work for six weeks and then went into weekly therapy for the next six months, that is to say, for almost the entire period of engagement. She suffered from insomnia during that time. She was very weak, could not drive a car during the entire period, and was not strong enough to go out evenings with Vincent. She was taking valium that was prescribed for her and any stress would cause a tachycardia attack.

There seem to have been several stressful events in the early seventies that precipitated Elizabeth's anxiety reaction. Her father had died in October of 1971 at which time the role of principal breadwinner and family manager had been thrust on Elizabeth. In the summer of 1972 she broke off her relationship with the "other" man in her life; and that September a beloved uncle died after a long bout with lung cancer. The following month Elizabeth's first tachycardia attack occured.

After the May 20 marriage Elizabeth, still weak, took the rest of the summer off in an attempt to regain her strength. She relaxed and engaged in some sports (she had always been a kind of tomboy) and to some extent did build up her strength. But at the same time the marriage was an enervating experience for her. The sex life of the couple was not good and quickly deteriorated to the point almost of non-existence. In October Elizabeth returned to McKenzie General Hospital for further therapy but one of the witnesses, who actually lived under the same roof as Elizabeth and

Vincent during the first year of marriage, noted that by the Spring of 1974, only nine months after marriage, Vincent and Elizabeth were like a couple of strangers who had developed separate life styles.

Elizabeth, who had been very dependent on Vincent, tolerated his absence from the home several nights a week, guessing that he was being unfaithful but "keeping everything in" and suffering periodic attacks of tachycardia. Her self-esteem plummeted until, as she said, she felt both sexless and brainless.

Finally, in January of 1976, Vincent told Elizabeth he wanted a divorce and even though she knew the marriage was a failure, she was crushed and defeated by his request. She moved out the following month.

Our expert, Doctor Limpkin, considers Elizabeth's anxiety severe and pathological, not just a case of chronic low self-esteem but an actual neurotic process triggered most probably by the losses of her father and uncle and resulting in a repetitive need for support from her therapist and in an inability to function at many levels.

I am satisfied that the evidence shows that Elizabeth's pathology deprived her of the capacity to enter an intimate give-and-take relationship with Vincent Veery in 1973.

WHEREFORE

I

The Facts

Betty Quaglia and James Macreuse, both Catholic, were married at the Church of St. John, Athens, Connecticut in the Archdiocese of Hartford on the 12th day of August 1952. At the time Betty was twenty years old and James was twenty-two.

Betty and James lived together for sixteen years and had six children. James, however, was in and out of psychiatric hospitals over those sixteen years and even while he was at home his behavior was often strange, bizarre and sometimes threatening. Betty finally decided to leave him in 1968. A divorce was granted in New Haven on September 3, 1970.

On February 7, 1983 Betty petitioned this Court to declare the marriage null. The Revered Thomas Lynch was appointed Guardian for the respondent; Betty's petition was accepted and on April 2, 1983 the *Contestatio Litis* was conducted, at which the Judge declared that the grounds on which the validity of the marriage would be investigated and adjudged would be lack of due competence on the part of James.

II

The Law

A. C. 1095 3° notes that "they are incapable of contracting marriage who, because of psychological reasons, are not strong enough to assume the essential obligations of marriage." It is generally recognized that these essential obligations include some personalist elements. Many recent Rotal decisions, notably by Lefebvre, Ewers, Anné, Parisella, DiFelice and Serrano have taken this position. And, in a decision of July 15, 1977, (*Monitor Ecclesiasticus*, 1978, 2, pp. 145-157) even Monsignor Jose Pinto, who for some time was "the most visible opponent" of that position (see David Fellhauer's thesis, *Studia Canonica*, 1979, 1, p. 143) admitted that a person contracts marriage invalidly if he or she is antecedently and perpetually incapable of exchanging the right to those interpersonal relations without which a conjugal society would be morally impossible.

B. Marriage cases involving a person with an affective disorder are fairly uncommon these days but occasionally it will happen that the marriage will occur before the first episode, or perhaps between episodes, and that after marriage the episodes will be so frequent and severe that they are disruptive of marital life.

C. In making a judgment on validity, all four of the standard areas of investigation regarding incompetence must be considered.

1. *Severity*

These disorders can range anywhere from mild to psychotic. A mild depressive disorder might involve a feeling of being down in the dumps, a weight change, sleepless nights, a loss of interest in sex and other pleasurable activities. A mild manic disorder could involve inflated self-esteem, buying sprees, reckless driving and being more talkative or more active than usual. At the psychotic stage the person would experience delusions and/or hallucinations.

In order to determine whether the disorder involves incompetence the judge must decide whether it in fact destroys the capacity for community of life, i.e. the basic capacity for self revelation, understanding and caring.

2. *Antecedence*

The precise etiology of the episodic affective disorders is not clear. Perhaps hereditary, constitutional, biological and psychological factors all play a part. It seems clear, however, that some kind of predisposition for the severe disorder certainly exists. Therefore, even when the first episode occurs after marriage, antecedence may be presumed.

3. *Perpetuity*

Although some cases of episodic affective disorders become chronic, there is rarely marked deterioration in functioning or personality in between episodes. It should be noted also that in many cases the disorder can be controlled by the use of chemotherapy. Such therapy, if successful, can prevent florid episodic manic attacks and often episodic depressions. Though the chemotherapy may have to be continued indefinitely, when successful, a relatively normal life is possible.

Relative to the marriage, however, it is still possible that the disorder would destroy the marriage before it could be cured, in which case it would be considered legally perpetual. This matter must, of course, be investigated by the Court.

4. *Relativity*

It may be that, in the case at bar, the "other party," usually the petitioner, is a walking precipitating factor for the respondent's disorder. Should this be true, it is possible that the respondent could function in another marriage but not in the marriage under consideration.

James Macreuse was one of four children. Although his parents were protective of James and reluctant to divulge any information about him, an uncle of his described James as a "nervous and irritable little boy." He did quite well in school, however, was active and proficient in several sports and graduated from high school in 1948.

About a year after graduation James became very disturbed, caused a commotion in the house and was brought to a psychiatrist by his parents. The psychiatrist quickly hospitalized him at McKenzie Hospital and he remained in that institution for nine months. James was nineteen years old on admission to that facility. Records from McKenzie, obtained by Betty in 1969 for possible future use, reveal the following about that 1949 admission. James was described as silly and facetious. He was seen frequently talking and laughing to himself. He would answer questions by repeating either the whole question or the last part of it and usually made little or no sense. He was incoherent, in poor contact, distractible, preoccupied and quite scattered in his behavior. He would say things like, "Keep it up, boys, it hurts but it's going to be some fun. Am I imitating myself? Irritated, it hurts." At times he would be noisy and destructive. He would move around shadow boxing. He would put his head into his plate and throw his food around. He tore some bed linen, took a shade from the window and started to eat it, tried to eat a mattress, was denudative, masturbated frequently on the ward, smeared feces on the wall, destroyed a loud speaker and was "totally out of contact with his environment."

By July of 1950 James' condition was much improved and he was discharged from the hospital. He obtained work as a mechanic and in November of 1951 he met Betty Quaglia and they began to date. To Betty, James seemed entirely normal, except perhaps that he was very aggressive sexually and was constantly after her to have sex with him. But he was outgoing and charming. Occasionally he was irritable but Betty did not regard this as a serious problem. James, during the courtship, did not clearly recollect his stay at the hospital and at any rate was convinced that he was completely cured. James mentioned to Betty that he had had some treatment at McKenzie but the whole episode was belittled and did not dissuade Betty from marrying the man she loved.

After marriage James became more and more irritable and he also wanted sex more often than Betty would have liked, sometimes several times a day. Apart from this, however, Betty saw nothing unusual in James' behavior and she was quite content with her marriage.

But around Christmas time of 1953, about a year and a half after marriage, James started causing trouble at work. He was rude to customers and became rather obnoxious. He started writing to his congressman and even to the President of the United States offering advice on a variety of matters about which he knew very little, and he wrote regularly to Archbishop O'Brien outlining wondrous schemes for raising funds and saving souls. He also spent a great deal of time drawing strange pictures, and he began to send flowers and love letters to Betty's sister.

By the summer of 1954 James was back in McKenzie Hospital, where he remained for six months. Over the next fourteen years, until 1968 when Betty finally left him, he was admitted seven more times, each time for a period of several months.

This Court has in its possession records from McKenzie Hospital and these records constitute the principal evidence in this case. Also of value was the testimony of Betty Quaglia, an honest, simple, long suffering woman and that of Philip Macreuse, James' uncle. James himself is presently hospitalized but he was represented in this hearing by his Guardian, the Reverend Thomas J. Lynch.

The hospital records consistently diagnose James as suffering from a Manic-Depressive Psychosis, that is to say, a Bipolar Episodic Affective Disorder, and it is clear that an acute episode of that disorder occurred three years before James' marriage to Betty, and that several episodes occurred later.

It is clear, therefore, that the predisposition for the disorder existed at the time of the marriage and that it deprived James Macreuse of the ability to enter a true marital partnership with Betty Quaglia and to undertake the responsibilities and obligations of marriage.

WHEREFORE

I
The Facts

Yvonne Cormorant and Lionel Skowronek, both twenty-seven years old and both Catholic (Lionel was received into the Church on the same day as the marriage) had their civil union validated on November 18, 1967 at the Church of the Holy Rosary, Billings, Connecticut in the Archdiocese of Hartford.

Yvonne and Lionel lived together for five years after the validation and had no children of their own. During those years Lionel was often intoxicated, lost several jobs and was physically abusive to Yvonne. She left him in March of 1972 and obtained a divorce in Billings County on February 12, 1973.

On September 20, 1979 Yvonne petitioned this Court to declare the marriage null. Her petition was accepted and the *Contestatio Litis* was conducted on November 24, assigning Lionel's lack of due competence as the grounds on which the validity of the marriage would be investigated and adjudged.

II
The Law

A. Definition

Alcoholism may be defined as a chronic behavioral disorder manifested by a dependence on alcohol and by repeated drinking of alcoholic beverages in excess of the dietary and social uses of the community and to an extent that interferes with the drinker's health or his social or economic function.

B. Alcoholism vs. Alcohol Abuse

DSM III identifies alcoholism as Alcohol Dependence, and, in a distinction very important to jurisprudence, differentiates it from Alcohol Abuse.

1. *Alcohol Abuse*

The two diagnostic criteria for Alcohol Abuse are:

a. *Pattern of Pathological Use* — need for daily use of alcohol for adequate functioning; inability to cut down or stop drinking; repeated efforts to control or reduce excess drinking by "going on the wagon'' (periods of temporary abstinence) or restricting drinking to certain times of the day; binges (remaining intoxicated throughout the day for at least two days); occasional consumption of a fifth of spirits (or its equivalent in wine or beer); amnesic periods for events occurring while intoxicated (blackouts); continuation of drinking despite a serious physical disorder that the individual knows is exacerbated by alcohol use; drinking of non-beverage alcohol.

b. *Impairment in Social or Occupational Functioning* — e.g., violence while intoxicated, absence from work, loss of job, legal difficulties (e.g., arrest for intoxicated behavior, traffic accidents while intoxicated), arguments or difficulties with family or friends because of excessive alcohol use.

2. *Alcohol Dependence* (Alcoholism)

There are, in effect, three diagnostic criteria for Alcohol Dependence, namely:

a. *Pattern of Pathological Use* — as described under Alcohol Abuse

b. *Impairment in Social or Occupational Functioning* — as described under Alcohol Abuse

c. *Either Tolerance or Withdrawal*

1) *Tolerance* — need for markedly increased amounts of alcohol to achieve the desired effect, or markedly diminished effect with regular use of the same amount.

2) *Withdrawal* — within several hours after cessation of or reduction in drinking, a coarse tremor of hands, tongue and eyelids plus at least one of the following: nausea and vomiting, malaise or weakness, autonomic hyperactivity (tachycardia, sweating, elevated blood pressure), anxiety, depressed mood or irritability, orthostatic hypotension.

C. A Jurisprudence

1. Marriage cases in which alcoholism is the only diagnosis are very rare. Generally the psychiatric expert sees the alcoholism as one aspect of a larger syndrome. Occasionally, however, the drinking is so heavy and frequent that there is no clear picture of how the person functions when sober, so that a broader diagnosis would not be justified by the evidence.

2. In determining whether alcoholism is invalidating of a marriage, the usual four areas must be investigated.

a. *Severity*

Alcoholism is profoundly disruptive of marriage life. Members of an alcoholic's family often live in fear, embarrassment and deprivation. And, almost by definition, the alcoholic lacks the capacity for those specifically marital acts of self revelation, understanding and caring; he is too self centered or bottle centered for that.

Alcohol abuse, it should be mentioned, can be equally disruptive of married life.

b. *Antecedence*

Generally, in cases that come before a Tribunal, the alcoholic party was either already drinking excessively during the courtship but the other party believed she could cure him, or the alcoholic had a drinking problem earlier in his life but had managed to bring it under control prior to the marriage only to have it flare up again afterwards. In such cases it may be presumed that the incompetence resulting from the alcoholism was at least causally antecedent.

Occasionally the person whose alcoholism eventually destroys the marriage never drank at all before marriage. In such cases a rule of thumb might be that if alcohol abuse began in the first few years of marriage then the incompetence may be presumed to have been virtually antecedent, i.e., the proximate disposition to alcoholism and the proximate causes of its onset were present at the time of marriage. If, however, alcohol abuse began only after several years of marriage, then the legal presumption would be against antecedence.

The same presumptions would apply to alcohol abuse.

c. *Perpetuity*

Alcoholism, as defined above, includes as one of its essential elements disruptive drinking. It was so defined because controlled alcoholism is neither an impediment to a future marriage nor a source of nullity for a past marriage.

The issue, therefore, concerns disruptive drinking. The question here is whether the drinking of the alcoholic in the case under consideration was legally uncontrollable, i.e., legally incurable, i.e., perpetual at the time of marriage.

Generally it can be said that alcoholism is absolutely curable. Given the right circumstances, in other words, given the right therapist or facility, given enough money to avail oneself of the needed assistance, given a miracle of grace and perhaps a truly superhuman, extraordinary effort, the drinking can be controlled.

This is not to say, however, that it is legally curable. It is only regarded as legally curable when it can be controlled by ordinary means. A fair presumption here would be that where true alcohol dependence exists at the time of marriage, the incompetence should be considered perpetual, whereas if it can only be determined that alcohol abuse existed at the time of marriage, the legal presumption would be that the abuse could have been controlled by ordinary effort or means, and that the incompetence was therefore temporary.

To repeat, this does not mean that every alcoholic is presumed to have a legally uncontrollable drinking problem. It only means that when, post factum, alcohol dependence has in fact been coupled with disruptive drinking, then the law is ready to presume that the drinking was controllable only by extraordinary means.

d. *Relativity*

The alcoholic's choice of partner can be critical. It could happen, for example, that a man who was abusing alcohol at the time of marriage but was not dependent on it, married a woman whose own problems would certainly exacerbate the man's attachment to alcohol. In such a case it could be argued that the drug abuse plus the exacerbating spouse would constitute uncontrollable incompetence. Thus the man would presumptively be competent for marriage in general but incompetent for this particular marriage.

III
The Argument

Lionel Skowronek has now been in and out of three marriages. His first marriage was to Doris Lynch, a Catholic, in 1960, when Lionel was twenty years old. He lived with Doris for about three and a half years and had two children by her, separating from her in late 1963. On June 14, 1965, Lionel married Yvonne Cormorant before a Justice of the Peace. This marriage was validated in November of 1967 (after Lionel's marriage to Doris was declared null by the Hartford Tribunal by reason of Lack of Form - P.N. 14382) and all told, including the two years of cohabitation prior to validation, Lionel and Yvonne lived together for seven years. After being divorced from Yvonne in 1973 Lionel married a third woman, this one about a dozen years his junior; he moved to Pennsylvania with this woman but that marriage ended in divorce after about a year and a half. Lionel is now back in Connecticut and there is some talk about his having entered a fourth marriage.

Lionel himself would not cooperate in these proceedings but spoke briefly with the Instructor on the telephone and then abruptly hung up.

However three knowledgeable witnesses testified and the facts seem reasonably clear. A Court-appointed expert, Walter Taube, M.D., also provided the Tribunal with a report and diagnosis.

Lionel Skowronek grew up in a family where the father was quiet, indecisive and a fence sitter, and the mother was negative, aggressive and manipulative. Lionel had one brother, Stanley, who was much favored by the mother, and because of this favoritism Lionel both resented his brother and hated his mother. In 1966 (after Yvonne and Lionel were civilly married but before the validation) Lionel's brother was killed in an accident. The mother supposedly said that Lionel should have died instead of Stanley. Lionel, at any rate, was much affected by his brother's death.

At fourteen years of age Lionel began to drink and during his youth, according to one witness who knew him, he drank as often and as much as he could afford to, "always beyond reasonable limits."

At sixteen years of age Lionel quit school to go to work and help support the family (neither parent worked a great deal). In his early years Lionel was an industrious worker but as the drinking increased there was more and more absenteeism and, in the seven years that Yvonne was with him, he changed jobs two or three times a year, usually because he was fired. Often he was unemployed but he was an auto body repairman and quite skilled at his work so he was fairly successful at finding new work.

Yvonne and Lionel first met in 1957 when they were seventeen years old and Yvonne was in high school. They dated and when Yvonne graduated from high school Lionel wanted to marry her. Yvonne, however, had her mind set on becoming a nurse and she went off to nursing school. They broke up and five years passed before they saw each other again. In the meantime Lionel married Doris Lynch and was only recently separated from her when, in late 1963 or early 1964, he re-met Yvonne Cormorant, by this time a practicing nurse. Yvonne felt sorry for him, and especially for his two children (Doris had a drinking problem and Yvonne, and later the Court apparently, regarded her as an unfit mother). Yvonne and Lionel began dating, married before a Justice of the Peace in June of 1965 and, later that year, gained custody of Lionel's two boys.

From the beginning of the marriage Lionel drank a great deal. When he was out of work he would sit around the house during the day and drink, and the drinking became progressively worse. Just about a year after the validation, in October or November of 1968, he signed himself into McKenzie Hospital for ten days for detoxification and for the next two months he visited a psychiatrist on a weekly basis but then stopped and began to drink again.

Throughout the marriage Lionel was also suspicious of people. He always thought friendly people were using him and so withdrew from any friends he had.

Although it has not been established that Lionel was actually unfaithful to Yvonne, one of the witnesses, Susan Murphy, testified that Lionel did proposition her and other women as well, and that the women she knew were very wary of Lionel, especially when he was drinking.

Lionel was also abusive during the marriage. Generally the abuse was only verbal but on three occasions it was physical and the third time involved Lionel's choking Yvonne to the point where she blacked out. It was shortly after that that Yvonne left him.

Our expert, Doctor Walter Taube, has diagnosed Lionel as suffering from true Alcoholism. It is clear that this alcoholism was both antecedent and legally perpetual. Lionel had been drinking since he was fourteen. He concealed his drinking to a large extent from Yvonne during the courtship but within a year of the validation he was hospitalized. Disruptive drinking continued throughout the marriage and therapy was undertaken but apparently and presumably, according to the jurisprudence stated in the law section, Lionel's drinking could not be controlled by ordinary means.

I am satisfied, therefore, that because of Lionel's antecedent and perpetual alcoholism, he lacked the due competence for marriage and that this has been adequately demonstrated by the evidence presented to the Court.

WHEREFORE

SEAL - ALOUETTE

```
      I
  The Facts
```

Henrietta Seal, Catholic, and Philip Alouette, unbaptized, were married at the Church of St. Henry, Kerrville, Connecticut, in the Archdiocese of Hartford, on the seventh day of September, 1970. At the time of marriage Philip was twenty or twenty one years old (his year of birth is variously listed as either 1949 or 1950) and Henrietta was eighteen. A dispensation from the impediment of disparity of cult was granted by the Hartford Chancery on August 13, 1970 but Father George Wilson erroneously listed Henrietta's age as nineteen when asking for the dispensation, and, as a result, the "Under Nineteen Procedures" were not followed.

The couple lived together for a year and seven months, and then separated because of Philip's addiction to alcohol and drugs. No children were born of the marriage. The separation was in April of 1972. The divorce was granted in Hartford on February 24, 1973.

On April 20, 1978 Henrietta petitioned this Court to declare the marriage null. Her petition was accepted and on July 8, 1978 the Issue in Pleading was declared to be whether the marriage was proved invalid on the grounds of Philip's lack of due competence.

```
      II
  The Law
```

As indicated in *Annulments,* the jurisprudence on Drug Use Disorders would follow the same principles of law that would prevail in a case involving alcoholism.

Briefly those principles are that, in order to be invalidating, the disorder:

1. *Must be Antecedent,* i.e. that at least the proximate disposition to the drug dependence and the proximate causes of its onset were present at the time of marriage — and

2. *Must be Perpetual,* i.e. the disruptive use of the drug was, at the time of marriage, legally uncontrollable, that is to say, not controllable by ordinary means. The reigning presumption here is that if true *dependence* existed at the time of marriage the disorder should be considered (at least following a final marital breakdown) perpetual, whereas if only drug *abuse* existed at the time of marriage, the disorder would, presumably, be controllable by ordinary means, and therefore not perpetual and not invalidating.

The respondent, Philip Alouette, could not be notified of these proceedings for want of an address. A letter was sent to him in care of his mother at her last known address in Kerrville but the letter was returned indicating that the mother had moved and left no forwarding address.

The available evidence, therefore, consists of 1) the testimony of the petitioner, 2) the testimony of the petitioner's mother and sister and 3) a report from James Oriole, M.D., the court-appointed psychiatric expert.

The evidence shows that Philip Alouette was the youngest of six children. His father died when Philip was nine years old, and after the father's death, the mother, who had a severe drinking problem, lost all control over the children and they ran wild. Several of them, including Philip, wound up with drinking problems.

When Philip was sixteen he met Henrietta Seal, who was only thirteen. They dated occasionally but the next year Philip quit school and joined the Army. He remained in the Army for only a year and a half and was discharged, but the circumstances and classification of his discharge are unknown.

After Philip was discharged from the Army, he and Henrietta started dating again and eight months later they married. Henrietta's mother was opposed to their marrying so young but the couple was determined and the marriage took place in September.

After leaving the service Philip had a *part time* job with a trucking firm but, according to him, had a promise of *full time* employment from the company, and Henrietta was already working full time, so it appeared that there was some financial stability. Shortly after the marriage, however, Philip was fired by the company and for the next year and a half, the duration of the marriage, Philip only worked a total of about six weeks.

The major problem was that he was addicted to alcohol and other drugs. He had overdosed on barbiturates once before marriage and was hospitalized on that occasion but whether that was while he was in the Army or perhaps even before is unclear. At any rate, alcohol and drugs were his life during the marriage. Eleven days after the wedding he went on a two week binge involving both alcohol and drugs and during that time he told Henrietta he no longer wanted to be married. Then, throughout the marriage, he would leave the house at ten o'clock in the morning, saying he was going out for a newspaper or to look for a job, and he would return drunk at two or three o'clock the next morning.

He lied constantly. His only friends were his drinking buddies with whom he hung around the bar or the park drinking. He had a violent temper when he was home, throwing clothes around and punching holes in the wall or punching the door. As the weeks passed he became more and more grubby looking. He wore his hair long and grew a mustache and he was dirty looking. He was drunk or on drugs most of the time and, on one occasion, Henrietta saw him use a heroin needle.

After the separation Philip was arrested on several occasions for disorderly conduct and for driving a vehicle under the influence, and he lost his driver's license. He got another girl pregnant and married her, and they are, reportedly, on welfare.

Our expert, Doctor James Oriole, has diagnosed Philip as suffering from severe multiple substance dependence. It is clear from the anamnesis and from the brevity of the marriage that the disorder is both *antecedant* (he had OD'd before marriage and went on his first binge only eleven days after marriage) and *perpetual* (the disorder has been diagnosed as true dependence and was clearly resistant to being brought under control by ordinary means — Doctor Oriole, indeed, is fairly certain that Philip suffered as well from some underlying personality disorder that diminished his control).

It has, therefore, been demonstrated that Philip Alouette, because of his disorder, lacked the due competence for marriage.

WHEREFORE

```
┌─────────────────────────┐
│            I            │
│        The Facts        │
│                         │
└─────────────────────────┘
```

Magda Eider and Douglas Perdrix, both Catholic, were married at St. Anselm's Church, Towson, Connecticut in the Archdiocese of Hartford, on the fourteenth day of October, 1970. At the time Magda was nineteen years old and Douglas was twenty-one.

Magda and Douglas lived together for seven years and three children were born of the marriage but Douglas was a homosexual who was completely preoccupied with his male lovers, and Magda finally left Douglas in June of 1977. A divorce was obtained in New Haven on November 18, 1977.

On February 27, 1978 Magda petitioned this Court to declare the marriage null. Her petition was accepted on March 11, 1978, and on April 7, 1978 the grounds of lack of due competence were established by the Judge at the *Contestatio Litis*.

```
┌─────────────────────────┐
│            II           │
│        The Law          │
│                         │
└─────────────────────────┘
```

The jurisprudence regarding the effect of homosexuality on marriage is well summarized in the following brief excerpt of Lefebvre's decision of December 2, 1967 (59, 799):

> A homosexual person is incapable of marriage both because of a defect of discretion of judgment and also because of an inability to assume conjugal responsibilities.

> Those people are to be regarded as homosexual who, either exclusively or prevalently, desire sexual relations with a partner of the same sex because they feel a kind of aversion to the opposite sex.

```
┌─────────────────────────┐
│            III          │
│      The Argument       │
│                         │
└─────────────────────────┘
```

Douglas Perdrix, though notified by the Tribunal that Magda had petitioned for an annulment, indicated by return letter simply that he had nothing to say and did not wish to be bothered further regarding this matter.

Minus Douglas' testimony, therefore, the evidence in this case consists of 1) the testimony of the petitioner, 2) the testimony of three witnesses (the parents of the petitioner, and Phyllis Dorchester, a neighbor of the Perdrixes during the marriage) and 3) a copy of the decree of divorce granted by Judge G. Richard Maloney in New Haven on November 18, 1977.

The evidence shows the following:

Magda knew Douglas for only about six months before marriage but he was a steady worker at the time, and was very "polite and respectful."

A couple of months after marriage Douglas took a young man into the house as a boarder and he showered all his attention on this young man while virtually ignoring Magda, with whom he almost never had marital relations. Actually Douglas and Magda had intercourse only five times in the seven years they lived together, and on one of those occasions Douglas was intoxicated.

The young male boarder remained in the house for about two years at which time he announced he was leaving. Shortly thereafter another young man was invited by Douglas to board with them. He, too, remained a couple of years, and finally a third boy did the same.

The divorce record shows that, in the civil hearing, Phyllis Dorchester (who also acted as a witness in these ecclesiastical hearings) testified, as she did before our Court, that Douglas had attempted to seduce her eleven year old son in 1973. In light of this, it would take extreme naivete to imagine that, as regards the other three boys (two of whom worked part time but never actually paid any board), Douglas was merely extending Christian hospitality. It seems clear that those boys were Douglas' lovers.

As part of the divorce decree Judge Maloney ruled that Douglas' visitation privileges regarding his three sons would be restricted to between the hours of one o'clock and three o'clock on Sunday afternoon, not outside the city of Towson, where they lived with their mother. The Judge also ruled that "the children will not be placed in the company of the defendant's male friends."

Homosexuality was clearly a problem. It was indeed the major but not the only problem. For the first five years of marriage, even though Douglas was steadily employed, he nevertheless failed to support his wife and children. He spent a great deal of money on his young boyfriends but Magda's parents had to see to it that the Perdrix children were fed and clothed.

But after five years things got even worse. Douglas lost his job for embezzling money from the company that employed him and he then went through a whole series of jobs. He stayed away from home more and more and for the last year of marriage he stayed out all night every night.

Finally, in 1977, Magda gave up all hope that the marriage could ever amount to anything, and she left Douglas.

Considering all the evidence, I am convinced that Douglas Perdrix, because of his demonstrated homosexuality, was constitutionally incapable of sustaining a heterosexual community of life and that he therefore lacked the capacity to exchange the formal object of the marriage covenant.

WHEREFORE

I

The Facts

Linda Turnstone, a professed atheist, and Anthony Corvidae, a non practicing Protestant, were married on the fourth day of June 1974 in their apartment in Cushing, Connecticut in the Archdiocese of Hartford before a Unitarian minister. At the time Linda was twenty-two years old and Anthony was twenty-three.

They had lived together for about six months prior to that and they continued to live together for another eight months after the ceremony at which time they decided it was over and Linda filed for divorce. The divorce was granted in New Haven, Connecticut on September 18, 1975.

On December 18, 1982 Linda petitioned this Court to declare her marriage null. Her petition was accepted and the *Contestatio Litis* was conducted on February 3, 1983 with ignorance being assigned as the grounds on which the validity of the marriage would be investigated and adjudged.

II

The Law

A. The Pertinent Canon

C 1096 § 1. In order that matrimonial consent may be possible, it is necessary that the contracting parties be at least not ignorant that marriage is a permanent partnership between a man and a woman ordered to the procreation of children through some bodily cooperation.

§ 2. This ignorance is not presumed after puberty.

B. Some Observations On The Canon

1. The ignorance spoken of in this canon may refer to one of two elements.
   a. The *Personalist* Element — "that marriage is a permanent partnership between a man and a woman."
   b. The *Procreational* Element — "ordered to the procreation of children through some bodily cooperation."

2. In the case at bar (and perhaps in most cases involving invalidating ignorance in our culture) the alleged ignorance involves the personalist element.

In order to prove invalidity, then, it must be shown that one of the partners was, in effect, ignorant (or in error - see C. 126) regarding the nature of marriage as a permanent partnership of spouses involving them in a partner-type relationship, i.e., one in which the spouses are seen as joint principals having joint rights and responsibilities.

3. When the evidence points more to the person's intentions than to his or her ignorance, then the case is usually handled under the rubric of total simulation rather than ignorance. See, for example, the decision coram Sincero in AAS VII, pp. 51-56, and the decisions coram Anné and Pucci in SRRD 55, 764 and 57, 29.

III
The Argument

The evidence in this case consists of the testimony of both Linda and Anthony, the principals in this case, along with that of three knowledgeable witnesses. The testimonies are entirely concordant and deal with the following points:

1. *The Ceremony.* Linda steadfastly and adamantly refused to refer to the ceremony she went through on June 4, 1974 as a wedding or a marriage. She would not permit invitations or flowers or anything that might connote marriage. She wore a simple green dress. The ceremony was in the home rather than in a church. At her insistence, God was not mentioned. Although there was a party afterwards, Linda would not call it a reception, and there was no honeymoon because a honeymoon follows a wedding and this was not a wedding as far as she was concerned. When asked whether it was like what her relatives and friends did when they married, Linda said that there was no comparison, that her ceremony and the weddings of her friends and relatives were as different as night and day. She preferred to view hers as a kind of graduation ceremony or a social rite that would make her cohabitation with Anthony acceptable, particularly to her parents. Other marriages, she said, created a spiritual bond; hers did not. Hers was completely secular. She did not believe in marriage. She wanted things to be no different from what they were when she was in college and living with Anthony. Linda's mother, who had been a rigorous Baptist, was shocked that God was not mentioned in the ceremony. Linda's brother-in-law, Francis O'Brien, called the whole thing a "farce."

2. *The Motive.* Linda's motive in going through with the ceremony was only to win acceptance from her parents. She had already been living with Anthony for some months but she was graduating from college on the sixth of June and her parents were coming then for the graduation. Her mother was ill and Linda was reluctant to hurt or offend her by her lifestyle so it seemed to Linda that the only thing to do was for her to move out, even though she resented having to do it. Anthony offered getting married as an alternative and Linda liked that idea except

that she wouldn't view it as marriage because she didn't believe in marriage. But it was the first day of April when they had this discussion and it seemed like an appropriate April Fools' Day decision.

3. *Rebellion*. In the early '70s, Linda was in a general state of rebellion. Her father, though a brilliant man, had been cold and aloof in the home while the mother had imposed her strict Baptist beliefs on her children and had not permitted them to attend dances or play cards or to engage in other similarly sinful behavior. Linda grew up very dependent on her mother, always taking her side and without any real personality of her own. At the same time, part of her disliked her mother, and Linda always resented being compared unfavorably to her All American sisters. So in college Linda rebelled against all this and became a kind of hippie. She did not bathe or comb her hair and she wore ugly clothes and academically she performed far below her potential. She was against the war in Vietnam, our corrupt government and the phony hypocrisy of the American middle class. Marriage was a repressive institution and part of all this.

4. *Atheism*. Part of Linda's general rebellion was against religion in general and the Baptist religion of her mother in particular. Even now she regards all full-time ministers of religion as hypocrites, and, during her meetings with the Instructor, Father Gianelli, she refused to call him "Father" but always addressed him as "Doctor" or "Sir." Since marriage has traditionally, even popularly, been associated with religion and church (it consists of getting a person "down the aisle" or "to the altar"), Linda's atheism reinforced her antipathy to the institution of marriage.

5. *Confusion*. The months, and even years, prior to the ceremony had been hectic for Linda and she was confused. For some time she had suffered from nightmares about hell fire and damnation, perhaps because of the Baptist influence of her mother. She also suffered from hypoglycemia (low blood glucose) and seems to have presented some of the classical clinical features of that condition like confusion, blackouts, apathy and depression. She found it difficult to relate to her peers in college. She switched majors three times and then in her junior year she was brutally raped, an experience that was, of course, traumatic for her. Shortly after this her cousin George, who was probably a homosexual and is now a full-blown alcoholic, offered her support and she became extremely dependent on him, sometimes staying with him overnight, to the point where some people thought they were man and wife. In the beginning of Linda's senior year George introduced her to Anthony Corvidae who was living with a homosexual though Anthony claimed that, at the time, he did not realize that his roommate was homosexual. At any rate, Anthony and Linda were attracted to each other and began to date—which offended cousin George. In November or so Linda decided to join a commune. A few weeks later Anthony joined the commune but since the rules of the commune did not permit sex between members, Anthony and Linda left in December and took an apartment of their own. After they started to live together George poutingly thought they should get married but the couple themselves did not really consider it until the April Fools' Day decision was made. Finally, on the

night before the wedding George arrived begging their forgiveness if he had offended them. George and Anthony stayed together that night. As for what went on between them, Linda thought that was none of her business. Her whole approach, in other words, was not what one might expect of one entering a genuine marriage.

6. *Attitudes*. Linda's attitudes towards both children and permanence in respect to the arrangement also bespoke an erroneous concept of marriage, or more accurately, it suggested that what Linda was doing in going through the ceremony was not what we call marrying. Contraceptives had been in use since the beginning of the cohabitation period and would continue to be used. If a child was perchance conceived it would definitely be viewed as a "mistake." Children were not considered part of the deal. And as regards permanence it was understood between them that they would live together as long as they both wanted to and that was the sum total of their commitment.

7. *Cohabitation*. For the eight months that the couple lived together following the ceremony, Anthony's work kept him away about seventy-five percent of the time. He also drank to excess and was openly unfaithful and obviously did not comport himself like a married man. Linda, meanwhile, was depressed and took no interest in keeping up the apartment. They maintained separate checking accounts, partly, no doubt, because Anthony was financially irresponsible and partly because they did not really see themselves as husband and wife. After eight months they agreed that it was pointless to continue and Linda sued for divorce. The "marriage" was over.

The total evidence, in the opinion of the undersigned, demonstrates that the ceremony of June 4, 1974 was not understood or viewed by Linda Turnstone as a marriage. Canonically she was in ignorance about the nature of the action in which she was engaging. She did not see it as the establishment of a bond between spouses, entitling them to a permanent partnership of life together. And since Linda, one of the contractants, was in ignorance about the nature of marriage, the marriage is therefore null.

WHEREFORE

WRONA - CARACARA

```
        I
   The Facts
```

Jane Wrona and Henry Caracara, both Catholic, were married on September 13, 1948 at St. Bridget Church, Parkersburg, Connecticut, in the Archdiocese of Hartford. Both parties were twenty-three years old at the time.

The marriage went along reasonably well for a few years, and one child was born to the couple.

However, in December of 1951, Jane opened and read what she thought was a business letter (they operated a trucking firm), to discover that Henry had been in a previous marriage. The letter was from a sheriff requiring that Henry pay support for the two children he had fathered from his previous marriage.

Jane confronted Henry with the letter, and Henry admitted that he was previously married. Jane then called Catholic Family Services. Their eventual advice was that she separate, and Jane did this. On December 19, 1951, Jane filed for a civil annulment, granted finally on December 24, 1953.

On January 21, 1983 Jane petitioned this Court to declare the marriage null ecclesiastically. The petition was accepted, and on March 7, 1983 it was agreed by the Court that the grounds would be substantial error.

```
       II
   The Law
```

The jurisprudence in this case is summarized in a decision dated March 26, 1977, coram DiFelice, as found in *Monitor Ecclesiasticus,* 1978, III, pp. 266-268:

> 2). A condition properly so called, as discussed in Canon 1092, 4°, affects marital consent, and is entirely distinct from a postulate, otherwise known as a prerequisite, which does not affect consent. The *object* of a condition and of a postulate is the same; it usually refers to a quality of the other party. But these two institutes differ in the *force* of the will by which this quality is intended. The contractant who, by a positive act of the will, makes his consent depend on the existence of the quality states a true condition. But he who only requires the quality in the party, but at the same time in no way wishes his marital consent to depend on that quality, contracts marriage simply and in no way places a condition.

Consequently, in order to prove a condition, one ought to establish that the marriage itself was, by a positive act of the will, subordinated to that required quality. This can be established by the excessive estimation of the object that is desired which causes the contractant to renounce the marriage rather than the quality; by a doubt about the existence of the desired quality by which one is induced to place a condition; by the way in which a person conducts himself when he discovers that the condition has not been fulfilled; and by all other conclusive circumstances.

3) However, the wished for quality in the other party, when it does not exist, can also give rise to an error on account of which the marriage is contracted. This is stated in Canon 1083, § 2 as follows: "Error regarding a quality of the person, even though it is the cause of the contract, invalidates marriage in the following cases only: 1° if the error regarding the quality amounts to an error regarding the person; 2° if a free person contracts marriage with a person whom he or she believes to be free but who is, on the contrary, in a condition of slavery in the proper sense."

An error of quality which amounts to an error of person may be understood either in a strict or in a broad sense, depending on whether the quality is an individual and unique one which identifies the physical person or whether it is a moral, juridic, social quality which, although shared by other people, nevertheless specifically designates a particular person in his or her own individual nature.

The doctrine about that error of quality "which amounts to an error of person" taught by St. Thomas (S. Theol., p. III, Suppl., q. 51, art. 2, ad 5) was interpreted strictly by Sanchez who, considering the essence, nature and circumstances of the contract, concluded: "Since, therefore, the error of quality refers only to accidentals connected with marriage, it will not vitiate it" (Sanchez, De sancto matrimonii sacramento - Lib. VII, disp. 18, n. 18). This Sanchezian interpretation came to be regarded by canonists as a kind of principle of law and it was still considered to be such at the time of the Code of Canon Law, although it was explained in different ways by different authors. St. Alphonsus, however, in his third rule for determining the error that amounts to error of person, held: "If the consent is given directly and principally to the quality and less principally to the person, then the error in the quality amounts to an error in substance" (Theol. Mor., IV, n. 1016, p. 179) and this Alphonsian interpretation of the words of Canon 1083, § 2, 1° is now being revived by many authors. (Cir. O. DiJorio - Errore di qualità ridondante in errore di persona nel consenso matrimoniale - in "Il Diritto ecclesiastico" 1970, n. 5, ss., p. 8).

As long as the teaching remained uncertain, the jurisprudence of our tribunals in judging the validity of a marriage was generally inclined to consider a condition about a desired quality in a partner rather than error of quality amounting to an error of person. There were, however, some decisions which proposed that the third rule of St. Alphonsus about an error of quality amounting to an error of person be used in deciding such questions. A Rotal decision, coram Mannucci, of June 20, 1932 declared: "As regards an error about an accidental quality amounting to an error of person, our judgment is that nullity has not been proved . . . Error giving rise to the contract was definitely present; but it has by no means been proved that that error of quality amounted to an error of person. It has not been proved that the stated quality entered directly, principally and precisely into the marital consent defining and positively limiting it" (24, 236).

A decision of the Rota in a case from the Diocese of Dinajpur [which at the time was located in Bengal, the northeast province of India, later to become East Pakistan and still later, Bangladesh], handed down by Monsignor Heard on June 21, 1941, stated, after quoting the third rule of St. Alphonsus in its entirety: "It is indeed true that, in the external forum, such an intention could scarcely be proved and admitted without it having been drawn into the contract as a condition or pact; nevertheless, it is at least conceivable that in a given case, given the right circumstances, the prevailing intention could be demonstrated. Canon 1083 simply says that an error about the quality of a person can invalidate a marriage whenever 'the error of quality amounts to an error of person'. It makes no mention whatever of the necessity of having a condition or a pact in order to prove that, and it therefore clearly insinuates that there must be another way of showing, even in the external forum, that an error of quality can amount to an error of person" (33, 530). This decision was an affirmative one on the grounds of error regarding the wife's virginity.

Recently a decision in a case emanating from the Diocese of Niteroi in Brazil, handed down by Canals on April 21, 1970, stated: "The third notion is when a moral, juridic, social quality is regarded as being so intimately connected with the physical person that, when that quality is absent, the physical person is somebody entirely different" (62, 371).

A subsequent sentence, coram Ferraro, dated July 18, 1972, in a case from Cambrai in France, after tracing the history of the doctrine and jurisprudence about an error of quality which amounts to an error in person, draws this conclusion regarding the principles of law as stated by Canals: "A redounding error [i.e., an error which amounts to an error of person - error qualitatis redundans in errorem personae] can be invalidating even when the quality is not a physical quality but a moral, juridic, social quality." Ferraro, in other words, seems to be in basic agreement with Canals. Finally, there is Pinto's decision of November 12, 1973, in a Montevideo (Uruguay) case in which he opts for the stricter interpretation of an error of quality amounting to an error of person, denying that, even after the Second Vatican Council, the broader interpretation can be admitted.

4) It should be noted, of course, that Canon 1083, § 2, 1° neither defines nor specifies the force of the quality which can amount to an error of person.

135

However, § 2 of the Canon cannot be completely absorbed by § 1 [which states that error regarding the person invalidates the marriage], since it is not to be presumed that the legislator intended to be redundant. Besides, if one pays attention to 2° of the second paragraph, it is clear that it is not referring just to a physical quality which is inherent in a concrete person, because slavery is obviously not a quality that identifies a single physical person and designates him or her as a unique individual. Therefore, even a quality which is not so unique and individual that it can be confused with a single physical person can also be included in the meaning of this canon. Nor can it be held that the legislator, in stating that an error of quality *about slavery* invalidates a marriage, thereby wished to exclude from having any invalidating force errors *about other qualities,* which, like slavery, could apply to many persons. When, indeed, the canon explicitly stated that an error about slavery could be invalidating, it implicitly suggested that other errors, at least when they are errors about equally personal qualities which motivate one to marry, can be invalidating, providing always that they amount to an error of person.

Anyone who knows a given individual in the concrete, endowed with his or her own special qualities, knows also that some of those qualities are of only moderate importance while other qualities are so serious that they are critical in determining exactly who the person is, such as the social, economic, familial and marital status of the person. These qualities, at least in the society in which we live, are considered of great importance and can actually identify persons as individuals. And we must not forget that we are dealing here with the province of error and, therefore, great attention must be paid to the mind of the contractant himself, that is, to the value and importance which the contractant attributes to a determined quality for individuating that person with whom he wishes to contract.

5) In interpreting the law of Canon 1083, a judge, especially since Vatican II, must not overlook any of these things, because, in his office, he is to be, as it were, "justice personified," as St. Thomas, quoting Aristotle, said (II, II, 60, 1); and he ought to have constantly in mind the magnificent teachings of the Council regarding the family and marriage. Cfr. *The Allocutions of Pope Paul VI to the Auditors, Officials and Advocates of the Sacred Roman Rota* of January 28, 1971 (AAS LXIII, 140) and of January 28, 1972 (AAS LXIV, 205).

The dignity of the human person, as extolled in the teaching of Vatican II, stems not only from his physical qualities but from his ethical, juridic and social qualities as well. Recall, for example, what the Council Fathers taught about the interdependence of the human person and human society: "Life in society is not something accessory to man himself; through his dealings with others, through mutual service, and through fraternal dialogue, man develops all his talents and becomes able to rise to his destiny. Among the social ties necessary for man's development, some correspond more immediately to his innermost nature — the family, for instance, and the political community" (*Gaudium et Spes,* n. 25). And the Council also taught as regards the family and marriage: "The wellbeing of the individual person and Christian society is closely bound up with the healthy state of conjugal and family life .... thus the man and woman who 'are no longer two but one' (Matthew 19, 6) help and serve each other by their marriage partnership; they become conscious of their unity and experience it more deeply from day to day" (*Gaudium et Spes* nn. 47-48).

Since, therefore, a person is, as it were, the sum of "all his talents" as the Council said, and since he ought to hand himself over as such to his spouse in the intimate union of the marital covenant, an error of quality, even though it is not individual and unique but rather common to other persons but still identifying this person in a special way, can, when it motivates a person to marry, amount to "an error of person" according to Canon 1083, § 2, 1°, and can, therefore, invalidate marriage.

III
The Argument

It is generally agreed that, in order for imposed error or "error dolosus", as it is called, (C. 1098) to be invalidating, the quality must be:
1. True
2. Present at the time of marriage
3. Unknown
4. Grave (potentially seriously disruptive)
5. Fraudulently concealed to obtain consent

All five criteria are judged present in the case at bar.

1) *True.* Although the Court was unable to locate an actual marriage record for Henry Caracara's first marriage, the Court does have in its possession a copy of the Decree of Annulment issued by Judge Thomas J. Frequent in the Hartford Superior Court on December 24, 1953 in which it is stated that the marriage of Jane and Henry "was void for the reason that the defendant at the time of the marriage herein alleged was married to another woman."

The Instructor, John F. Edwards, asked two experts, Attorney Francis X. Murphy and Judge James Pierino, about this decree. Attorney Murphy said that a Judge would almost certainly have had documentary proof of the first marriage before he would issue a decree declaring the person guilty of the crime of bigamy. Judge Pierino said that, although the file behind the decree would have been liquidated by now, there is no question in his mind but that Judge Frequent certainly had the first marriage record.

Furthermore, the annulment decree indicates that Henry Caracara was present at the proceedings and filed a "no contest" which is an implicit admission of the truth of the grounds.

The Tribunal also has in its possession a copy of the dispensation from the banns relative to the Wrona-Caracara marriage which is also suggestive that there might have been something to hide. Two reasons were given by the parish priest for requesting the dispensation: the fact that both parties were twenty-three (which is a non reason if ever there was one) and "family objection." In fact it appears that this was not really a reason to *dispense* from the banns but a reason to *announce* them. Apparently, if the banns were announced, some family member might have objected to the Wrona-Caracara marriage on the grounds that Caracara was already married to someone else.

Lastly we have the testimony of two witnesses, Jane's sister and her brother-in-law, that Henry Caracara was married before, that he deserted his former wife and children, and without ever obtaining a divorce, listed himself as single and entered a marriage with Jane.

2) *Present at the time of marriage.* The proof of the previous marriage came to light only two years after the Wrona-Caracara marriage. Clearly at that time the wife and children were still alive and insistent upon their claim to support by Henry Caracara.

This, too, is the whole point of the civil annulment.

3) *Unknown.* The two witnesses testify to the fact that Jane was completely unaware of Henry's previous marriage on September 13, 1948. The Court also has in its possession the marriage license issued in Parkersburg on September 13, 1948 (interestingly, the dispensation from banns was also issued that day) in which Henry lists himself as single and never married. Given, then, the evidence both of the witnesses and of the document, it may be considered proved that Jane was unaware of Henry's marital status. She was, in other words, deceived, and she, of course, attests to this herself. It is the burden of her testimony.

That the quality was unknown to Jane is further corroborated by her reaction on learning of it. The witnesses describe her as being shocked on discovering that Henry was in a previous marriage. She immediately called Henry's aunt to try to verify the fact, and the aunt admitted that she had known that Henry was in a previous marriage but refrained from telling her because Jane and Henry seemed in love and the aunt didn't want to spoil things. Jane then called Catholic Family Services, and almost immediately separated and filed for annulment.

4) *Grave.* A previous, still existing civil marriage is recognized as an objectively grave quality by our jurisprudence. This is the gist of the Canals decision. See D1, p. 133.

5) *Fraudulently concealed to obtain marital consent.* All the witnesses agree that, if Jane had known that Henry was married, she never would have married him. She was an excellent Catholic but, even apart from that, she was only twenty-three years old, and there is every reason to believe that she would not have chosen a

man already married with two children. The fact that she was not married in her home parish but rather in St. Bridget's in Parkersburg, then a mission of St. Francis of Assisi; the fact that the license and the Church dispensation were issued on the day of the marriage itself suggests that Henry, who is described by everyone as a pathological liar, must have contrived a hasty marriage precisely to prevent Jane from knowing his background.

Since, therefore, all five criteria are verified in this case, the Court judges this marriage to be null on the grounds of imposed error.

WHEREFORE

I
The Facts

Ladislas Strzyzyk and Mercy Corbeau, both Catholic, were married at St. Anne's Church, Freeport, Connecticut in the Archdiocese of Hartford on the fourteenth day of May 1975. At the time Ladislas was twenty-four years old and Mercy was twenty-three.

With a few separations Ladislas and Mercy lived under the same roof for two years although there was no sex between them after four weeks. They separated finally in April of 1977. No children were born of the marriage. A divorce was obtained in Freeport on November 30, 1977.

On October 10, 1981, Ladislas petitioned this Court to declare the marriage null. His petition was accepted on October 29 and on November 15, 1981 the Issue in Pleading was declared to be the proved invalidity of the marriage based on Mercy Corbeau's total simulation.

II
The Law

The jurisprudence on total simulation, as summarized by Stankiewicz in his decision of January 29, 1981 (*Monitor Ecclesiasticus,* 1981, II, pp. 198-200), may be rendered in English as follows:

> 4. In order to enter "the intimate community of conjugal life and love" which is marriage, the parties must bestow themselves and receive each other by an irrevocable personal consent, that is to say, by a truly human act (*Gaudium et Spes,* n. 48).
>
> This human act, which is *externally* manifested by "the words or signs used in celebrating marriage" (Canon 1086 § 1), ought to include as well the *"internal* consent of the mind" (*Ibid.*).
>
> Consequently, as often as there is a discrepancy between the internal intent and the external manifestation of that intent, that is, "when one thing is done and another thing is pretended to have been done" (Ulp D. 2, 14, 9), then a valid "sacred bond which takes into consideration the good of the spouses, of the children and of society" (*Gaudium et Spes,* n.

140

48) in no way arises. It is an ancient legal principle that "a simulated marriage is of no importance" (Gai. D. 23, 2, 30).

Consequently, "if either or both parties, by a positive act of the will, exclude either marriage itself or every right to the conjugal act or some essential property of marriage, that person contracts invalidly" (Canon 1086 § 2).

Since the object of simulation is two-fold, that is, either marriage itself or some essential good of marriage, the prevailing jurisprudence of our Court recognizes two different kinds of simulation, namely, total simulation and partial simulation. See, for example, the following decisions:

Staffa	June 15, 1948	40, 245
Caiazzo	June 13, 1949	41, 293
Canestri	November 29, 1951	43, 736
Wynen	January 31, 1952	44, 46-47
Fidecicchi	January 11, 1955	47, 9
Lefebvre	March 12, 1960	52, 171
Anné	November 8, 1963	55, 764
Pucci	March 23, 1966	58, 168
Bejan	March 1, 1967	59, 137
Raad	June 27, 1973	
Pinto	October 20, 1975	
DiFelice	February 21, 1976	
Ewers	July 26, 1980	

This is the prevailing jurisprudence though a few decisions can be found which do not accept a distinction between total and partial simulation. See, for example:

Felici	May 9, 1951	43, 370
Rogers	July 8, 1969	61, 748

5. In *total* simulation, the contractant willingly and knowingly intends to enter an imitation marriage while excluding marriage itself, whereas, in *partial* simulation, he intends to enter a sort of marriage (a pseudo marriage), one accommodated to his own wishes; and oftentimes he does not realize that this results in the nullity of the marriage.

Consequently, both in canon law (which accepts the fact that simulation need not be in the form of an agreement by the two parties but can be done unilaterally) and in civil law (cfr. Perego E., *La simulazione nel matrimonio civile*, Milano 1980, p. 92 ss.), a marital intention is considered to be entirely lacking in *total* simulation, whereas, in *partial* simulation, there is present a kind of marital intent but an atypical one which is openly opposed to the substance of marriage as established by

God the Creator in his laws. An atypical marital intent, however, cannot produce a valid conjugal bond since some essential good, that is, children, fidelity, or perpetuity, is withheld from marriage (see n. 5 of my decision in a Roman case dated June 26, 1980).

Consequently, a marriage case cannot be accepted and defined on the grounds of both total simulation and partial simulation except when one ground is heard subordinately to the other, because it cannot happen that a person both altogether excludes marriage and, at the same time, intends a certain kind of marriage (see the decision coram Ewers of October 18, 1978).

Although the juridic figure of total simulation means exactly the same thing as the exclusion of marriage itself (C. 1086 § 2), nevertheless, in practice it is often phrased in slightly different ways:

a) The usual approaches are that one totally simulates marriage "when he in no way consents to it" (coram Bejan of July 29, 1970 [62, 861]; coram De Jorio of April 29, 1964 [56, 314]) or "when he does not intend positively to give consent while he can" (coram Abbo of February 8, 1968 [60, 81]) or, "when he does not have the intention of contracting," but, rather, as they say, "wishes to put on an act" (coram Parisella of December 18, 1980).

b) In order to understand more clearly the object of simulation, other rotal decisions note that one totally simulates "when a person excludes either marriage itself or his or her spouse" (coram Ferraro of April 26, 1978; coram Fagiolo of April 28, 1971, and coram Mercieca of June 15, 1973). For, as Innocent III said, when a man "does not propose to take this particular woman as his wife and in no way consents to that person, a marriage in no way results because in that sort of intention neither the substance nor the form of the marital contract can be found. The only thing that is present is deceit; absent entirely is marital consent and without marital consent a conjugal covenant cannot arise." (Innocent III c. 26, X, IV, I).

c) Exclusion of marriage itself is *properly* present when the contractant, by a positive act of the will, excludes a permanent society between a man and a woman for procreating children (C. 1082 § 1; and the decision coram Pinto of July 9, 1970 [62, 768]), that is to say, the intimate communion of one's whole life ordered for the good of the spouses and of the children (Canon 243 of the Schema on marriage, and *Communicationes* 9, 1977, p. 122-3). It is *improperly* present "when the contractant absolutely intends to exclude the sacrament in such a way that he does not want to contract marriage if at the same time he has to contract a sacrament (see the 1975 decision of Pasquazi in a case from Belley) or, in what amounts to the same thing, if "a marriage is entered in a pro forma way" whenever this is, in fact, tantamount to excluding marriage itself (coram Canestri of July 15, 1941 [33, 621]; coram Bonet of July 12, 1956 [48, 664]; and coram De Jorio of January 20, 1960 [52, 10]).

7. Total simulation is, finally, also present not only through the exclusion of the marriage itself (or of the other party) but also through the inclusion of an element which totally takes the place of marriage insofar as it is "an intimate community of conjugal life and love founded by the Creator and endowed with certain laws" (*Gaudium et Spes,* n. 48). For, when a person celebrates a nuptial rite *only and exclusively* "for his own purposes which are different from marriage" (coram Rogers of December 16, 1963 [55, 892]), that person "exclusively intends to attain something which is essentially different from marriage" and thereby "undermines the contract itself" (coram Anné of November 8, 1963 [55, 764]).

It should be noted, however, that a simple *absence of the intention to contract,* which, for example, would be verified if one were to enter marriage as a joke, is in no way sufficient, because the external manifestation of the consent is eliminated only through a contrary positive act by which one either excludes marriage itself or intends something else to serve as the only and exclusive substitute for marriage (or pseudo marriage).

III
The Argument

The evidence in this case consists of the testimony of both principals along with that of four witnesses, including Francine Gagliardi, a close friend and confidante of Mercy Corbeau.

The total evidence, I am convinced, demonstrates satisfactorily that Mercy Corbeau did indeed totally simulate her marriage to Ladislas Strzyzyk.

First of all the circumstantial evidence.

Antecedent Circumstances. In 1971, when Mercy was nineteen years old, she fell in love with a certain Frank Rogers. In April of 1973 Frank ended their relationship and entered the service. Just around that time Mercy saw a young man by the name of Ladislas Strzyzyk who was an exact look-a-like of Frank. Shortly thereafter Mercy decided that she would get to know this Ladislas and marry him, not for himself, but in order to spite Frank. All the time that Mercy dated Ladislas she pined for Frank and wrote him letters but Frank meanwhile became involved with another woman and married her early in January of 1975. Mercy, against the advice of friends, attended that wedding, sat in the back of the church and planned to get even with Frank by marrying Ladislas. She became engaged to Ladislas in February of 1975.

Concomitant Circumstances. Three days before their wedding, Mercy, feeling guilty about what she was doing, told Ladislas they should "split," i.e., call off the wedding, but Ladislas, thinking Mercy had the usual premarital jitters, would not hear of it. At the wedding itself, Mercy had the very same music played that Frank had had at his wedding. She cried all day: on the way to church, throughout the wedding and at the reception. At the wedding she could not bring herself to state her vows and, as she remembers it, the priest had to do it for her. At the reception she did not want Ladislas near her and she refused to kiss him.

Subsequent Circumstances. On the honeymoon, Mercy continued to cry. The thought of Ladislas touching her made her want to vomit. She refused to consummate the marriage and, finally, on the third or fourth night Ladislas forced himself on her, after which Mercy again wept. On the honeymoon she told Ladislas she wished she hadn't married him, and the honeymoon was cut short. The last few nights of the honeymoon Ladislas slept on the floor.

For a few weeks Mercy did some domestic chores, cooking, laundry, etc., making believe she was doing them for Frank but she could not sustain the charade and after a few weeks she quit these chores altogether. The same was true of sex. For a month she had sex a few times with Ladislas and got through it by making believe Ladislas was Frank. But after the first month, she never again permitted Ladislas to have sex with her.

After about nine or ten months Ladislas heard rumors from several sources that Mercy was seen often with a black man, and he left her for a time. According to Mercy, she never did have sex with that man but she was, meanwhile, having an affair with her employer. By this time Ladislas had heard about Frank and he knew why Mercy had married him. They lived under the same roof off and on for another year and separated finally in April of 1977.

Apart from this very weighty antecedent, concomitant and subsequent circumstantial evidence, the Tribunal is also faced with the fact that Mercy's *motive for marrying* (to be vindictive to Frank) was tawdry and contributed to her *motive for simulating* (because she still loved only Frank and could not give herself to another man).

There was also an implicit extrajudicial confession when Mercy told her friend Francine Gagliardi (who testified to this in Court) that she, Mercy, was being a "phony." Francine even tried to dissuade Mercy from marrying because she knew it was wrong and an injustice to Ladislas but Francine was not successful.

All of this evidence, taken together, the circumstances, motive, and confession are, in my judgment, probative of the nullity of the marriage on the grounds of Mercy's total simulation.

WHEREFORE

CIGNO - ANITRA

John Cigno and Dorothy Anitra, both Catholic, were married at Incarnation Church, Merrill, Connecticut, in the Archdiocese of Hartford, on the tenth day of May 1977. John was twenty-three years old at the time; Dorothy was twenty-two.

John and Dorothy lived together for only about a year. During the course of the marriage John discovered that Dorothy intended to exclude children from the marriage. He attempted to dissuade her from this conviction but, when it became apparent to him that Dorothy was adamant on the issue, he left her. It was June of 1978. A divorce was obtained in Merrill on March 12, 1979.

On February 18, 1982, John petitioned this Tribunal to declare the marriage null. His petition was accepted and Dorothy's intention *contra bonum prolis* was assigned by the Judge on March 3rd as the source of nullity for investigation and adjudication.

II
The Law

The jurisprudence regarding an intention against children is well explained in a decision of December 22, 1969, coram Pompedda (61, 1188-1189):

> Well known, because frequently and illuminatingly discussed in our jurisprudence, are the principles regarding the good of children, viewed either as the *end* to which marriage is, by its nature, ordered, or as a *right* to intercourse which constitutes the object of consent between the spouses. It goes without saying that the nullity of a marriage necessarily results from a substantial and radical defect of either of these aspects, that is, either when the *end* is excluded or when the *right* is not exchanged.

> As judges in the Church of Christ, whose duty it is to set forth a jurisprudence which both coincides with the natural law and contributes to the supreme good of souls, part of our function is to examine the opinions of others lest we seem, by our silence, to approve of or rashly ignore certain erroneous statements which are being made, either out of malice or ignorance or misunderstanding, both by judges and by other clerics.

> Appropriate importance should be given to the teaching which was so forthrightly and neatly set forth in Canon 1013 § 1, namely, that the end of

marriage includes the mutual assistance of the spouses and the remedy of concupiscence. This is listed as a secondary end not to belittle it, or to imply that it does not pertain to the essence of marriage, or to suggest that it is not sufficient, in itself, for conferring the goodness and honesty necessary for the great sacrament of marriage. The Church furthermore has always and constantly clung to the teaching that was so beautifully stated by the Apostle Paul about the intimate and essential likeness of the *marital* union (both physical and amorous) of the spouses with the *mystical* union of Christ and his Church.

It would be erroneous to say that only the so-called material aspect of marriage, or, if you like, the sexual donation, is included in the canonical definition of marital consent. Because the two aspects ought not to be separated, nor should we speak of two ends of marriage. These days, especially, we ought to preach clearly and without ambiguity that primarily and principally, in the objective order of things and by the intent of the Creator, *children* are the end of marriage. But this very special end of marriage *includes* conjugal love. For it is obvious that even the purest love of man and woman often, perhaps always, assumes some self-centeredness, in that it closes the spouses off into a circle of only two people. But, through procreation, a person becomes a collaborator with divine providence, greatly contributes to the good of human society and communicates the inestimable gift of his or her own life to other creatures.

This point was made clear by our latest Ecumenical Council. While the other ends of marriage are not, according to Vatican II, of lesser importance than the procreation and education of children, nevertheless marriage and conjugal love, itself, "are by nature *ordered* to the procreation and education of children"; true conjugal love, therefore, and the whole structure of family life "is directed to disposing the spouses to cooperate valiantly with the love of the Creator and Savior who through them will increase and enrich his family from day to day" (*Gaudium et Spes* n. 50). Regarding this point, the so-called Dutch Catechism noted:

> "When we survey the history of marriage, the question cannot but be raised: why did man and woman come together and stay together in marriage in the first place? Was it to give themselves to each other or to have and to educate children? But this is a question which puts asunder things that are united and should remain united. Fruitfulness is something that naturally springs from love, and love is always life-giving—even in other realms of human life. Where there is love, there is always new life.
>
> But the characteristic of sexual love is that it is intrinsically connected with a particular and lofty form of fruitfulness—the origin of new human life. This is so intimately connected with married love that a marriage where the condition is laid down from

the start that a child must be excluded is not regarded as valid by the Church. Obviously, this does not mean that sexual intercourse is only right when it is directly intended for the begetting of children. No one holds that. But it means that in the projected matrimony as a whole the child may not be expressly excluded."

"A New Catechism: Catholic Faith for Adults," Herder and Herder, 1967, pp. 401-402.

It is clear, therefore, that marital consent includes not just the handing over and receiving of the right to intercourse but also, as a necessary and juridically important consequence of that, the right to an intimate communion (both spiritual and physical) intended by the spouses in their exchange of consent.

III
The Argument

Dorothy Anitra has been plagued with poor health and a variety of rather serious illnesses from the time she was a little girl.

As her marriage date approached Dorothy became more and more concerned about the effect that bearing children might have on her health. It even seemed to her that, if she did have children, she would not live long enough to nurture them through adolescence.

So three weeks before the scheduled wedding, Dorothy visited Doctor Ivan Sunderhauf, and was fitted for a diaphragm. The acts of this case include a report from Doctor Sunderhauf attesting to this fact.

Dorothy never advised John that she was wearing a diaphragm but, after a few months of marriage, John discovered the diaphragm in a drawer and asked Dorothy what it was. Dorothy confessed to John at that point that she had been using the contraceptive from the beginning of the marriage because of her fear of having children. John felt betrayed and told Dorothy that, if she had had any love for him at all, she would, at the very least, have discussed the matter with him before marriage.

For the next several months John attempted to talk with Dorothy about the issue of children but Dorothy would only say, "I have made up my mind. Please leave me alone."

All of the three witnesses in the case (including Dorothy's mother) testified that they heard, shortly after John did, about the diaphragm and about John's vain efforts to persuade Dorothy to at least discuss the matter of children. Two of the witnesses knew of Dorothy's serious concern for her health. Dorothy herself testified under oath that she always wore the contraceptive during intercourse and that she would not have had intercourse without it. She has not remarried.

Dorothy's judical confession was clear and peremptory and was corroborated by the testimony of the witnesses. Dorothy had a serious motive for simulating; she was fitted for a diaphragm before marriage and after marriage always used it. Her behavior subsequent to marriage, beginning with the very first moment of conjugal existence, may be presumed to be the logical consequence of a prenuptial intention.

In the opinion of the Court, therefore, Dorothy's invalidating intention *contra bonum prolis* has been demonstrated.

WHEREFORE

I
The Facts

Leah Kestrel, Catholic, and Miles Whistler, baptized a Catholic but not reared in any faith, were married at the Church of St. Jude, Huntsville, Connecticut in the Archdiocese of Hartford on the twenty-eighth day of June, 1973. At the time both parties were twenty years old.

Leah and Miles lived together (with one separation lasting several months) for just about two years, separating finally in June of 1975. Throughout the marriage Miles steadfastly refused to have children. A divorce was granted at Huntsville on March 18, 1976.

On September 24, 1979 Leah petitioned this Court to declare the marriage null. Her petition was accepted and on November 13, 1979 the Doubt was Formulated as follows:

> Whether the Kestrel-Whistler marriage has been proved null on the grounds of Miles Whistler's intention contra bonum prolis.

II
The Law

The law regarding an intention against children is clearly summarized in the following excerpt from a decision coram Davino dated December 13, 1978, as reported in *Monitor Ecclesiasticus,* 1979, II, pp. 199-202:

> 5. *The Constitution on the Church in the Modern World (Gaudium et Spes,* n. 48) says: "By its very nature the institution of marriage and married love is ordered to the procreation and education of the offspring and it is in them that it finds its crowning glory."
>
> If, however, by a positive act of the will, a person *either* excludes children, i.e., positively rejects the idea of children (Suppl., q. XLIX, art. 3) *or* denies, in marriage, the mutual right to those acts which are per se apt for the generation of children, then that person contracts invalidly. In the *former* instance the nullity of marriage is derived from the rejection of the purpose of marriage, as indicated in C. 1013 § 1, whereas, in the *latter* case, the nullity of marriage stems from the prescriptions of C. 1086, § 2.

6. The exclusion of *children,* or of the end of marriage, only invalidates a marriage when it is perpetual, not when children are only excluded for a time, whereas the denial of *the right to conjugal acts* can be had, although with difficulty, even when the right is denied only for a time.

As Ferraro noted, in a decision of October 12, 1976, "whenever the exclusion of children is perpetual, the exclusion of the *right* is involved, whereas a temporary exclusion of children generally indicates an exclusion only of the *exercise* of the right. There is, however, no question but that even a temporary exclusion of the right results in the invalidity of marriage, because in such a case the perpetuity of the right is limited, and perpetuity belongs to the essence of the nuptial covenant."

Bejan noted, in a decision of April 24, 1968, that "where the contractant, by spurning and positively rejecting the law of nature, presumes to pass himself off as the only source of rights in marriage and consequently decides that the right to intercourse may be used according to his own lights and for his own purposes, and where indeed that can be juridically demonstrated, it cannot be doubted that such a position can wound the very essence of conjugal consent."

Ewers, in a decision of April 10, 1965, noted "It should be added here that even a temporary exclusion of the right suffices to induce the nullity of marriage for, as Staffa (*De conditione contra matrimonii substantiam,* 1955, p. 38, n. 14) noted, 'Since the right flowing from marital consent is by its nature exclusive and perpetual and therefore admits of no limits, a condition interrupting that right even briefly, indeed even for one single act, suffices to destroy it completely: and the same may be said concerning the positive act of the will'. C. 1081, indeed, expressly says that in marital consent a perpetual right to the body is given and received." (57, 357)

This is our standard jurisprudence. Dean Brennan, for example, noted, in his decision of February 19, 1965, "Even a temporary restriction of the right brings about the nullity of marriage or of marital consent for, as C. 1081 § 2 indicates, the right that is to be handed over and received ought to be perpetual and, therefore, without any limitation of time." (57, 170)

And, as De Jorio said in the sentence of December 14, 1966, "We leave unsolved the question of *whether,* by postponing to a later date the handing over and receiving of the right to the body for those acts which are per se apt for the generation of offspring, marriage is entered invalidly, or *whether* its validity is only suspended . . . for, if at a later time this right is handed over and received, no one will demand that the marriage be declared null, whereas, if it is not handed over at a later time, then certainly the marriage will be invalid." (58, 921) See also Filipiak's decision of November 5, 1965 (57, 784).

7. Since we are talking here about a temporary exclusion of children, we should keep in mind that there are two possibilities. Either children are excluded for a determined period of time (consider here the doctrine on responsible parenthood) or children are excluded conditionally, that is to say, the right to children is handed over depending on some condition. As Dean Brennan noted, in his October 24, 1966 decision, "If in contracting marriage one withholds the handing over of the right until some specific future circumstances occur, then the right is obviously not handed over at the time of the wedding and, consequently, that kind of consent restricts the object of marriage." (58, 724)

Or, as De Jorio said, in his decision of March 6, 1968, "If one decides that he is not handing over to his partner the right to those acts which are per se apt for the generation of offspring until such time as the compatibility of the parties is experientially tested, then that person is giving marital consent only on a condition and, if that condition is not fulfilled, then the bond of marriage never comes to be. If, afterwards, the marriage breaks down without any hope of reconciliation, then the party who gave the conditional consent revokes it, and without consent he cannot enter marriage. In this hypothesis, therefore, the marriage bond never arises." (60, 182, n. 5)

8. As regards proving simulation, it is important to keep two things in mind: (a) The existence of a motive for simulating, which should be at least subjectively grave in order to result in the exclusion of offspring or the restriction of the right; and (b) the confession of the simulator which should be understood not only in the context of the words themselves, but in light of the sum total of all the elements of proof.

Actually, as Dean Brennan noted in his December 5, 1966 decision, "There are many serious difficulties involved in proving a temporary exclusion of a conjugal right. To demonstrate that a temporary denial of this kind reaches to the right itself must be collected from the facts and from unequivocal circumstances, since the contractant himself rarely understands the niceties of the law and, therefore, does not enter marriage making fine distinctions. The difficulties are increased where there is no expressed agreement between the parties and no clear condition to exclude children." (58, 887)

The prudent judge will therefore conduct his investigation not in an abstract way but by carefully giving his consideration to all of the proofs in their complex singularity.

As Anné noted, in his decision of June 27, 1972, "Every marriage case should be viewed according to its own peculiarities, considering all the existential circumstances in which the contractants are involved. Each case must be decided on the basis of its own special complexion resulting from the confession of the parties, the deposition of the witnesses concerning the alleged simulation, and also from all of the information provided by the acts regarding the people and the circumstances."

```
   III
The Argument
```

The evidence in this case consists of the testimony of both principals and that of two witnesses: Margaret Little, who was the maid of honor at the wedding, and George Hart, who was the best man. The witnesses were knowledgeable and impressed the Court with their honesty. The respondent, though not a practicing Catholic was cooperative and forthright. The total evidence demonstrates beyond reasonable doubt that the marriage was null because of Miles Whistler's intention *contra bonum prolis*. The evidence may be summarized as follows:

1. *Circumstantial Evidence*. Miles came from a troubled home. He was born out of wedlock and was reared as an infant by his grandparents. When he was three his parents finally married and he then went with them but they divorced four years later and Miles returned to his grandparents. Though baptized he had no religious rearing. He was in trouble as a teenager, did poorly in school and finally quit school in his senior year. He was considered selfish and unethical and he used some drugs. Because of his own unhappy childhood Miles was loathe to bring children of his own into the world, and he had little esteem for women as mothers.

2. *Motives*. Besides a general reluctance to bring children into the world, Miles was also interested in maintaining his own freedom and did not wish to be burdened with a child while he was in his early twenties. The two witnesses saw Miles' desire for freedom as his principal motivation in not wanting children and they noted that Miles sought freedom in other areas as well: he floated from job to job and he spent a great deal of time away from home with his "drinking buddies."

3. *Extrajudicial Confession*. A couple of weeks before the marriage Miles told his best friend, George Hart (who testified to this in Court), that he and Leah had had an argument over children. Although they had agreed some months before that they would postpone children for a couple of years, Leah was now (two weeks before the marriage) wondering whether they couldn't have a child after a year or so. Miles said "No way." They quarrelled over it but finally settled on a rather vague agreement that they would have children as soon as they got their feet on the ground. This is what they agreed on but, in fact, Miles told George, Miles himself had no intention of having children for at least seven years. This was a clear extrajudicial confession that Miles, without telling Leah, intended to avoid children for several years.

4. *Judicial Confession.* Much to Leah's surprise, Miles agreed to offer testimony to the Court. He did so, he said, because Leah is a "good woman" and because he "felt bad for having deceived her." In Court, Miles corroborated his conversation with George a couple of weeks prior to marriage as well as the following two points.

5. *The Presumption of Cause.* Miles said that if Leah had not at least agreed to postpone children until they got their feet on the ground, he wouldn't have married her. He was not, he said, going to put up with a big hassle about children right from the beginning. The fact that he would have cancelled the wedding unless a postponement of children could be arranged demonstrates where Miles' priorities lay and shows the intensity of his intention to avoid children.

6. *The Presumption of Tenacity.* Leah took the contraceptive pill during the first four or five months of the marriage but they made her ill and the doctor recommended she discontinue them. Miles then convinced her to use a contraceptive foam but by the end of the year Leah became more and more interested in having a child and the couple became embroiled in bitter quarrels over this "almost every week." Miles, however, would not relent, suggesting again that he was determined to avoid children. Finally the couple separated, mostly because there were so many arguments over children. Leah, however, loved Miles and after six months pleaded with him to return. He did and the couple lived together peacefully for another couple of months. But then Leah began to bring up the subject of children again and Miles at that point left for good.

The Court is convinced that the total evidence shows that Miles' intent, even though it involved only a temporary exclusion of children, was nevertheless so firm, intense, inflexible and non-negotiable that it cannot be viewed as a mere side agreement subordinate to the marriage covenant but that, on the contrary, it invaded the heart of the covenant itself and limited the terms of the covenant, thereby rendering it a contract different from the marriage covenant.

WHEREFORE

```
        I
    The Facts
```

Marshall Grebe and Colette Avocet, both Catholic, were married at the Church of St. Louis, Marion, Connecticut in the Archdiocese of Hartford on the twenty-fourth day of June 1978. At the time both parties were twenty-five years old.

Marshall and Colette lived together for only a few months. In October Marshall discovered that Colette was unfaithful to him and he left her. He absolutely refused reconciliation, at least on Colette's terms, and he quickly applied for a divorce, which was granted on March 3, 1979 in Marion County.

On May 17, 1979 Marshall petitioned this Court to declare the marriage null. His petition was accepted on May 29, and on June 20, 1979 the Issue in Pleading was declared to be:

> Whether the Grebe-Avocet marriage has been proved null on
> the grounds of an intention contra bonum fidei.

```
        II
    The Law
```

The law regarding an intention against fidelity is clearly expressed in the following excerpts from two rotal decisions. The first decision, given by Palazzini on July 26, 1966 (58, 663-664), reads:

> A rule of law states: what a person does is of more importance than what he secretly has in mind. Which explains why the Code of Canon Law says: "If either or both parties, by a positive act of the will, exclude marriage itself or all right to the conjugal act or some essential property of marriage, they contract invalidly." (Canon 1086 § 2)

> He who excludes marriage itself is said to simulate *totally*, whereas he who denies one or other of the goods of marriage, is said to simulate *partially*. As regards the bonum fidei, we read in a decision coram Wynen: "One's juridic status remains unchanged when the intention of retaining one's lover is combined with the intention of not fulfilling the obligation of fidelity. For such intention, though it be evil, does not necessarily indicate that the contractant intended to deprive his wife of

any right. . . . Even if he promised his lover before marriage that he would remain faithful to her, even this does not necessarily mean that in contracting marriage he intended to deprive his wife of her right and that he gave this right, instead, to his lover. The distinction between legitimate conjugal union and cohabitation with a lover resides so firmly in the minds of Christians, even those of weaker morals, that a confusion of concepts as regards conjugal rights cannot be admitted." (31, 255)

Nevertheless, Monsignor Mattioli has wisely noted: "When a person, caught in the dilemma of having to say goodbye either to marriage or to his lover, is more inclined to renounce marriage (either explicitly or implicitly) than his lover, but does, in fact, go through the ceremony, it seems that he has reserved to himself the right to have sex with his lover.

In other words, the exclusive right is undoubtedly damaged, that is to say, excluded when:

> a. some limitation contrary to the obligation of fidelity is imposed on the consent;

> b. the intention is made of not entering marriage except under a certain condition, namely, that one not be restricted from having sex with others;

> c. a positive obligation is contracted with a third party;

> d. the right of not observing fidelity is reserved." (45, 641-642)

The other decision, given by DiFelice on November 3, 1971 (*Monitor Ecclesiasticus*, 1972, II, pp. 187-188) reads:

> It is of the greatest importance, in proving the nullity of marriage on the grounds of the exclusion of the bonum fidei, that it be shown that the very exclusivity of the right to those acts which are per se apt for the generation of offspring was refused.

> The *simple* right to those acts constitutes the bonum prolis, but the *exclusivity* of that right constitutes the bonum fidei. The distinction between these two bona comes from Canon 1081, paragraph 2, which says that marital consent is an act of the will by which the parties hand over and receive the perpetual and exclusive right to the body for those acts which are per se apt for the generation of offspring. A party is obliged to hand over and receive that exclusive right; otherwise he contracts invalidly according to Canon 1086, paragraph 2, since in denying the exclusivity of the right, he thereby denies the unity of marriage, and unity is one of the essential properties of marriage.

Our jurisprudence, which has always recognized the distinction between the excluded *right* and the excluded *exercise* of the right, has often said that simple adultery, insofar as it involves only the denied *exercise* of the right, does not invalidate the marriage.

Nevertheless, when it is a question not of simple adultery but of an intention to continue a premarital affair after marriage, then the matter ought to be carefully investigated so that it can be properly determined whether it is just the exercise of the right or rather the very exclusivity of the right that is being denied. In this case, in order to determine precisely whether it is a question of the denied exclusivity of the right, the Court ought to investigate whether the party, in giving his marital consent, wished to assume the obligation of fidelity, that is to say, whether he was handing over to his wife the exclusivity of the right to those acts which are per se apt for generation. If it was his intention not to assume any obligation of belonging exclusively to his wife, then he was rejecting, by a positive act of will, the bonum fidei, and he was therefore contracting invalidly. Because he who accepts no obligation is not giving to his partner the right that is involved.

When therefore, in entering marriage, a man presumes to reserve to himself the right to give his body to another person besides his wife in such a way that he intends to enter marriage on no other terms, then he is setting aside from the usual marital obligations the exclusivity of the right, and he is denying the bonum fidei.

On the other hand, the mere intention of pursuing after marriage a love affair that went on before, does not demonstrate the exclusion of the right to the bonum fidei. The exclusion of the right should be proved by weighty arguments which show that the party would have preferred not to have entered marriage at all than to have entered a marriage that obligated him to observe fidelity. Besides, therefore, the intention of breaking the covenant, it is further required in order to prove invalidity, that the exclusion of the right to the bonum fidei be adequately demonstrated from the prevailing intent to hand over one's body to a third person, and also from the circumstances that make it clear that the party did not marry with the obligation of fidelity towards his wife but rather that he intended to deny fidelity and not enter marriage with integral consent.

See the following rotal decisions: *Vol. 47*, pg. 241; *Vol. 50,* pg. 65; and the five decisions given in 1959, found in *Vol. 51* on the following pages, 10, 161, 397, 503 and 610.

Finally, it should be pointed out that those circumstances which demonstrate particularly well that the bonum fidei was denied and that a proper marriage was not entered, generally regard two things, first the *motive* for simulating, and secondly, the *manner* in which the simulator conducts himself. If the motive for simulating seems more important than the motive for marrying, then it ought to be presumed that the right to the bonum fidei was excluded. Likewise, if the party conducted himself in such a way as to show that he had practically no regard for fidelity and wished only to maintain a liaison, then it must be concluded that he never accepted the obligation of the bonum fidei and that he never handed over the exclusive right to his wife. Because on the basis of these circumstances, one can safely presume that the party would have entered marriage only if the bonum fidei was excluded.

III
The Argument

The evidence in this case consists of the testimony of both principals, Marshall and Colette, plus that of three witnesses: Colette's lover, Craig Nagh; her girlfriend and confidante, Robin Sand; and Marshall Grebe's father.

The facts are as follows:

Colette Avocet majored in drama while in college and became an actress of some talent. She worked in a repertory company and did summer stock. In the summer of 1976 she played the lead, opposite Craig Nagh, in Bernard Slade's play, *Same Time Next Year,* the play about the man and woman, both married to other parties, who spend the same weekend each year together for many years.

Craig, a man five years Colette's senior, was already married at that time and had two children, but Colette fell madly in love with him and they had sex together often that summer. Colette had had a couple of affairs before, while in college, but she saw Craig as altogether unique, the man of her dreams. They had a great deal in common, could talk readily about each other's feelings, and Colette had a fierce sexual passion for Craig.

Craig was less involved. He had a summer infatuation with Colette, was captivated by her beauty and wit and artistry. He enjoyed her as a companion and as a sexual partner. But he was married and was not about to divorce his wife.

As summer drew to an end, Colette was determined that it would not mean the end of their romance. She made Craig promise that, like the couple they played in *Same Time Next Year,* they, too, would have at least a weekend together for the rest of their lives. It was, for Colette, a solemn commitment. They would begin that October and, come hell or high water, they would do so every year thereafter. Craig liked the idea. He did not take it as seriously as Colette. Nor was he sure that he would sustain the commitment. But he liked the idea and he did not mind promising Colette that, come hell or high water, they would spend a weekend together every October. The meeting of October 1976 was wonderful as far as Colette was concerned. It exceeded her expectations.

Colette met Marshall Grebe at a New Year's Eve party in New York a couple of months later. Marshall was a conservative young businessman, a partner in his father's construction firm. Colette was not much attracted to him but Marshall was very taken with Colette and pursued her. Colette and Marshall were often separated by hundreds of miles but Marshall wrote to her, telephoned her, and frequently flew to wherever Colette was and took her to dinner and the theater. Colette remained rather cool to Marshall but began to admire his stability and persistence. He had money; he was a church-going Catholic and would undoubtedly make a good husband and father. That summer Marshall proposed marriage but Colette declined saying that they did not yet know each other well enough.

In October of '77 she rendezvoused with Craig and once again was transported into the world of her dreams. She told Craig about Marshall and about how he had proposed but she swore on the motel bible that even if she did marry Marshall she would always belong, at least on that one weekend a year, not to Marshall but to Craig.

On returning from that weekend Colette told her friend, Robin Sand, of the marvelous weekend she had had with Craig and of her renewed commitment to him.

At Christmas time Marshall proposed marriage again and this time she accepted. Craig was really her man but he still had no intention of divorcing his wife; she, Colette, was not getting any younger; and she did really admire and respect Marshall. They agreed to a June wedding.

They returned to Colette's home town of Marion, Connecticut for the wedding and then took a place at Cape Cod where Colette was working that summer.

The early months of marriage went quite well. Marshall spent about three and a half days each week with the company and he found the commuting tiresome but he loved his time at the Cape with Colette, and their time together was pleasant for Colette too. At summer's end they returned to New York.

One day in late September, Marshall picked up the downstairs phone to make a call and, by sheer accident, overheard the tail end of a telephone conversation on the upstairs phone between Colette and a man. Colette said, "See you on the thirteenth, darling. I love you." The man said, "I love you too," and they hung up.

Marshall's whole world collapsed. Colette had no idea that Marshall had overheard the conversation, and Marshall felt that he successfully concealed that fact from Colette. But inside, his stomach was churning and he was bewildered. For three days he said nothing to anyone, thinking perhaps he was mistaken. But he *had* to talk with someone, and on the morning of the fourth day he told his father and asked his advice. The father advised hiring a detective, and when Marshall demurred, the father said, "Well if you don't I will, so which is it?"

A week or so later Colette asked Marshall if she could accompany her parents to visit her grandmother in New Hampshire on the weekend of October 13, Marshall said it was OK by him.

On Saturday, the 14th, the detective reported that Colette had spent the previous night in a motel with a man.

On Colette's return, Marshall told her what he knew and also told her the marriage was over. Colette pleaded with Marshall not to end the marriage. She told him the whole story about Craig, promised Marshall that she would be a good wife to him and mother to his children for 363 days a year but on that one weekend she belonged to Craig. Marshall saw a lawyer the next day.

These are all established facts, sworn to by the two principals and corroborated by the three witnesses. They demonstrate that when Colette married Marshall, she harbored an intention *contra bonum fidei,* that she had made a firm, irrevocable commitment to hand over her body to a third party for a limited but specific time each year and that she was therefore excluding from the commitment an essential property of marriage (C. 1101 § 2), namely unity (C. 1056).

WHEREFORE

```
┌─────────────────────────┐
│            I            │
│        The Facts        │
│                         │
└─────────────────────────┘
```

Amy Petrel, Catholic, and Eric Fulmar, unbaptized, were married at the Church of St. Raymond, Bordley, Connecticut, in the Archdiocese of Hartford, on the fourteenth day of September, 1973. Amy was twenty-three years old at the time; Eric was twenty-five.

Amy and Eric lived together for seven years. At times Eric complained that Amy was not quite adventurous enough for him but basically they had a good life together and were good parents to their only child, Eric Jr., born in 1975. In 1980, however, Eric left Amy. A divorce was granted in New Haven on March 3, 1981.

On August 29, 1981, Amy petitioned this Tribunal to declare the marriage null. Her petition was accepted and on September 19, 1981 the Judge assigned Eric's error and intention *contra bonum sacramenti* as the *caput nullitatis investigandum*.

```
┌─────────────────────────┐
│            II           │
│        The Law          │
│                         │
└─────────────────────────┘
```

The law on an intention against indissolubility as affected by error is summarized in the law section of January 23, 1971, coram Pompedda (63, 53-54):

> Canon 1084, because of its high relevance to such a large number of cases is well known and understood by all. Lest, however, it be applied indiscriminately to an excessive number of cases, the undersigned judges wish to offer the following observations: The canon suggests two points, the former more general, the latter more specific. The more general point is that not all marriages contracted *with* or even *from* simple error about the unity or indissolubility or sacramental dignity of marriage are, because of that fact and only because of that fact, invalid, in accordance with Canon 1086, § 2. The more specific point is that we must always distinguish between the *error* (as it remains in the intellect) and the *will* (as it is strongly influenced by that error).

> The former, more general point, is useful in preventing the facile annulment of a great number of marriages, especially marriages of non-Catholics, non believers and those who do not, at least in practice, adhere to the faith. But a judge must also take the second, more specific point into consideration as well, so that, in individual cases, he carefully inquires

into the force and influence of error on the act of the will, through which the consent, and therefore the marriage, comes about (Canon 1081).

In our judgment it is not a legitimate conclusion from Canon 1084 to say that there exists a presumption in favor of marriage for those people who, perhaps largely because of their religious beliefs or secular education, are laboring under a misunderstanding of the essential properties of marriage. This is especially true since such a presumption is arrived at only by gratuitously conjecturing to a second presumption, namely, that it never occurs to such people, when they enter marriage, to apply their intellectual error to their intention. It would seem, therefore, as regards both Catholics and others, that the principle should be retained that, the more deeply and radically an error is ingrained and endorsed, the easier it is to establish a presumption in favor of an essential property of marriage being excluded. Because the will, which is a kind of blind faculty of the soul, generally goes along with whatever is presented to it by the intellect. Therefore, the deeper, more vehement and more conscious is the fixation and attraction of the intellect to its object, the more difficult it is (although not impossible, because of the influence of the passions) for the will to be turned away from the object presented to it by the intellect. Indeed, it sometimes happens that a person holds an opinion (rightly or wrongly) with such intense conviction that the opinion becomes, as it were, part of his or her personality and when that happens, the will follows along almost irresistibly.

The phrase "simple error," furthermore, was not used gratuitously by the legislator. The phrase, it should be noted, seems to contain a double meaning, the one logical, illustrating the distinction between error and will, the other ontological, suggesting the force and influence of error on the will.

When all this is taken into consideration, it should be apparent that it is unworthy of a judge, when faced with a difficult case, to take refuge in the statement that, since marriage enjoys the favor of law, as noted in C. 1014, it is always simple error that is present and not a positive intention of the will elicited by the contractants.

```
┌─────────────────────┐
│         III         │
│    The Argument     │
└─────────────────────┘
```

Although the invalidating force of error pervicax seu radicatus (radical, intransigent error) is disputed (see, for example, the decision of March 19, 1978 coram Pinto in E.I.C. 1979, pp. 249-252), still Pompedda's observations are well made and are applicable to this case.

Eric Fulmar certainly held, as an ingrained conviction, that marriage was a limited, qualified commitment. Eric himself chose not to offer testimony but the four witnesses (including an aunt of Eric) made it clear that, given Eric's often stated attitude regarding marriage, it would have been virtually impossible for him to enter a marital union that could only be terminated by the death of one of the partners.

Eric's own parents were divorced and two of the witnesses were aware that it was Eric himself, then twelve years old, who urged them to separate. Prior to that time, both parents had, for some years, had extramarital lovers. Between themselves, meanwhile, the parents fought constantly and let Eric know that they were staying together for his sake only. In 1960 Eric told them to forget it, that he would be much happier in a different environment. The parents, at that point, did divorce and both married other partners.

For the next six years Eric lived in his mother's custody but visited his father often. Both second marriages were reasonably happy and Eric enjoyed both his mother and his father more than he ever had in the years prior to their divorce. Eventually, however, the father divorced his second wife as well, when she refused to accompany him to California where an employment opportunity opened up for him. Eric, at the time, supported his father in his request for a divorce.

All this became known to Amy Petrel during the course of her two year courtship with Eric but she was always afraid to bring it up because she feared that Eric would be honest with her about his convictions and she didn't wish to hear them.

Amy also had apprehensions about how Eric would get along with the priest when the time came to make arrangements for the marriage. Eric had grown up with an intense dislike for organized religion of any kind but he had a particular antipathy for the Catholic Church (which he considered oppressive) and for Catholic priests (whom he regarded as hypocrites). As it turned out, however, there was no confrontation between Eric and the priest. The priest was extremely conciliatory and made practically no demands and Eric even took a liking to him because they were both avid fans of the same football team.

After marriage both Eric and Amy worked outside the home (except for a leave Amy took around the time the baby was born) and they both helped with household chores as well.

Eric, however, came to feel that he was intellectually superior to Amy. He was, for one thing, a college graduate whereas Amy had attended only one year of college. According to the witnesses, Eric also felt that their different experiences broadened the gap between them. Amy saw just a few of her old high school friends whereas Eric was meeting people from all over the country and was periodically receiving job offers from other sections of the country. Amy, however, preferred to stay close to home and to her parents, so the couple remained in Connecticut. But Eric came to feel more and more that life was passing him by and that Amy was an albatross, holding him back from his destiny, limiting his potential.

On several occasions during the marriage Eric told Amy that for a marriage to be useful, it had to work for the benefit of *both* partners and that it was becoming more and more apparent that their own marriage was not mutually beneficial. "Perhaps it was time," he would say, "for us to go our separate ways." Over the years Amy told a couple of her friends about these discussions and these friends have corroborated the tenor of those discussions in their testimony before the Tribunal.

After Eric Jr. was born, Eric seemed happy for a time but then seemed to feel more and more trapped. He was off on frequent business trips and became involved quite seriously with another woman.

Finally in 1980 Eric was offered a position in Dallas. His friend, Cynthia, was most willing to go along with him but when he discussed the matter with Amy, she was reluctant to go. Eric told Amy, therefore, that he thought they should part amicably. It was not that their marriage had been a mistake, he said; it was simply that it was time to move on. Some things last longer than others; nothing is forever; and this relationship, he felt, had enjoyed a reasonable longevity. He promised to assume a suitable responsibility for Eric Jr. and he moved out shortly thereafter.

Given Eric's background, attitudes and convictions and given his consistent behavior throughout the marriage, it is obvious to this Court that his error regarding the indissolubility of marriage did determine his will at the time of marriage (C. 1099) and therefore vitiated his matrimonial consent and was tantamount to an exclusion, albeit virtual and implicit, of an essential property of marriage (C. 1101 § 2), namely indissolubility (C. 1056).

WHEREFORE

163

```
┌─────────────────────┐
│           I         │
│      The Facts      │
│                     │
└─────────────────────┘
```

David Gazza and Charlotte Epervier, both Catholic, were married on May 12, 1975 at St. Mark's Church in Hamilton, Maine. David was twenty-four years old at the time and Charlotte was twenty-one.

This couple met briefly, for one day only, in July of 1972 when David was vacationing in Maine. Two years later, in July of 1974, after serving with the United States Navy, David returned to Maine and began courting Charlotte. David lived in Johnstown, Connecticut and Charlotte in Hamilton, Maine but David travelled to Maine on the average of three weekends a month and on November 24 of that year, at Thanksgiving time, they became engaged.

There was some discussion as to where they would live and on January 9 and 10 of 1975, Charlotte wrote to David saying, "I've been so miserable and unhappy ever since you said that you had made up your mind that we are going to live in Connecticut. . . . As much as I love you, I'm not leaving the State. . . . Hon, please try to understand that I just don't want to leave the people I love. . . . I want to see as much of them as I can—not only once or twice a month." In both of these letters, Charlotte offered to return the engagement ring. David, however, telephoned Charlotte, talked to her for two hours, and the wedding was on again. They married on May 12.

The couple was unhappy right from the beginning. Charlotte was lonely. There were accusations that David did not spend enough time at home and that his parents interfered. After a few weeks, they visited Father Anthony D'Angelo for counsel but without any resultant improvement in the relationship.

Finally, on July 2, less than two months after the wedding, there was a violent argument involving the parents of David, and Charlotte left and returned to Hamilton.

In September, Charlotte returned to Johnstown to pick up some of her belongings and informed David at that time that she was pregnant but the situation had deteriorated to such an extent that reconciliation no longer appeared possible.

On March 23, 1977, Charlotte obtained a civil divorce in Hartford and on March 7, 1983 David petitioned this Court, competent by reason of the petitioner's residence, to declare his marriage null.

On April 26, it was officially agreed at the Contestatio Litis, with Charlotte denying the allegation by letter, that the case would be heard on the grounds of a condition attached to and limiting the marriage contract, namely that Charlotte intended to marry David if he would live in Maine.

```
┌─────────────────────┐
│         II          │
│      The Law        │
│                     │
└─────────────────────┘
```

A. C. 1102 says that a marriage cannot be validly contracted under a *future* condition (§ 1), whereas a marriage entered under a *past* or *present* condition is valid or not depending on whether the matter concerning which the condition is made, exists or not (§ 2).

B. As far as the qualities of a condition are concerned, it is well known that an interpretative, generic or habitual condition does not suffice. On the other hand, it is not required that a condition be either actual or explicit. Rather it suffices if it is a positive act of the will, if it is virtually perduring and if it is implicit, that is to say, if it is expressed implicitly as, for example, when a woman would say, "The man I marry must absolutely be a practicing Catholic."

C. As regards the contractant's awareness of the juridical effect of a condition, the common jurisprudence used to hold that, when a person truly places a condition, he is aware at least vaguely that if the condition is not verified, the marriage is null, that, to some extent, in other words, the person must want the validity of the covenant to depend upon the existence of the circumstance (40, 251). The terms "at least vaguely" and "to some extent" were meant to take into consideration the fact that people are not after all canon lawyers and would not have a precise or explicit knowledge of the canonical implications of a condition but would nevertheless have at least some kind of fuzzy notion that in placing a condition they would be tampering with the covenant itself and hedging it.

Now, however, there is increasing support for the fact that a person does not even have to have a vague knowledge or intention of nullity. The general idea is that in this matter there are two will acts, one to marriage sic et simpliciter and the other to marriage with a person endowed with a specific quality. In order to be invalidating the second must prevail (Felici, 43, 569). The first must be subordinate and therefore rendered inefficacious (Mattioli, 51, 631. See also 42, 150). Or to put it another way, the marital consent has to be subordinated to the quality in a nexus subordinationis (Lefebvre, 51, 117).

So, if in fact, the circumstance is *prevailingly* important (i.e., prevails over the pure, uncluttered, integral covenant of marriage) then the contractant doesn't really have to know or intend even vaguely the legal effects of his action on the validity of the bond (Felici 43, 570).

D. As regards proving the existence of a condition it must be remembered that a condition often presents an extremely low profile so that a most careful scrutiny of the acts is required by the judge. This is true partly because the word "condition" is an ambiguous one so that the judge should look more to the subject's whole frame of mind rather than to the word itself; partly because a condition so closely resembles the other non invalidating situations of mode, demonstration, cause and postulate (this latter being a condition which refers primarily to the original decision to marry but which may also be regarded as an initial step towards a matrimonial condition, 49, 420); and partly because it is not really required, since a condition may be expressed implicitly, that the contractant grasp the canonical implications of his action.

As a consequence of all this, the following presumptions, as recognized in our jurisprudence, can be most helpful in determining whether or not a true condition has been placed.

1. Objective

If the circumstance is something which will play a significant part in the future life of the couple then more than likely it was not just a mode, demonstration, cause or postulate but a real condition that was attached to the covenant. Such circumstances would be immunity from venereal disease, the virginity of the woman, the absence of any grave and contagious disease, the absence of epilepsy or some sexual perversion.

If, on the other hand, the circumstance is of minor importance and only indirectly affects conjugal life such as a man's job or social status, then the contrary presumption would be operative (50, 73).

2. Subjective
a. Principal
1) Prenuptial

a) The contractant's estimate of the importance of the circumstance— more often than not this will be in accord with the objective importance of the circumstance but sometimes a person will attach more than ordinary importance to a given factor, e.g., the conversion of one's spouse to the Catholic religion, and this should be adverted to and weighed.

b) The contractant's doubt about some circumstance—normally a person will not stipulate as a condition what never occurs to him to doubt in the first place. So that generally if the person did not have some doubt about a given quality, e.g., heterosexuality, he would not place a condition making the validity of the marriage hinge on that quality. Like all presumptions, however, this cedes to the truth and where it can be shown that a given person has a kind of obsession about some quality, a condition can be proved even when no specific doubt is present (49, 442).

2) Postnuptial

The general presumption here is that the quicker a person declares his marriage null because of an unfulfilled condition and effects a separation, the easier it is to conclude to the presence of a true condition. Here again, though, the criterion is not absolute since sometimes a condition is fulfilled only gradually or equivocally and sometimes it demands injuring the reputation of the other party, in which cases a delay is more than understandable (50, 74).

b. Accessory

Other less important but still significant criteria are the degree of seriousness or solemnity used in expressing the condition, whether it was expressed only once or repeated, whether there was an attempt to impose it on the other party and so forth (34, 819).

III
The Argument

There is no indication in the acts that, *if* Charlotte entered the marriage conditionally, she did so *explicitly* or with the realization that her intentions would invalidate the marriage. The only question, therefore, is whether Charlotte married David with an *implicit* condition, saying to herself, "The man I marry must absolutely and above all permit me to live in Maine. This is more important to me than marriage itself."

Unfortunately, in attempting to discern the facts, the testimony of Charlotte herself is not very helpful, perhaps because she is confused or perhaps because she does not wish to be helpful. She did, after all, admit that she once told David that she would do everything she could to prevent his getting an annulment. But for whatever reason, her testimony is shot through with contradictions. For example:

1. Despite the letters of January 9 and 10, in which Charlotte said with much anguish and pain that she simply couldn't stand being separated from her parents, nevertheless in her testimony she says that it really wasn't that important, that she merely wanted "to keep in touch," that she "didn't want to be a stranger."

2. Despite the fact that, according to Charlotte's testimony, she got along fine with Mr. and Mrs. Gazza prior to July 2 and that according to Mrs. Gazza they saw each other only twice, nevertheless Charlotte testified that she "could have adjusted if his parents had not interfered. But they didn't give me a chance."

3. Despite the fact that Charlotte complained about David being out all the time, nevertheless she testified that she was happy and content until July 2.

4. Despite the fact that Charlotte and David discussed the question of residence "several times" before marriage and despite the fact that according to Charlotte there was an arrangement a) about her visiting Maine as often as she wanted and b) about their returning to live there if she could not adjust to Connecticut, nevertheless Charlotte unhesitatingly said not once but several times that this had absolutely no bearing on her decision to marry David and that she would have married him regardless.

5. Despite the fact that Father Anthony D'Angelo was called in during the marriage about the residence issue, nevertheless Charlotte testified that there was no serious discussion about residence during the marriage, that there was no problem at all until July 2 and that the only thing they quarreled about was David's golfing.

So Charlotte's testimony is a veritable maze of inconsistencies and of little value. Father Ralph Franklin, the Auditor, perhaps put it most charitably when he said that he accepted "the sincerity of the Respondent's deposition while recognizing that she definitely minimizes the question of residence in her marital history."

Consequently, in order to prove the allegation, attention must be given to the two letters of January 9 and 10 and to the testimony of the petitioner and witnesses.

Although living in the neighborhood of one's parents rather than a couple of hundred miles away would *objectively* probably not be considered a circumstance of major importance, nevertheless the letters of January 9 and 10 indicate that *subjectively* living in Maine was of vital importance to Charlotte Epervier.

In the letter of January 9, for example, Charlotte wrote, "Please forgive me for what I'm about to say, but it is very important to me. Hon, I just don't want to leave my home town." This is an explicit statement that not leaving Hamilton was "very important" to Charlotte. The subjective importance of remaining in Maine is further borne out first by the fact that Charlotte was ready to call off the marriage in favor of it and secondly by the fact that Charlotte sat down the next day with the obvious intention of writing a retraction but only managed one paragraph before her compulsive immobility from Maine once again prevailed and consumed her and she retreated to her position of yesterday, writing several more paragraphs in which she simply reiterated her sentiments of the day before. She was, in other words, unable to sustain a retraction and what began as a retraction finished as a vigorous confirmation.

What happened between January 10 and May 12 is not entirely clear. Charlotte says that David agreed that they would return to Maine if she could not adjust to living in Connecticut (and such an agreement would surely strengthen the case) but David denies this saying that he merely assured her that Maine wasn't really that far away and besides they could make frequent visits. At any rate there is no evidence that Charlotte had any real change of heart. Indeed, the evidence indicates quite the contrary.

Mr. Gazza noted that Charlotte did not show the usual joyful attitude of a bride in shopping for furniture and looking for a rent. Mrs. Gazza said that Charlotte was "cold" during the wedding ceremony and Charlotte's sister said that at one point Charlotte was crying. On the honeymoon, Charlotte wrote to her mother while on the plane saying that she would telephone from Florida and in general wanted to go home, and she was unhappy and crying on the honeymoon. Charlotte made no effort to obtain a job in Johnstown though she apparently had ample opportunity to do so. She declined to associate with the Gazzas, even failing to attend parties to welcome David's brother home from the army. She kept hounding David to move to Maine. She complained of loneliness. She telephoned to Maine with excessive frequency, running up a telephone bill of something like forty-five or fifty dollars in one month, even though they visited Maine at least six times in the brief time they lived together. In the opinion of John Law, David took Charlotte to Maine "too often" and as Mrs. Gazza said, "she was in Hamilton as much as in Johnstown." When David and Charlotte visited Father D'Angelo regarding their problems over place of residence, Father D'Angelo concluded, "It seems that she'd be willing to make the marriage go if she could have her own way and live in Maine. I really wasn't anxious to meet with her again because there was no communication—her mind was made up." And finally, the marriage lasted less than two months and terminated, according to John Law, because, "I don't think she ever doubted the fact that she'd be back in Maine. She was confident that she'd get him there. But when reality came and David proved headstrong, she just left him."

The evidence, therefore, is that living in Maine was prevailingly important to Charlotte, that marriage was subordinate to that circumstance and that this was true before, during and after marriage. As Mrs. Gazza said, as far as Charlotte is concerned, "Hamilton is really God Almighty."

Two witnesses should be singled out for their probative value, Father D'Angelo and John Law, the former being a "testis qualificatus" and the latter being recommended by a professor at the University of Hartford as being "far above average in matters of moral judgment and reliability" and recommended especially for his "judgment and insight into human behavior."

According to Father D'Angelo, when Charlotte came to see him a few weeks after the wedding, she was uncommunicative, did not respond at all, was very cold and offered no justification but "just figured she belonged in Maine and that was it. She wasn't prepared to leave her own family and make a new life." And when asked how important to Charlotte was living in Maine, Father D'Angelo responded, "I think it was absolutely important because this was the only condition she offered him on which the marriage could be continued. I think it was of prime importance to her."

John Law, for his part, said that he met Charlotte right after the honeymoon and "gathered that she went along with him, figuring she could persuade him after they got married." He said, moreover, that Charlotte on that occasion said that she didn't want to be here, she wasn't happy and "that she wasn't about to live here."

She just didn't want to make any effort. She had an inward confidence, as if she'd be able to take care of everything. . . . She had her own ideas and was not going to conform to David"and, in response to a later question, Mr. Law added, "Family ties meant more to her than marriage. . . . she had one thing in mind—go home to Maine—by hook or crook she'd do this and David was to come along with her. . . . When you talk to someone and she's quiet and confident like Charlotte was, she gave me the impression through smirks and grins that they would not be in Connecticut long. . . . She said she was bored, wanted to go home, didn't want to stay here, was homesick and wanted to live in Maine and not here." In Mr. Law's opinion, Charlotte did not get on with the Gazzas because "she didn't accept them." Charlotte's plan, according to Mr. Law, was to wear David down, and, he said "living in Hamilton was more important to Charlotte than David was."

It has, therefore, been proved that living in Maine was prevailingly important to Charlotte both before and right after marriage, that she certainly had serious doubts about the likelihood of that circumstance being verified, that she effected a separation as soon as it became apparent that her condition was not going to be fulfilled and that a host of accessory criteria are also present: the repeated attempts to impose her will on David, her obsessive attachment to home, her unwillingness to make any attempt at adjusting, etc.

WHEREFORE

I
The Facts

Janet Rail and Joseph Pavone, both Catholic, were married on August 28, 1968 at the Church of St. Margaret, Woodsfield, Connecticut in the Archdiocese of Hartford. Janet was, at the time, twenty years old, and Joseph was twenty-three.

Janet and Joseph had met some six years earlier, when they were in high school. They dated during their high school years, became engaged in June of 1967, and married about a year later. Two children were born of the marriage, the first less than ten months after the marriage, the second about fourteen months after the first.

The marriage went fairly well for the first few years, except for the fact that, as one witness said, Joseph was more a third child in the marriage than a parent. He just didn't want to get involved in disciplining the children or in assuming responsibility for them.

By early 1973 Joseph was seeing another woman, and he proposed to Janet that they both engage in extramarital liaisons. As one witness said, "he wanted to spend weekends with some woman and he expected Janet to agree to this; however he found that Janet was not about to compromise the goals of marriage to satisfy Joseph."

In May, however, Joseph left Janet in order to cohabit with this woman. Over the summer there were a couple of brief reconciliations, but in September Joseph left for good.

About a year later, in June of 1974 a divorce was granted, and a year after that, on June 8, 1975, Janet petitioned this Tribunal to declare null her marriage to Joseph on the grounds that he "never realized the sacredness of marital vows and therefore was not committed to them."

Although, strictly speaking, no such ground exists in canon law, the Court judged the phrase in the petition to be a non juridical way of expressing the recognized ground of a conditioned marriage (C. 1092, 3°). On July 5, therefore, the Court accepted Janet's petition, and on July 29, at the *Contestatio Litis*, it declared the Issue in Pleading to be:

> Whether the Rail-Pavone marriage has been proved invalid on the grounds of Joseph's condition that the marriage be fulfilling.

For a more complete discussion of the conditioned marriage, see "A New Condition Limiting Marriage" in *The Jurist,* 1974, pages 292-315, but the following 1956 Rotal decision coram Mattioli (48, 742-743) is an excellent resume of the pertinent jurisprudence:

In order that consent to a marriage contract be placed conditionally, it is necessary and it suffices that either party wishes that the marriage be regarded as valid if a "certain something" of great value is realized, and that it be regarded as invalid if that "certain something" is not realized.

Needless to say that "certain something" can be a characteristic, or a quality, or a past or present fact not yet known to or even readily knowable by the parties. It can also be something that refers to the future but is contingent and verifiable within a certain determined period of time. And so a condition can refer to past, present or future.

When speaking of a future condition, we limit ourselves here to the future *contingent* condition. That is to say, we will not discuss here the future *necessary* condition or a future condition *against the substance* of marriage. In a future contingent condition, the consensual effect is suspended until the verification of the event. For example, "I am marrying you providing you obtain your doctoral degree within a year," or "I am marrying you if surgery makes it possible for you to have children," and so forth.

In a past or present condition, the consent is immediately valid when the circumstance is true and real (even though unknown at the time) and it is immediately invalid when the circumstance is not verified. Because, when not verified, the matrimonial consent, which can be supplied by no human power (Canon 1081 § 1) is totally defective because it is entirely absent. Canon 1092 clearly summarizes all of this.

One thing always to be kept in mind is that conditions which vitiate consent are most often placed by people who are not lawyers and who do not understand juridical terms and their force and effect. Consequently, it comes as no surprise that such people sometimes express a condition inexactly and ambiguously, that is, in words that perhaps suggest a cause rather than a condition, or perhaps an extremely important postulate or prerequisite (so important that if it is present the marriage will be contracted absolutely, and if it is absent the marriage will not be contracted at all). Or perhaps such persons will express themselves in words which may suggest either an interpretive intention or perhaps an error giving rise to the contract.

Moreover those who place a condition are often unaware of the invalidating effect of a condition, since most people entering marriage conditionally are not thinking about entering an invalid marriage but only about entering a happy marriage or at least an agreeable one, because they are convinced, rightly or wrongly, that they cannot find peace in their marriage if that "certain something" is lacking (42, 149-152).

Consequently, it is often difficult to distinguish true from false conditions. It can sometimes happen, as we know, that people who never really conditioned their marriage, will suggest, whether in good or bad faith, that, in fact, they have. In order to distinguish true from false conditions, rotal jurisprudence has, from its earliest days, developed wise and equitable norms designed to ferret out and understand the actual mind of the one placing the condition rather than the mere words spoken. A review of all of these norms, however, would serve no purpose here since they have been discussed at length in other decisions (42, 149-152).

Besides, certain of those norms should be emphasized in one case and certain others of them in another case, depending on the circumstances. For example, sometimes too much attention is paid to the fact that the marriage was consummated even though it had been earlier suggested that, in fact, consummation had not taken place: and sometimes too much attention is given to the fact that the spouse continues on with the marriage even after the circumstance has been verified. Oftentimes the spouse's reaction on attainment of the circumstance should be taken with a grain of salt, because, particularly among young people, emotions often override reason; and we must always keep in mind that love is a very powerful force, and that people are often ignorant of their rights and duties and of the practical avenues open to them in order to vindicate their rights publicly. Also to be kept in mind is that frequently they receive inept and positively erroneous advice.

Consequently, rather than trying to investigate a whole series of circumstances one by one, it is better to assess the total picture with a view to understanding the mind of the person. Otherwise excessive attention might be given to specific elements. It is important to bear in mind that the mere fact that one or other element (whose presence might have been corroborative) is absent, cannot be regarded as proof that the marriage was not, in fact, conditioned, and certainly does not mean that the nullity of the marriage has not been proved.

Mattioli is insistent on understanding the mind of the person because oftentimes marriages are conditioned not explicitly, that is to say, in so many words, but implicitly. As Monsignor Pinto said in his decision of June 26, 1971 (*Ephemerides Iuris Canonici*, XXVIII, 328-329), sometimes all these people know is that

a particular circumstance is so important to them that they rate it higher than marriage itself, and that, if they can't have the circumstance, they don't really want the marriage either.

Or, as Mattioli said in his 1950 decision (42, 150),

> conditioning a marriage involves a kind of contradiction. The person wants to marry, but on the one hand he wants to marry a person who is, say, endowed with a certain quality, and, on the other hand, he is marrying a person who perhaps lacks that quality. The task of the Court, therefore, is to determine which is the genuine intent and which is the subordinate and inefficacious one.

III
The Argument

When the facts of this case are seen in the light of the law, it is clear that Joseph Pavone's mind set was such that, even as he entered marriage in 1968, his own personal freedom and fulfillment were much more important to him than marriage itself, that he wanted marriage *only if* it was fulfilling, that personal fulfillment was that "certain something" for Joseph Pavone that constituted the object of his prevailing and genuine intent, and which, if unrealized, would render the marriage invalid, because his marital intent was subordinate to it.

This is proved first of all from Joseph's general personality structure and attitude towards life. He had been overindulged as a child and had, therefore, an extremely low threshold or tolerance for hardship and difficulty. He was, said one witness, a "taker, not a giver," and, when real life became a little difficult, Joseph's inevitable reaction was to run away from it. Perhaps the best example of this is Joseph's behavior in college. Studying involved work and was unpleasant for Joseph so he found himself a large closet, put a mattress in there and slept away most of his college life. His former roommate, Philip Goetz, estimated that Joseph slept 50% of the time. Eventually, of course, he flunked out. Goetz commented, "Joseph was the type of guy who at times went along with things in the system up to the point that it satisfied his needs." As Janet Rail said about Joseph, "anything hard wouldn't fit . . . when something got to mean responsibility or got too hard, he dropped it."

The two really excellent witnesses, Loretta Gorman and Philip Goetz, agreed that Joseph was not representative of his age group. Goetz said that Joseph, much more than other young people of the time, lived only for the day, had no long range goals at all, satisfied himself only for the moment and had little or no long range commitment.

The other witness, Dorothy Ryan, who repeatedly said that she did not really know Joseph Pavone very well, thought that he changed towards the end of the marriage. She said, "It was like a kid going four years to college and ending up a hippy." But, besides the fact that Joseph did not really attend four years of college, it is apparent from the more knowledgeable witnesses that Joseph did not really change towards the end of the marriage but was, in fact, like that all along. Long before the marriage.

174

A second proof of the alleged conditioning of the marriage is Joseph's attitude towards marriage in general and towards the special firmness of Christian marriage. According to Janet Rail, Joseph had stated that marriage is nothing more than a piece of paper, and that the term, "the sanctity of marriage" was found only in catechisms. Janet and Loretta Gorman are in agreement that Joseph never took religion seriously, and they agree, too, on Joseph's basic understanding of and attitudes towards marriage. Janet said that Joseph had the same belief about both marriage and living together, namely, that "if it gets to be a hassle, then split up," that "if people are having a hard time together, then forget it and do something else." Joseph, according to Janet, thought it was dumb of Janet's parents to go on living together since they didn't have all that great a marriage. Loretta Gorman concurred in this assessment of Joseph's attitude towards marriage. According to Loretta, Joseph's attitude was "If something is too difficult you flunk out or leave; in marriage you get a divorce."

A third and final proof of the fact that the Rail-Pavone marriage was conditioned by Joseph is in the circumstances of the marriage itself. Janet Rail said that if Joseph had any idea of the work involved in making a marriage work, he wouldn't have married in the first place. Philip Goetz said that Joseph had very little determination to make the marriage a success, that he was in no way prepared to sacrifice his personal contentment in order to make the marriage work, and that, in a sense, therefore, Joseph was entering a trial marriage. Loretta Gorman agrees that this was, in effect, a trial marriage for Joseph. Joseph, in other words, would try out the marriage. If it contributed to his fulfillment, fine. But if not, then Joseph did not really want the marriage. This is what is known as conditioning the marriage. Janet said that it was "very important to him to be happy, to be carefree," that "a sense of freedom and his personal satisfaction were more important to him than a successful marriage."

In point of fact, the marriage went fairly well for a while. Joseph played with the children and was like a "third child" in the family. But as all the witnesses testified, Joseph had not really married for better or for worse, and as soon as marriage began to cramp his style, he moved out. Before it came to that, actually, he made a couple of attempts to have his cake and eat it too, and apparently felt totally justified in doing that, but when Janet would not agree to that, he moved out.

Joseph himself declined to testify in these proceedings but he did tell the Instructor on the telephone that the most important thing in the world to him was his own freedom and that, "if you can't hold on to that in marriage you just have to move on."

It is regrettable that the Court was unable to obtain more detailed testimony from Joseph but, based on the available testimony, the Court is nevertheless convinced that when the situation is viewed as a whole, as Mattioli recommends, and when the mind set of Joseph Pavone is understood, it is adequately demonstrated that Joseph's intent to marry was subordinate to his intent to find personal fulfillment, and that his intent to marry was therefore inefficacious and invalid.

WHEREFORE

175

```
    I
The Facts
```

Ida, our petitioner, was born in 1935 and was adopted two years later by Mr. and Mrs. Gelinotte. The Gelinottes were Catholic and Ida became an exemplary young Catholic girl, receiving the sacraments almost daily when she was in high school. Mrs. Gelinotte dominated the family, partly by force and partly by wile, and her word was law in the family.

On Memorial Day, 1952, when Ida was seventeen years old, she met Luke Orzel, who was in the Navy and about five years older and she became infatuated with him.

During the next year, Ida and Luke corresponded and saw each other perhaps a half dozen times. During this year, Luke was AWOL on more than one occasion and spent time in the brig but Ida was not less infatuated.

In June of 1953, Ida graduated from high school and the next month, when Luke was visiting Ida at her aunt's house in Temple, Connecticut, Luke raped her.

Although Ida remained somewhat infatuated with Luke after the rape, her basic attitude toward him changed to one of hate, particularly when he reacted with indifference to the news that she was pregnant.

But it was hardly with indifference that Mrs. Gelinotte received the news. On the contrary, she became very upset and angry and she wept and told Ida that she had to marry Luke. And Ida felt she had no other choice. She married Luke in Saint Edward's Rectory in Temple, Connecticut in the Archdiocese of Hartford on September 28, 1953.

The marriage was very unhappy. Luke drank a lot, abused Ida and once even threatened to kill her. There was a temporary separation or two and they finally separated in April of 1955, about a year and a half after the marriage. The divorce was granted on November 12, of the same year in Hartford.

On October 16, 1970, Ida petitioned this court to declare her marriage null and on December 4, 1970, the issue was joined in the following terms: Whether there is evidence of the nullity of the Gelinotte-Orzel marriage on the grounds of force and fear.

A. The Two Arguments

"Fear is difficult to prove both because the passive party experiences it in the recesses of his soul, and because the active party, especially where it is a parent acting in respect to a child, is almost always acting in equal secrecy. In coming to a judgment, the usual arguments in a force and fear case are two, namely, *aversion* on the part of the passive party and *coercion* on the part of the active party. The *first* argument proves that the mind of the party was alien to the imposed marriage and the *second* argument shows that some grave, extrinsic, unjust evil was pressing the contractant and that he could free himself from it only by going through the marriage. Where it is proved that grave aversion was overcome by some coercion, it is not, strictly speaking, presumed that the coercion was grave but the point can be easily conceded. And, by the same token, if it is proved that grave force was used to overcome some aversion, then it is not really presumed that the aversion was grave but again it is easily granted." (Holbock, pg. 188)

B. The First Argument - Aversion

"When signs of aversion are in evidence at the very time of the marriage, then the presumption of either a forced or a simulated marriage is especially strong. Aversion doesn't come up overnight. Tears and complaints preceding the marriage, weeping, protestations, sadness and pallor at the time of the marriage plus a denial of any signs of love after the marriage are arguments in favor of the presence of fear. If after the marriage *signs* of grave aversion are not present, this does not really prove that the party is not experiencing aversion, because it could happen that the party did not realize that the marriage was null and consequently was just resigning himself to his irreparable fate. . . . That aversion before and after marriage about which we just spoke doesn't have to be an aversion to *any* marriage or even an aversion to the person *as such,* but it suffices if there is an aversion to *marrying* that person. So even a friendship between a young man and woman would not necessarily rule out grave, unjust fear, for it is one thing to be a friend and another to wish to marry that person. Consequently, love and aversion regarding the same person are not necessarily incompatible. It is certainly possible that young people could be friends or even be sleeping together but still not want to marry each other. But where an argument of aversion to a person or at least a repugnance to marrying that person is entirely lacking, then a judge is not able to say that the person was entering the marriage out of grave fear and the marriage may not therefore be declared null." (Holbock, pgs. 188-189)

C. The Second Argument - Coercion

After succinctly explaining the nature of reverential fear in a decision of 1961, Fiore goes on to say, "Harshness, physical beatings and reprimands are *not necessary* to constitute coercion and on the other hand encouragement, advice and recommendations are *not sufficient*. But a grim appearance, a genuine command, repeated, insistent requests that wear the person down, these are the things that can remove the freedom of will that is necessary for marital consent. All of which are, of course, more effective on women than on men, on younger people than on the more mature and on children who are entirely dependent than on those who have gained some independence, especially economic independence." (53, 6)

In a similar decision, Heard wrote: "The point at issue in this case is reverential fear which, like common fear, renders marriage null whenever the qualities mentioned in C. 1087 are verified. Per se, reverential fear is light but it becomes grave through circumstances. In order to bring this about, however, because of the reverence which a child has for his parents, which is accompanied by a kind of natural submission, violence or threats are not required but it is sufficient if there are inordinate requests by the parents or a command by the parents which the child does not dare to resist because of a reasonable fear of it resulting in their grave and prolonged indignation. In making a judgment, attention should be paid to the age and the sex of the child. Fear is easily created in a young girl. But the young person should also give evidence of some aversion for otherwise one cannot really speak of force, and the fear, if it is present, is intrinsic. And also parents can legitimately offer advice to their children and even moderately urge them to enter what seems to be a good marriage." (51, 421)

D. The Implications of Rape

Regarding the implications of rape, the following "in iure" section of Pasquazi is interesting:

Fear induced on the contractants carries with it the nullity of the marriage only if it be grave, unjustly and extrinsically induced and if the one who is afraid cannot free himself from the fear in any other way (Canon 1087). It is certain that the fear of losing one's good name is ordinarily grave because the loss of public esteem is most often considered and in fact is a grave evil. And besides that, it is also considered a grave sin to deprive one of his good name. Also, the disclosure of an occult crime without a just and grave cause constitutes a genuine villainy and the fear which is inflicted by threats of disclosure is unjustly induced.

The question at hand concerns a lady petitioner's fear of losing her good name on account of the disclosure of sexual relations with the male respondent at least on one occasion and from which the petitioner thought that she had become pregnant. The fear resulting from the disclosure of a sin of this kind is ordinarily grave but the question is, is it also extrinsically and unjustly induced? Let us discuss the various possibilities.

A certain woman willingly has sexual relations. Knowing or thinking that she is pregnant, she fears the loss of her good name and therefore decides to contract marriage. If nobody induced fear into her by threats of disclosing the sin that she committed then her fear is intrinsic. She acted on account of objective circumstances, resolving to enter a marriage and without anybody externally compelling her to do so. 'But the fear would be intrinsic if the woman who had relations with a man feared that her sin would be disclosed if she didn't marry him. In this case nobody externally forced her to marriage and she is compelled only by an internal pressure on account of the fault that she committed.' (38, 525)

On the other hand, the fear of infamy on account of sexual relations, even though they were freely indulged in, would be *extrinsic* if the man with whom the woman had intercourse, or other people, in order to promote the marriage, threatened the woman with the disclosure of the sin she had committed. Because in this case, the woman was also externally compelled to enter the marriage by the threats of being defamed.

If the fear from threats of disclosure induced on a woman who freely indulged in premarital intercourse is extrinsic, then all the more is it extrinsic if the man used force or deceit to have sexual relations. But what should be said if the man actually raped the woman in order to promote the marriage even though he did not threaten the woman with disclosure of any kind? In this case too, the fear would be extrinsic because it would be from an external cause, that is to say, from a fact caused by somebody else and indeed for the purpose of promoting the marriage. (50, 613-614)

The final phrase: "for the purpose of promoting the marriage," should not be understood, of course, as being absolutely necessary in order to invalidate the marriage. Gasparri (856) and many others after him have pointed out that force in order to be invalidating, need not be *direct*, "ad extorquendum consensum" as a rejected draft of the 1917 Code had phrased it, but *indirect* force suffices, "a quo, ut quis se liberet, eligere cogatur matrimonium" as the 1917 Code reads.

It is not required, in other words, that the rapist commit the act in order to extort consent. It suffices that the raped woman feels that her only choice is to marry.

III
The Argument

In the petition Ida says, "Once I found out that I was pregnant, my first thought was that I had to marry Luke because of religion. I believed that God had joined us and was afraid to look ahead. I also wanted my baby to have a name." She says again in her testimony, "Finding out I was pregnant, I felt there was nothing else I could do."

179

It is the opinion of this Court that the acts offer adequate evidence that the pregnancy of which Ida is speaking was the result of her being raped by Luke Orzel. Her mother spontaneously testified to this and her aunt Florence said that she learned of the rape on the day of the marriage.

What Ida is saying, therefore, is that Luke Orzel forced her to marry by raping her and causing her to become pregnant. This allegation may be true. It is in many ways supported by the circumstantial evidence, particularly Ida's feeling of guilt and her somewhat compulsive religious attitudes. But that allegation has hardly been demonstrated, probably because it was simply overshadowed by the force inflicted on Ida by *her mother*. There was, in other words, no period of time when Ida had to live only with the force exerted by the rape cum pregnancy. Had some period of time elapsed between Ida's learning of the pregnancy and her mother's learning of it, then perhaps the coercive gravity of the rape could have been measured as a separate unit. But in fact, Ida's mother learned of the pregnancy almost as soon as Ida herself did and Mrs. Gelinotte immediately ordered Ida to marry.

This is not to say that the force of the rape was insignificant or should be discounted but only that it has not been proved that, *taken by itself*, the rape cum pregnancy was sufficient to force Ida into marriage. On the other hand, it surely was part of the combined force that induced in Ida an invalidating fear.

The major and prime force, however, seems to have been caused by Ida's mother. The testimony proves that Ida's mother used grave, unjust force on Ida to extort consent. Even though Ida told her mother that she didn't want to marry Luke and even though Mrs. Gelinotte knew that the pregnancy was due not to an indiscretion but to rape and even though Mrs. Gelinotte knew or could easily have found out that Luke would make a very poor husband for Ida, despite all these things, Mrs. Gelinotte ordered her daughter to marry Luke, and badgered her incessantly because Mrs. Gelinotte "couldn't stand the disgrace." As is apparent from several sources, Mrs. Gelinotte became angry and excited when she heard about Ida's pregnancy, she wept and carried on and, as Ida said, every time she turned around, her mother was weeping and telling her she had to marry Luke.

It should further be borne in mind that Mrs. Gelinotte was "bossy" and domineering anyway, that she was far and away the dominant figure in the household, that when she said to do something, one did it—she had that way about her—and that Ida in particular, as an adopted child, did everything her mother told her like a "puppy dog."

Ida felt that if she had disobeyed her mother on this occasion, her mother would have become indignant and would have "thrown it up in my face whenever I moved," and Mrs. LaPlante agrees that the mother would have been pretty harsh.

So the evidence adequately demonstrates that the extrinsic force exerted by Mrs. Gelinotte (particularly when coupled with that caused by Luke) was grave and unjust (metus reverentialis est semper iniustus) and also causative, that Ida did not want to marry Luke, that she was crying "most of the time," that she was sick and numb during the ceremony, and that her "first" reason for marrying was that her mother had ordered her to.

WHEREFORE

Brendan Kite and Laura Osprey, both Catholic, were married at the Church of St. Stephen, Edgewood, Connecticut, in the Archdiocese of Hartford, on the twelfth day of December, 1965. Brendan was twenty-two at the time; Laura was twenty-three.

The couple lived together for only a few months, separating in April of 1966 because Laura found living with Brendan to be impossible for her. A divorce was granted in Edgewood on February 19, 1970.

On March 12, 1982 Brendan petitioned this Court to declare the marriage null. His petition was accepted and the Issue in Pleading was, on April 10, 1982, declared by the Judge to be the proven nullity of the Kite-Osprey marriage on the grounds of force and fear.

┌─────────────────┐
│   II   │
│   The Law   │
└─────────────────┘

The jurisprudence pertinent to this case is summarized in the following law section of a decision dated April 20, 1978, coram Parisella, as found in *Monitor Ecclesiasticus*, 1978, IV, pp. 387-389:

> 2) Reverential fear, which is at issue in this case, insofar as it is distinct from common fear, is defined as "the estimate of a future evil which we fear will be imposed on us by those in whose legitimate power we are and to whom we owe respect and honor" (B. Pontius, *De Sacramenti matrimonio Tractatus*, Lib. IV, c. V, n. 1).

> Which definition, as everybody knows, is found, practically verbatim, in all of the approved authors (D'Annibale, Summula Theol. Mor., I, § 138, 16; Cappello, *De matrimonio*, n. 605).

> 3) According to the well known jurisprudence of this Court, reverential fear, as it affects both young men and young women, is, in general, to be presumed as *light*; nevertheless it is able to become *grave* if it is qualified either through beatings or threats or insistent and rude requests or even through paternal indignation.

As C. Jemolo says, "It is clear that paternal (or maternal) indignation, even if it is without threats or beatings, can constitute grave reverential fear whenever, by itself, it constitutes a grave evil" (C. A. Jemolo, *Il matrimonio nel diritto canonico,* Milano, 1941, p. 232).

This is understandable. For, as the Angelic doctor says, "Since in marriage one is, as it were, in perpetual service, a father can never order a child to marry since marriage must be a matter of free status" (*Suppl.,* q. 47, a. 5, c).

Furthermore, as the jurisprudence of this Court has always taught, the gravity of reverential fear is to be measured in light of the character of the one who is alleged to have inflicted the fear, with consideration given to whether or not he would be ready, willing and able to carry out the threats.

4) One should also pay very careful attention to the character of the one who is suffering the fear, since reverential fear should always be viewed not in the abstract but in the certain special circumstances of the events and the people involved.

It is a fact that the gravity of reverential fear is more easily verified than the gravity of common fear "since in reverential fear, besides the external force, the honor and reverence due to parents is an ever present and compelling factor" (S. R. *Rotae Decisiones,* vol. 35, pag. 178, a; conf. sententiam coram Czapla diei 6 novembris 1967, vol. 59, pag. 769).

5) Finally, as regards the matter of proof, the well known double argument is to be considered, the one indirect, namely, the *aversion* that the person has towards the other party, or at least towards marrying the other party, and the other, the direct argument, namely, the *force* itself.

"In both arguments, importance is to be attached both to the character of the one suffering the fear and also to judicial and extra judicial confessions made by that person" (S. R. *Rotae Decisiones,* vol. 48, pag. 215, n. 3) since we are talking about investigating one's inner state of mind, which cannot be known by anyone more fully than it is by the person who himself is experiencing the fear. Which confession should be confirmed by trustworthy witnesses and other circumstances properly understood.

Finally it should be noted that the mere fact that the couple initiated domestic life and even continued that life for some time, ought not by its nature to be considered as undermining proof of the presence of fear, since there could be many reasons for the couple to have cohabited; mere cohabitation in no way suggests that the marriage was entered free of fear.

In order for a marriage to be proved null on the grounds of force and fear (C. 1103) it must be shown that the force exerted at the time of marriage was grave, extrinsic and causative. In the judgment of this Court, the available evidence in the case at bar, namely the testimony of both principals and of four witnesses, does indeed show precisely that.

1. *Grave.* It is clear that the force exerted in this case was not *absolutely* grave (there was no threat of death or serious harm). It is equally clear, however, that the fear which Laura Osprey, the respondent, experienced was not purely subjective or imaginary, that it was, rather, real and *relatively* grave, and that Laura experienced it as such.

All of this is clear from the circumstances, from the personalities of Laura and her father, and from their relationship to each other.

a) The circumstances are as follows: in 1960, when Laura was eighteen years old she met and fell in love with Jim Fredericks. Four years later she conceived a child out of wedlock by Jim, but when he learned that Laura was pregnant he left town. After some months, Laura too moved out of town and into the Edgewood home for unwed mothers, where the child was born in January of 1965.

After the birth of the child Laura lived with a family in Edgewood, and in April of that year she met Brendan Kite who had recently been discharged from the Navy. In June, Brendan began asking Laura to marry him. Laura was not really attracted to Brendan and kept putting him off. Finally, however, she began to feel that life would be easier for her and better for the baby if there were a father in the house. In November she agreed to marry Brendan and arrangements were made.

On the night before the wedding, however, Laura realized that she was making a terrible mistake and she told her parents, who had come almost a hundred miles to attend the wedding, that she couldn't go through with it. Her father told her that she couldn't back out now; it was too late; cancelling the wedding was out of the question.

b) Mr. Osprey was a long distance trucker who was absent from the home for lengthy periods. He had fathered twelve children, many of whom were retarded, by his emotionally disturbed wife. When he was home he was distant, demanding and insensitive.

c) Laura Osprey was the second oldest of the twelve children who, throughout her childhood and adolescence, had been largely responsible for the younger children. It was a weighty responsibility and Laura was an extremely dutiful and nervous young woman. After she had the child out of wedlock, she was depressed and, according to one witness, almost had a nervous breakdown.

d) The relationship between father and daughter had never been affectionate and was very strained after Laura became pregnant. Laura was, indeed, so intimidated by her father that, after learning of the pregnancy, she could not bring herself to discuss the matter at all with him. She told only her mother about the pregnancy and left it up to her to break the news to the father.

During the time that Laura was in Edgewood (from July of 1964 to December of 1965) Mr. Osprey made no direct contact with Laura at all. Laura knew that he was angry at her and that he felt she had already shamed the family. Up until a week before the wedding Laura was not even sure that her father would attend. But here he was and now she felt she was about to shame him a second time by a last minute cancellation of the wedding. When, therefore, Mr. Osprey told his daughter in no uncertain terms that a cancellation was out of the question, Laura was convinced that, if she did not go through with the wedding, her father would certainly be very very angry for a very very long time.

2. *Extrinsic.* There is no question about the fact that Mr. Osprey told his daughter immediately after the wedding rehearsal that a cancellation of the wedding was out of the question. Three of the witnesses actually overheard the conversation and attested to the fact that Mr. Osprey was angry. One witness said that Laura told her father that she couldn't stand Brendan Kite and didn't want to marry him, whereupon the father got "really angry" and said that she had dragged him all this way and she was not going to humiliate him twice in one year and that she was simply not in a position to back out now.

According to Laura, it seemed from the father's tone that it would be all over between them if she did not go through with the wedding, and so she did.

3. *Causative.* It is clear from the evidence that Laura Osprey entered this marriage not only *cum metu* but *ex metu*. Fear of her father's long lasting indignation was, in other words, the principal motive for her going through the ceremony.

This is corroborated by the presence of Laura's aversion to marrying Brendan Kite, which was attested to by all of the witnesses. After marriage Laura could scarcely stand to live under the same roof with Brendan let alone carry on an intimate relationship with him. Which explains the brevity of the marriage.

It is, therefore, clear from the entire evidence that even though the force in this case was not absolutely grave, and even though there was no screaming or badgering, nevertheless there was present in this case a force and fear that invalidated this marriage.

WHEREFORE

I
The Facts

Arnold Siskin, Catholic and Frida Wrobel, Lutheran, were married first in a Lutheran ceremony on the fourth day of August 1972. On the second anniversary of that ceremony, the marriage was validated at Our Lady of Hope Church, Claremont, Connecticut, in the Archdiocese of Hartford. Arnold was twenty-two at the time of the Lutheran ceremony; Frida was twenty.

Arnold and Frida lived together for three more years following the Catholic ceremony and had two children, both now in the custody of the mother. The separation took place in the fall of 1977. A divorce was granted in Claremont County on June 18, 1978.

On February 4, 1983, Arnold petitioned this Tribunal to declare the marriage null. His petition was accepted and, at the *Contestatio Litis* conducted on March 11, 1983, the Judge assigned Frida Wrobel's lack of renewal of consent at the time of the validation as the grounds for investigating possible nullity.

II
The Law

Both the Old Code (C. 1133 § 1) and the New Code (C. 1156 § 1) require, for the validity of a convalidation, that there be a truly new consent to the marriage being entered.

Both Codes, furthermore, in § 2 of the cited canons, note that that requirement of new consent is by ecclesiastical law.

The two Codes differ, however, regarding the *subject* of ecclesiastical laws. According to the Old Code (C. 12) all baptized people, including *Protestants,* are bound, unless otherwise noted. According to the New Code, however, (C. 11) only *Catholics* are bound to such laws.

Under the Old Code, therefore, it was required for validity that Protestant parties to a convalidation *first* of all recognize that the first ceremony (even if it was performed by their own Protestant pastor) was not a valid marriage, and *secondly,* that they give a new consent to the Catholic convalidation ceremony as the only true marriage. This unrealistic expectation, needless to say, resulted in many invalid convalidations. Once the New Code became effective, however, Protestants were no longer required to renew consent at the time of a convalidation. Their former marital consent is considered to perdure.

November 27, 1983 (the effective date of the New Code), therefore, becomes a key date in judging the validity of a convalidation, especially one involving a Protestant. In a convalidation *prior* to that date, it was required that both parties, including a Protestant party, recognize the first ceremony as invalid and therefore give new consent to the second ceremony (the convalidation). In a convalidation *after* that date, the Protestant party was not required to recognize the nullity of the first ceremony or give new consent to the second.

III
The Argument

Since the convalidation in question took place before November 27, 1983, it was required for validity that Frida Wrobel, at the time of the convalidation, *first* of all recognize the Lutheran ceremony as invalid, and *secondly* that she give new marital consent at the time of the Catholic ceremony, and that she recognize that ceremony as the only valid marriage.

The evidence shows that Frida Wrobel did not, in fact, meet those requirements. Frida herself testified in this hearing, saying that she certainly regarded the Lutheran wedding, performed by her pastor in her parish church, as entirely valid in every way and that, when she took the vows before the Luthern pastor, she regarded herself as married in the true sense before God and as a Christian. She was, she said, Arnold Siskin's wife following the Lutheran wedding and no thought to the contrary crossed her mind. As far as Frida was concerned, the convalidation was something she was asked to do and was happy to do for Arnold's sake so that he could be a member in good standing in his church.

The Tribunal also received the testimony of four witnesses, including Frida's mother and sister, the latter of whom was the maid of honor at the Lutheran ceremony. The witnesses were quite knowledgeable about Frida's attitude towards both ceremonies, and all confirmed, in considerable detail, Frida's own testimony.

The evidence, in short, specifically confirms in this particular case the common assumption (if not the legal presumption) that a Protestant marrying in her or his own church regards that ceremony as presumptively valid and is not disposed therefore to give new consent at a later convalidation.

It is clear, at any rate, that Frida Wrobel neither regarded the first ceremony as invalid nor gave new consent to the second.

WHEREFORE

```
┌─────────────────────┐
│          I          │
│      The Facts      │
└─────────────────────┘
```

Eric Noddy, Catholic, and Sylvia Junco, non-Catholic, were married at the Church of St. Joseph, Millerton, Michigan, on the twelfth day of December 1961. Eric was thirty-two years old at the time; Sylvia was thirty.

Eric and Sylvia lived together for only about six months. Eric was in the Navy at the time; Sylvia found life on a military base a most unhappy existence, and returned home to her parents in the summer of 1962. No children were born to the couple. A divorce was granted in Virginia on the eighth day of March 1964.

On March 9, 1982 Eric petitioned this Court to declare the marriage null. His petition was accepted and on April 3, 1982 the Doubt was Formulated as follows:

> Whether the Noddy-Junco marriage has been proved null on the grounds of lack of due discretion.

```
┌─────────────────────┐
│         II          │
│      The Law        │
└─────────────────────┘
```

C. 1060 says: "Marriage enjoys the favor of law, so that, in a case of doubt, one must hold for the validity of marriage until the contrary is proved."

This canon, which is one of the eight introductory canons to the section on marriage, is specifically applied to the procedural law of the Church in C. 1608, which speaks of the moral certitude required on the part of the judge in order to pass judgment. Paragraph four of that canon reads, "A judge who cannot arrive at this certitude, is to pronounce that the right of the petitioner is not established, and is to dismiss the respondent as absolved, unless there is question of a case which enjoys the favor of the law, in which case the decision must be in favor of it."

It is clear that, when the case at bar involves the alleged invalidity of a marriage, C. 1060 and C. 1608 § 4 are saying basically the same thing, namely that, when the judge is in doubt, when he is not morally certain about the alleged invalidity, then he must hold for the validity of marriage and issue a negative decision.

However, C. 1608 § 4 also contains an "unless" clause, an exceptive clause. It says that, when the judge is in doubt, he must issue a negative sentence *"unless there is question of a case which enjoys the favor of the law, in which case he must pronounce in favor of it."*

Besides C. 1060, which, as we have noted, has already been embodied in the *principal* statement of C. 1608 § 4, there is only one other marital situation which "enjoys the favor of the law" as the *exceptive* clause of C. 1068 § 4 says, and that is the one found in C. 1150 which states, "In a doubtful matter, the privilege of the faith enjoys the favor of the law."

It is clear that only the Holy See is competent to dissolve a marriage in favor of the faith. When, therefore, such a favor has been requested and the nonbaptism of one party has been certainly proved, the case should be forwarded to Rome for adjudication. Nevertheless, this Court's reading of the exceptive clause of C. 1608 § 4 is as follows: that when the moment arrives for a judge to pass sentence in a formal trial regarding the alleged nullity of a marriage, and when

1) the judge remains in doubt about the proven invalidity of the marriage (in practice, by the time a case progresses to the point of a sentence, even though nullity has not been proved, some positive doubt has, at least, been cast upon it) and

2) the judge likewise remains in doubt about the proven nonbaptism of one of the parties (the total evidence regarding the alleged nonbaptism must be submitted to the Court and must fall short of moral certitude but result in a positive doubt)

then the Court may not give an affirmative decision in favor of nullity but it must give (pronuntiandum est) an affirmative decision in favor of the doubtful privilege of the faith, thus freeing the petitioner to enter another marriage.

This reading of the Court would seem to be in accord with the decretal of Pope Lucius III (1181-1185) on which this canon is, to some extent, based (c. 3 X De probationibus, II, 19 - Friedberg II, 307). Pope Lucius wrote: "If, perhaps, the witnesses on both sides are equally impressive, then the witnesses of the party in possession should be preferred, since the rights to absolve are more urgent than the rights to condemn; however, in liberal cases, where the witnesses of both parties are equally probative, the sentence should always be rendered in behalf of freedom."

This reading also seems to be in accord with the observations of the Lega-Bartocetti commentary on procedural law (II, pp. 942-944). This commentary was, of course, on the Old Code but it is clear that the parallel canon in the Old Code (C. 1869 § 4) was not substantially different from the present C. 1608 § 4.

The evidence in this case is minimal. The respondent's whereabouts are unknown. Eric heard that she remarried sometime in the early 1970s but he has no more specific information about that. Letters were sent to Sylvia's parents but they never responded. Eric is a very reserved, private kind of person and he was unable to provide us with the names of any witnesses who would have first hand knowledge about the marriage in question — which took place more than twenty years ago while Eric was in the service. Affidavits were, however, obtained from three people: Mrs. Evelyn Richards (Eric's foster mother), John Richards (the petitioner's foster brother) and Thomas Campbell (a friend).

On the basis of the evidence the Court was unable to reach *moral certitude* regarding the alleged nullity of the marriage.

At the same time, however, the Court is of the opinion that a *positive doubt* exists both about the baptism of the respondent and about the validity of the marriage.

Regarding the Baptism of the Respondent. The evidence that casts a doubt on Sylvia Junco's baptism (but does not result in certitude about her nonbaptism) is as follows. Eric thinks that the Juncos were of Scandinavian descent but, as far as he knows, they had no church affiliation and were not church-going people. The Military Ordinariate issued a dispensation from the impediments of mixed religion and disparity of cult on November 28, 1961 but "no petition is available." The records at St. Joseph's in Millerton, Michigan indicate that "the bride was un-baptized" and that a dispensation simply from Disparity of Cult was granted. According to a letter to the Tribunal, from the pastor, dated June 23, 1978, however, "what is unusual is that the papers for this marriage are not on file here," despite the fact that, in general, at that time, the records were "meticulously kept." It must be concluded, therefore, that there is a doubt about Sylvia's baptismal status. Very probably she was not baptized. But there are no witnesses to that effect and no testimony from Sylvia herself, and the records are not entirely clear.

Regarding the Validity of the Marriage. Although Eric and Sylvia were thirty-two and thirty years old respectively, there are indications that both parties have rather substantial personality limitations which interfered with due discretion. Eric was abandoned by his parents when he was seven years old and reared in a foster family. He is a distant, extremely passive and avoidant person. He was a career military man from 1947 to 1967 and, since 1967, has lived by himself. He has been "dating" a woman for five years but works most of the time, sees her infrequently and seems apprehensive about marrying. Sylvia, on the other hand, was reared in a small community in Michigan and, although she appeared to Eric to be a good woman, her attitude towards marriage as a lifelong and genuine partnership seems seriously defective. When she married Eric, it was presumably clear to her that he was a career Navy man and that being his wife would, therefore, involve her in the special lifestyle of the military. After only six months, however, Sylvia asked Eric to leave the military because she was unhappy on the base and, when he declined, she left and returned to her parents.

All of which, to this Court, casts a doubt on the validity of the marriage.

WHEREFORE, in light of the jurisprudence stated in the "in iure" section, I the undersigned Judge of the Tribunal of Hartford render the following decision

AS REGARDS THE PROVEN NULLITY OF THE MARRIAGE — IN THE NEGATIVE, i.e. the marriage has not been proved null.

AS REGARDS THE PRIVILEGE OF THE FAITH — IN THE AFFIRMATIVE, i.e. since there is a positive doubt both about the baptism of the respondent and about the validity of the marriage, the privilege of the faith, insofar as it enjoys the favor of the law, is operative and the petitioner's freedom to marry is recognized.

APPENDICES

The following outline of a sentence satisfies the general requirements of the law:

IN THE NAME OF GOD, AMEN.

With Pope John Paul II as our Holy Father, and the Most Reverend John F. Whealon as Archbishop of Hartford, the Tribunal of Hartford, sitting as a Court of First Instance and consisting of the Reverend Lawrence G. Wrenn as Single Judge, issued on February 15, 1984 the following definitive decision in the case of Peter Egret, Petitioner, of 130 Circle Avenue, Laurel, Connecticut in the Archdiocese of Hartford and Claudia Lark, Respondent, of 19 Richard Drive, Carthage, Connecticut in the Archdiocese of Hartford, the Petitioner having attacked the validity of his marriage to the Respondent on the grounds of lack of due competence, the Reverend Gene E. Gianelli acting as Instructor, the Reverend Edward G. Pfnausch acting as Defender of the Bond and having contested the issue.

```
┌─────────────────────┐
│          I          │
│      The Facts      │
└─────────────────────┘
```

This section should include the baptismal status of the parties, their respective ages at the time of marriage, the place, diocese and date of marriage, the number of children born of the marriage, the duration of common life, and the date and jurisdiction of the civil divorce.

It should also indicate the basis for declaring competency (where this is not already evident from the addresses of the parties or place of marriage) and it should give a positive indication that the rights of the respondent were respected.

Finally this section should contain a concise but thorough, chronological narration of *all* pertinent events. Where it is possible to clarify with certainty factual discrepancies in the testimony, it should be done in this section, particularly where it might influence the final decision. Circumstantial evidence is, after all, one of the recognized proofs in law and can sometimes be critical to the case. The facts constitute the underpinnings of the case and the Court can never be satisfied with applying the law to a muddled and uncertain factual situation.

```
┌─────────────────────┐
│          II         │
│      The Law        │
└─────────────────────┘
```

Here the pertinent law contained either in this book or in other manuals can be copied, referred to or appropriately altered. It should be pointed out, though, that the legal outlines contained in this book contain only usual law. They will be found wanting for the unusual case.

III
The Argument

This section applies The Law (Section II) to The Facts (Section I) and reaches a conclusion. All evidence favoring the conclusion should be neatly marshalled and all contrary evidence should be forthrightly exposed with an evaluation that indicates why the Court did not consider it to disturb the balance of judgment.

The various proofs employed should be noted and specifically applied (e.g., judicial testimony of principals and witnesses, presumptions, documents, etc.). When the law demands it, the opinions of expert(s) are to be noted. When relevant, the opinion of the Defender of the Bond should be addressed.

WHEREFORE, I, the undersigned judge of the Tribunal of Hartford, having invoked the Divine Name, and having only God before my eyes, having considered the law and the facts pertaining to this case, define, declare and decree, answering the proposed doubt

IN THE AFFIRMATIVE
this is to say
THE NULLITY OF THIS MARRIAGE HAS BEEN PROVED

I order that the expenses of this trial, in the sum of $150.00, be paid by the Petitioner. I also order that this decision be published in accordance with the first method suggested in Canon 1615.

I further order that the Respondent, Claudia Lark, not be permitted to remarry in the Catholic Church without special clearance by the appropriate Chancery.

S/Lawrence G. Wrenn
Chief Judge

S/Susan Walsh
Notary

Given at Hartford, Connecticut
this 15th day of February 1984

SAMPLE DECREE OF RATIFICATION

The undersigned judges, having convened to consider the above entitled case, having examined the affirmative sentence of First Instance given by the Tribunal of the Diocese of Bridgeport on April 21, 1984, and having considered the observations of our own Defender of the Bond, the Reverend Thomas J. Barry, dated May 31, 1984, in accordance with C. 1682 § 2

DO HEREBY RATIFY
THE DECISION OF
FIRST INSTANCE

In compliance with C. 1617 and with the directives of February 14, 1974, October 15, 1974, and July 1, 1976, issued by the Holy See (CLD, 8, pp. 1109-1111) we offer the following reasons in law and in fact for this ratification:

Our jurisprudence recognizes that a marriage may be null by reason of the incapacity of a party to assume the essential obligations of marriage. Such incapacity can stem from a psychological reason that deprives the person of the competence for marriage. See, for example, C. 1095, 3° and the decision coram Dean Lefebvre of January 31, 1976, in D2 p. 75. In the present case, the incapacity of the Respondent was demonstrated in First Instance by the testimony of several witnesses and the observations of the Court-appointed psychiatric expert who diagnosed the Respondent as suffering from a Paranoid Personality Disorder which resulted in moodiness, depression, a suicide attempt, occasional confused, irrational and inappropriate behavior, denial, fault finding, rage and litigiousness.

This Court of Second Instance concurs that such evidence does indeed prove the nullity of the marriage and that the affirmative decision of the Court of First Instance should therefore be ratified.

_____
Judge

_____
Judge

_____
Judge

_____
Notary

Hartford, Connecticut
June 3, 1984

196

PROOF OF DEATH WITHOUT DOCUMENT

Decree

**I
The Facts**

The Reverend Henry Amsel, pastor of the Congregational Church in Mayfield, Connecticut was involved in an accident at sea on Friday, October 10, 1975.

Mr. Amsel, a respected minister, often went fishing with his wife. On October 10, 1975, however, Mrs. Amsel was recovering from recent surgery and was not able to accompany her husband. Accordingly, Mr. Amsel went off alone that morning, drove to Waterford, Connecticut where he parked his car, and put out to sea in his twelve foot aluminum boat. He was fifty-six years old.

When Mr. Amsel had not returned by one o'clock Saturday afternoon the police were notified but neither Mr. Amsel nor his boat was ever found.

**II
The Law**

1. The classical instruction on cases involving presumption of death is that of the Holy Office of May 13, 1868. The instruction indicates that the judgment is to be based on documentary proof, witnesses, hearsay evidence, presumptions, rumors and newspaper notices. Paragraph eleven of this instruction specifically indicates that the Ordinary (cf. C. 335 and 336) can decide such matters even where documentary proof and firsthand witnesses are lacking providing he is morally certain of the death.

2. Doheny notes that "ordinarily, cases involving the proof of the death of an absent consort are settled in administrative process." (*Canonical Procedure in Matrimonial Cases*, Vol. II, pg. 596)

3. C. 1707, in three paragraphs, reads as follows:

   C. 1707 § 1. Whenever the death of a spouse cannot be proven by an authentic ecclesiastical or civil document, the other spouse is not free from the bond of marriage until after a declaration of presumed death is made by the diocesan bishop.

§ 2. The diocesan bishop can make the declaration mentioned in § 1 only after he has attained moral certitude of the death of a spouse, having made opportune investigation from depositions of witnesses, reports and circumstantial evidence. The absence of a spouse, even for a long time, is not sufficient.

§ 3. The bishop shall consult the Apostolic See about uncertain and complex cases.

III
The Argument

---

1. Mr. James Hogan of the Coast Guard Station in New London reports that given the weather conditions prevailing at the time of the alleged accident, namely that a slight chop developed on the sea Saturday afternoon, that Sunday morning small craft warnings had been posted, that winds were gauged at 25-30 knots and waves at four to five feet, it would be "unusual but not unheard of" for neither body nor boat involved in an accident off Waterford to be found. Under such conditions, it was Mr. Hogan's opinion, the body could easily drift out into the ocean and the aluminum boat could sink.

2. It seems, furthermore, that the Reverend Amsel gave no evidence of wanting puposely to disappear. This fishing trip was in no way unusual for him. He led a good, Christian, family life. There was, according to the Reverend Edward J. Donnelly, who thoroughly discussed the matter with several knowledgeable people, "no hint of alcoholic or marital problems." Mr. Amsel had made plans for the services he was to conduct that coming Sunday. He had also made arrangements to bowl with some men from the Church on the night of the 10th. In short, there seems absolutely no reason to suspect anything but a tragic accident which took Mr. Amsel's life.

WHEREFORE, there seems no prudent reason to doubt that the Reverend Henry Amsel is now deceased. It is morally certain, in other words, on the basis of the foregoing presumptive evidence, that Henry Amsel is dead.

WHEREFORE, Betty Amsel is now declared free to marry.

Lawrence G. Wrenn
Officialis de mandato

Hartford, Connecticut
February 15, 1984

198

			First Edition	Second Edition
Anné	2/25/69	Competence	94	
Canals	4/21/70	Error	133	
Canestri	2/21/48	Competence	55	81
Colagiovanni	12/15/79	Personality Disorder		95
Davino	12/13/78	Children		149
DiFelice	7/22/70	Children	107	
DiFelice	11/3/71	Fidelity	112	155
DiFelice	1/17/76	Competence	37	63
DiFelice	3/26/77	Error		133
Doheny	5/4/56	Simulation	104	
Ewers	1/15/77	Competence	74	108
Felici	5/22/56	Competence	28	55
Ferraro	11/28/78	Competence	64	
Ferraro	11/28/78	Discretion	148	16
Filipiak	3/23/56	Perpetuity	117	
Fiore	1/16/61	Fear	169	178
Heard	1/30/54	Competence	28	55
Heard	7/30/59	Fear	170	178
Lefebvre	12/2/67	Homosexuality		126
Lefebvre	1/31/76	Competence	49	75
Mattioli	3/18/50	Condition	130	174
Mattioli	10/30/53	Fidelity	112	155
Mattioli	7/25/56	Condition	129	172
Morano	4/30/35	Peritior	56	82
Palazzini	7/26/66	Fidelity	111	154
Parisella	7/13/68	Expert	56	82
Parisella	4/20/78	Reverential Fear		182
Parisella	5/11/78	Competence	25	51
Pasquazi	11/25/58	Fear	170	178
Pinto	11/20/69	Schizophrenia		11
Pinto	3/18/71	Competence	43	69
Pinto	6/26/71	Condition	130	173
Pinto	2/4/74	Discretion	153	21
Pinto	7/15/77	Competence	84	113
Pinto	12/18/79	Competence		59
Pinto	12/18/79	Discretion		33
Pompedda	12/22/69	Children		145
Pompedda	1/23/71	Perpetuity		160
Raad	10/16/80	Female Impotence		5
Rogers	1/21/69	Convalidation	144	
Sabattani	6/21/57	Competence	55	81
Sabattani	2/24/61	Discretion	160	28
Serrano	4/5/73	Competence	8	
Stankiewicz	1/29/81	Simulation		140

	First Edition	Second Edition
Affective Disorder	84	113
Alcoholism	88	117
C. 1095, 3°		47
Condition	122	165
Convalidation		187
Death	180	197
Discretion		37
Discretion/Force	165	43
Draft Cc. 296, 297	32	
Elements of Community	59	
Error of Action	138	
Female Impotence	5	
Force - Two Arguments	168	177
Formal Object	28	55
Ignorance		129
Incompetence -Personal Element	55	81
Male Impotence 1	2	
Male Impotence 2		1
Naufragium		85
Navarrete	69	
Privilege/Administrative	177	
Privilege/Judical		189
Quality of Marriage		103
Schizophrenia	79	
Substance Dependence		123
Trichotomy		90